9

D0055391

9/11 Culture
America Under Construction

Jeffrey Melnick

A John Wiley & Sons, Ltd., Publication

This edition first published 2009
© 2009 Jeffrey Melnick

Blackwell Publishing was acquired by John Wiley & Sons in February 2007. Blackwell's publishing program has been merged with Wiley's global Scientific, Technical, and Medical business to form Wiley-Blackwell.

Registered Office
John Wiley & Sons Ltd, The Atrium, Southern Gate, Chichester, West Sussex, PO19 8SQ, United Kingdom

Editorial Offices
350 Main Street, Malden, MA 02148-5020, USA
9600 Garsington Road, Oxford, OX4 2DQ, UK
The Atrium, Southern Gate, Chichester, West Sussex, PO19 8SQ, UK

For details of our global editorial offices, for customer services, and for information about how to apply for permission to reuse the copyright material in this book please see our website at www.wiley.com/wiley-blackwell.

The right of Jeffrey Melnick to be identified as the author of this work has been asserted in accordance with the Copyright, Designs and Patents Act 1988.

All rights reserved. No part of this publication may be reproduced, stored in a retrieval system, or transmitted, in any form or by any means, electronic, mechanical, photocopying, recording or otherwise, except as permitted by the UK Copyright, Designs and Patents Act 1988, without the prior permission of the publisher.

Wiley also publishes its books in a variety of electronic formats. Some content that appears in print may not be available in electronic books.

Designations used by companies to distinguish their products are often claimed as trademarks. All brand names and product names used in this book are trade names, service marks, trademarks or registered trademarks of their respective owners. The publisher is not associated with any product or vendor mentioned in this book. This publication is designed to provide accurate and authoritative information in regard to the subject matter covered. It is sold on the understanding that the publisher is not engaged in rendering professional services. If professional advice or other expert assistance is required, the services of a competent professional should be sought.

Library of Congress Cataloging-in-Publication Data

Melnick, Jeffrey Paul.
    9/11 culture : America under construction / Jeffrey Melnick.
        p. cm.
      title: Nine/eleven culture
    Includes bibliographical references and index.
    ISBN 978-1-4051-7372-8 (hardcover : alk. paper) – ISBN 978-1-4051-7371-1 (pbk. : alk. paper) 1. September 11 Terrorist Attacks, 2001, in art. 2. September 11 Terrorist Attacks, 2001–Influence. 3. Popular culture–United States. 4. Popular culture–Social aspects. I. Title. II. Title: Nine/eleven culture.
    NX650.S49M44 2009
    700'.45873931–dc22

                                                            2008042455

A catalogue record for this book is available from the British Library.

Set in 10/13pt Sabon
by SPi Publisher Services, Pondicherry, India

001 2009

Contents

Acknowledgments

The work I have done in *9/11 Culture* grows from a course I have been teaching at Babson College for the past four years and it is my true pleasure to acknowledge the many ways my students have shaped this work. These students have contributed an enormous amount to *9/11 Culture* and I wish I had the space to thank the many who went beyond the class requirements to help push this book along. I do want to note how grateful I am to all those students who have sent me songs, clips from movies, television shows, stand-up comedy routines, and other 9/11-related materials, sometimes after graduating from college. It has made this work feel far less solitary than it might have been otherwise.

I am also happy to have the opportunity to thank the Babson Faculty Research Facility, which has supported the research and production of *9/11 Culture*. Susan Chern, at the BFRF, offered her usual expert support. I want to express my gratitude to Kate Buckley, formerly a research librarian at Babson, who answered many questions and hunted down many sources. Many others at Babson have supported the teaching and research related to this book: I want to make special mention of Kandice Hauf, chair of my division, Joyce Gordon, Barry Doucette, Mary Driscoll, and Sheila Dinsmoor. I also want to thank my friend and colleague at Babson, Marjorie Feld, who has made Babson a better place to be.

My work here has benefitted greatly from other scholars who have shared their work and insights with me. I am particularly grateful to Jonathan Ritter, who sent me an early copy of the excellent book he co-edited with J. Martin Daughtry (*Music in the Post-9/11 World*), and Greg Kornbluh, who started off as a research assistant – and an excellent one – but ended up reading and commenting on the entire manuscript and pushing me to make late-in-the-game improvements to the book. I also want to thank

Paul Watanabe at the University of Massachusetts Boston and Nina Tisch of the John F. Kennedy Library for giving me the chance to try out some of this material with their students at the 2008 Summer Institute. At Wiley-Blackwell I have been lucky to work with smart (and patient!) editors Jayne Fargnoli, Margot Morse, and Joanna Pyke.

It is my pleasure to have this chance to thank the artists who have allowed me to reproduce their work in these pages. David Rees, Matt Weber, Eric Fischl, and Vinnie Amessé have been wonderfully generous in sharing their art.

I am grateful to Larry Blum who reached into his amazing storehouse of film knowledge (and drafted the support of family members) as he helped me complete the filmography for the book. I also want to thank my "Boston Collective" colleagues at the *Journal of Popular Music Studies*: the work we did together on *JPMS* helped to energize the work I have done here. I have deep gratitude for my dear friend Cindy Weisbart who has asked wonderful questions and offered generative frameworks drawn from her own work as a teacher; she also sent me the link to the *Mad Men* credits, just under the wire. Aaron Lecklider, Gary Wilder, and Dan Itzkovitz have all been vitally important to me as colleagues and friends. I send my heartfelt thanks also to Judy Smith who has offered me crucial intellectual and professional guidance for over a decade.

Finally, and most centrally, there are three people named Rubin. Jessie Rubin is simply a wonder: she teaches me something new each day and her deep engagement with everything she does is thrilling. I am so grateful for her energetic companionship and I continue to be impressed with her ability to sort out the complicated messages the culture industries direct at her.

Jacob Rubin, with his rigorous refusal of conventional wisdom and his deep wells of empathy, has exerted a profound influence on this book. I have lost count of how many pieces in this book began as conversations with Jake, but I do know that I cannot even imagine doing this sort of work without him. How lucky I am to have him to help me find my way!

Rachel Rubin's scholarly work continues to set the bar for me. Her engaged interdisciplinary scholarship constitutes my primary academic model. That she has balanced this academic work with meaningful activism, as president of her union and elsewhere, is simply awe-inspiring. Rachel's influence is plain throughout this book, from the overall shape of it to numerous individual insights. Her intellectual generosity is a central fact of my own academic life. Taken together with all she shares me with me as co-parent and life partner, I just feel lucky.

Introduction: 9/11 Questions (and Answers)

It is risky, I know, to call this introductory chapter "9/11 Questions." At the time I am writing, putting "9/11" and "Questions" into a single, short phrase cannot help but tap into a very complex vein of American political and cultural expressive practices. The "9/11 questions" that shape the cyberculture of our time (you will see if you take a quick break from reading this and type "9/11 questions" into your favorite search engine) all grow from a shaky and contingent yet powerful consensus that has developed in the years since 2001 about how closely the official narrative of 9/11 matches what actually happened that day. Here is one neat summary of the authorized story of September 11, 2001, taken from what appears to be a self-published children's book, written by an author whose biographical note claims that she is "nationally known for her ability to simplify concepts":

> We Learned That These "Terrorists"
> Who did this horrible act are groups of people around the world who
> do not like the way we live or the freedoms we have.
> They do no like that we have many religions in America.
> They also think we are too rich and that we have too strong a military.
> These people want to take over the world. (Poffenberger, 2002: 10)

There is much to say about this children's book, most of which would not be suitable to say in front of children. But what is perhaps most striking about Nancy Poffenberger's *September 11th, 2001 (A Simple*

Account for Children) is how fully it participates in what novelist Lynne Sharon Schwartz (2005) has, in grief and anger, referred to as a post-9/11 "butchery" – the way that political leaders and media powers have ritually repeated the same key words and phrases in an attempt to control the possible meanings of the September 11 tragedy. Schwartz describes this collective effort as "not bloody but insidious, an assault on the common language" (78–9). The 9/11 questions that have received fullest play in the past few years fall under the general rubrics of "conspiracy theory" or "9/11 truth," depending on where you stand. Film actor Charlie Sheen has 9/11 questions and Iranian president Mahmoud Ahmadinejad has 9/11 questions. Television personality Rosie O'Donnell has 9/11 questions and rappers from Jadakiss to Immortal Technique to the Lost Children of Babylon (who made an entire record they called *The 911 Report: The Ultimate Conspiracy*) all have 9/11 questions.

These 9/11 questions are myriad and often quite technical, but in most cases the shape and content of the questions telegraph a few predictable, if politically satisfying, answers: George W. Bush at the very least knew ahead of time about the plan to attack the United States (or "knocked down the towers" himself, as numerous remixed versions of Immortal Technique and DJ Green Lantern's "Bin Laden" put it in 2005) and bin Laden had nothing to do with 9/11, or was on the payroll all along, so is not ultimately responsible. These now almost-mainstream 9/11 questions form a powerful river of cultural rhetoric, and at times branch off into unexpected tributaries; you know you are there when you hear or see references to the Illumanati or anything about the imagery on American paper money.

There is a *Doonesbury* comic strip from late December of 2003 that presents a fictionalized presidential press conference that lays out the cultural narrowcasting I am trying to describe here (see Figure 1). Press spokesperson "Scott" (McClellan) is taking questions from the assembled journalists, including longtime *Doonesbury* figure Roland Burton Hedley III. Scott never lets a full question get asked. One journalist begins "About the continuing chaos in Iraq," while another starts with "In regard to the ongoing gutting of our environmental laws ..." In each case, before the question is even finished, Scott says "9-11." Finally, Hedley asks "Uh ... Scott, is 9-11 the answer to every question now?" The answer?: "Yes, It's 9-11, 24-7." As a postscript, after Hedley asks "Until when?" this mouthpiece for George W. Bush says "11-2" (the date of the 2004 presidential election). I have been teaching a class on cultural

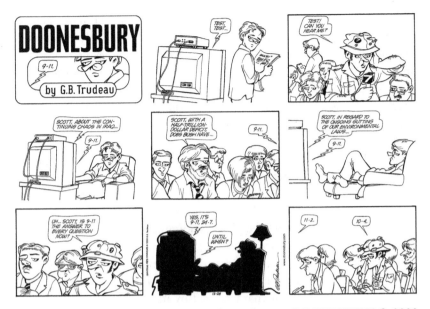

Figure 1 Doonesbury on 24/7 9/11 culture. Source: DOONESBURY © 2003 G. B. Trudeau. Reprinted with permission of UNIVERSAL PRESS SYNDICATE. All rights reserved.

responses to 9/11 for some 4 years now, at a small business college in the northeast of the United States, and my students have, at times, asked me Roland Burton Hedley's question with some exasperation. Bruce Springsteen's *The Rising* album? Sure. *"V" for Vendetta*? No doubt. Spike Lee's *25th Hour*? Yes. But the children's movie *Chicken Little*? Steven Spielberg's *Munich*? Television's *Lost*? The first major proposition of this book, then, is that 9/11 and its cultural and political fallout *have* functioned as the answer to countless questions of social import. We may not now be living "9-11, 24-7" but that seems an error only of degree and not of basic approach.

This book is *about* 9/11 questions, and also about 9/11 answers. Or, perhaps more accurately, it is about how 9/11 has served as a question and an answer on the cultural landscape of the United States in the years since September 11, 2001. The basic premise that will be explored in this book is that "9/11" has become the most important question and answer shaping American cultural discussions (in film and other visual arts, in music, in "high" and popular literature) – but not in the banal ways the official story or the "9/11 questions" of our own moment might suggest. Taking this task on means, of course, that we will likely have to be satisfied with hypotheses, possibilities, and even the occasional dead-end inquiry. The assumption here is that we historians, sociologists, musicologists, film scholars, literary critics, and teachers must begin tracking the resonances of 9/11 even as the apparatus used to support this cultural work is still being created: it is, as my subtitle suggests, "under construction."

What I am calling the "culture" of 9/11 is a multimedia culture; it has grown unpredictably, across space and genre, encompassing numerous demographic, affective, and affinity groups. The trajectory of the book – from 9/11 rumors to what I am calling 9/11 shout-outs – is meant to underscore the decentralized and anti-monumentalist nature of much of the most significant 9/11 art. To be sure, I discuss blockbuster Hollywood films, major-event novels and chart-topping popular songs in the pages that follow, but a central argument of this book is that the culture of 9/11 (*cultures*, really) has been characterized by its ad hoc willingness to get the job done now. American culture makers, from the celebrities who appeared at the *America: A Tribute to Heroes* telethon on September 21 to the "average" citizens who took pictures and passed rumors in the weeks following the attacks, contributed in remarkably functional ways to a new culture of grief, memorialization, and celebration too. Just above, I used the phrase "cultural work" and it is this concept, with its focus on what popular arts *do*, rather than what they *are* (in some purely aesthetic, non-social way), that guides *9/11 Culture*. While there have been predictable attempts by cultural gatekeepers to name this or that work as the great statement of post-9/11 consciousness (as with Bruce Springsteen's *The Rising* record and Don DeLillo's novel *Falling Man*), the people – bumper sticker logic notwithstanding – have not stood united.

Long ago the British cultural critic Raymond Williams explained that the word "culture" was one of the two or three most complicated words in the English language. I do not want to wade into the complex debates that have followed Williams about how to define "culture"; I want to encourage a reading of the "culture" in my title as a loose application of the scientific sense of the word – as having to do with material grown in special conditions for particular experimental or commercial purposes. The material of 9/11 culture(s) includes popular songs, comic strips, rumors, films, speeches, photographs, bumper stickers and t-shirts, along with novels and museum-ready visual arts, but is characterized above all by its on-the-fly practicality. While rules of genre and market (for instance) continued to matter after September 11, one central operating principle here is that as we begin to sift through the cultures of 9/11 we will have to develop appropriate interpretive paradigms that may be more particular to this event and its fallout than the standard frameworks for studying young adult "problem" novels or immigration literature on the one hand, and blockbuster disaster movies and animated television shows on the other. My intention here is less to survey the entire field of post-9/11 cultural expression than it is to create some provisional roadmaps for approaching that field. These "maps" are not drawn to scale; neither do they represent every major point of interest on the American cultural landscape since 9/11. It will no doubt strike some readers that I have over-focused on certain areas of cultural activity and neglected others. This "bias" grows not from any *a priori* belief that hip hop music, say, matters more than television drama, but from an evolving vision of where the most consistent and culturally significant action has been.

An accurate history of the present needs to begin to catalog how 9/11 has provided the obvious answer to expected cultural questions ("What happens to the people on the plane in the movie *United 93*?"), but it also needs to create proper lenses for looking at American cultural expression since the fall of 2001 that will reckon with how 9/11 might be the (less) obvious answer to apparently unrelated cultural questions (What happens to the people on the plane in *Red Eye*? Or *Flight Plan*? Or even *Snakes on a Plane*? Can this wave of airplane anxiety movies possibly be understood *outside* the framework of 9/11 sublimation?). If we are to uncover the deep structures that undergird the realities that we, in the United States, now inhabit, it will be important to approach 9/11 as a cultural readymade, the framing device of countless novels, the surprising answer to dozens of film conflicts, and the punchline to a thousand jokes. 9/11, as Mojo Nixon sang of Elvis a generation ago, is everywhere. In his comic song, Mojo Nixon took measure of what critic Greil Marcus called a "cultural obsession" (in his 2001 book *Dead Elvis*) and taught his listeners that Elvis built the pyramids and Stonehenge, and was the answer to the mystery of the Bermuda Triangle ("Elvis needs boats!"). This was a joke, of course, but it was a good one, the kind you can actually learn something from. Elvis may not have built the pyramids (his Memphis is in Tennessee, not Egypt) but what Mojo Nixon was getting at was how Elvis had come to be the "answer" to so many substantial questions – about race, sexuality, and region, for instance – on the American scene. Even, or especially, after his death.

Popular culture scholars often struggle with how to sift through the materials they "catch" in the nets they cast. Unlike literary scholars who have often worked to enshrine single great works of art, or historians who focus on great men or great battles, much of the most important work in the study of American popular culture has come from scholars studying dense forests, rather than tall, lone pine trees. From Constance Rourke's pioneering work in the early 1930s, in which she argues for three main "types" of American figures in popular culture (the minstrel, the backwoodsman, and the Yankee [Rourke, 2004]), to Michael Denning's (1987) work on nineteenth-century dime novels, to current scholarship on Asian American cyberzines by Rachel Rubin (2003), mid-twentieth-century "family stories" by Judith Smith (2006), or black-face minstrels by W. T. Lhamon (2000), very often the most convincing popular culture studies are those that embrace patterns, repetition, and ritualized expressions as the heart of the matter in American popular culture, rather than as an unfortunate cultural byproduct or incidental marketplace reality. Single articulations of this image or that political position, one instance of this style or that unanticipated line of questioning may certainly be consequential (or become so over time), but the ultimate significance of popular culture products comes when they meet with a mass audience – or at least with a significant subculture. The obsessive deployment of 9/11 as an "answer" – a way to talk about, say, proper gender roles, or racial and ethnic conflict in United States history – is a major cultural phenomenon of our time and will be treated here not as a hurdle to leap over but rather as what scholars in cultural studies call a "cultural formation." A cultural formation, in brief, is a site where important social and political institutions, rhetorical practices, and personal behaviors overlap and combine to create a threshold level of cultural energy that comes to help define its historical moment in some significant manner.

"9/11" is a language. It has its own vocabulary, grammar, and tonalities. While this language has certainly been spoken across all media, that fact should not obscure a more important reality – that 9/11 has exerted a more profound influence on certain forms of American cultural expression (e.g. Hollywood film and underground hip hop) while leaving other forms (network television, for instance) relatively unchanged. As a result, my strategy in *9/11 Culture: America Under Construction* is to offer a thematic investigation of some of the major ways that 9/11 has made itself felt in American cultural life, rather than to attempt a systematic overview of cultural institutions in the United States (e.g. "Hollywood" or "the Big Three television networks") and their responses to 9/11. The thematic chapters that follow represent an argument against more traditional scholarly attempts to catalog how 9/11 appears in film or television or music.

Using 9/11 is not, I want to be clear, a simple cultural bait-and-switch. The burden of this book is not to demonstrate that literary and popular artists are answering "9/11" when they really mean something else, or to reveal that loads of people are using 9/11 as a cheap shout-out – a way to establish authority, seriousness of purpose, marketability, and so on. Of course all that cynical activity surrounds us and forms a dense forest that needs attention as well. But what might be most culturally significant – and most affecting in so many ways – is exactly in what manner and to what degree "9/11" is becoming our cultural Esperanto: our language of grief and anger, of loss and steadfastness. In what is perhaps the most heartbreaking moment of *"V" for Vendetta* (2005), a character named Valerie narrates, via prison-house diaries, the story of her persecution as a lesbian living under a new fascist regime in England. Valerie and her lover Ruth, even after being spurned by Valerie's parents for their "sin" of homosexuality, still manage to create a little heaven on earth: in a romance-novel worthy sequence, *"V" for Vendetta* gives us vibrant flowers, glossy hair, and long, searching looks, to tell us that these two women have found a pure and authentic love together. That perfect romance is rent violently, of course, by the fascist revolution that comes to England on the heels of some offscreen trauma that has brought the United States to its knees. (And while America's decay is left mostly unseen, the filmmaker does give us a quick shot of protesters carrying anti-Bush signs, thereby rooting the crisis in its time – our time.) In a montage of the revolution, director James McTeigue makes sure that we understand gay people to be among the major targets of the nationalistic frenzy. Earlier in the film an evil newscaster has railed against "immigrants, Muslims, homosexuals, terrorists." (Of course in "real" life, fundamentalist Christian leader Jerry Falwell was quoted as saying that lesbians were among the dangerous groups that had conspired to bring 9/11 down on the United States).

In *"V" for Vendetta* Valerie (another "V," a double for the masked hero of the title) is left to wonder in her jailhouse narrative as she nears certain death, "why they hate us so much." Here the filmmakers are very pointedly making 9/11 the answer to many of the important questions, through this faked diary, of how the power of official rhetorics of national victimhood have served to obscure who is really being terrorized in the post-9/11 West. Some version of "Why do they hate us?" was repeated incessantly in the days and weeks following the 9/11 attacks, appearing in every public forum imaginable – from presidential pronouncements, to televised news, to person-on-the-street interviews, and to the children's book I quoted earlier in this introduction. The constituency of "us" was rarely called into question: "us" meant U.S. – the politically unified, culturally homogenized "heroes" and "victims" marching as to war by the early afternoon of September 11. But *"V" for Vendetta* has a different story to tell. The despised "immigrants, Muslims, homosexuals, terrorists" of the newscaster's rants will form the only "us" that matters by the film's end. Along with some disaffected teenagers, children, and other fellow-traveling citizens they will form a masked mob, all looking like "V" – the terrorist/hero engine of the movie. This army of the disempowered and despised is poised to overthrow the fascist regime and is ready to do so largely because they have come to recognize themselves and each other as a new, politically potent "us." When *"V" for Vendetta* brings 9/11 in as an answer to every question it raises, it does so in the service of an anti-militaristic, pro-democracy message. Inside of its own narrative, *"V" for Vendetta*'s ending turns the film, for our purposes, into a utopian fantasy. Such fantasy also shapes one of the other great cinematic achievements of the post-9/11 era, Spike Lee's *25th Hour* (2002).

25th Hour was well into production by the time of 9/11, but Lee, thinking on his directorial feet, managed to turn it into what film critic Ty Burr (2006) has rightly called the first movie to deal with "this new emotional landscape" after 9/11. Before viewers even see an image on screen they hear a dog's bark and car tires squealing. The opening scene shows us Montgomery Brogan (Ed Norton) and Kostya, his "fat Ukranian" sidekick, exiting a car to save a dog that has been badly abused by some unknown assailants. The conversation that ensues after Monty rescues the dog revolves around its indomitable spirit: "He wasn't lying down for anyone," Monty tells Kostya, who is puzzled by his friend's resolve in deciding to save the dog by bringing it to an animal hospital. This poetics of redemption established in the opening scene – the resurrection of this beaten but unbowed dog – is contextualized immediately as the title credits roll out over an image of the "towers of light," the two illuminated beams that stood in the place of the Twin Towers during the winter and spring of 2002.

25th Hour (on the most basic plot level) is about Monty Brogan's last day of freedom before he will begin a long jail term for selling drugs. The movie invites us to play with all kinds of theoretically triumphant parallelism – the redemption of the dog is the redemption of Monty is the redemption of New York is the simplest and most seductive equation – all of which collapses under the weight of Monty's ultimate reality. If Monty's adoption of the bloody Doyle allows us a few moments of "we're down but not out" pleasure, Lee quickly pulls the rug out. Soon after the title sequence Monty, out for a walk with Doyle, meets another dog, this one named Dante. It is hell that Monty now lives in.

Here is where Spike Lee, unlike so many of his American peers in the culture-making business, embraces the complexity of post-9/11 grief and mourning. No one is more clear than Monty that he is, or will soon be, fucked: a major subplot of the movie has to do with Monty's deep fear that his relative youth and good looks will make him a prime target for being raped in prison, and his desire to have his best friend Francis make him "ugly" before he goes off to prison the next day. The entire movie, as the *Washington Post*'s Ann Hornaday (2003) has put it, deals with "Monty's shame and self-loathing" and the "existential dilemma of a man whose once bright future is now a bleak smudge in his mind" in a city "knocked back on its heels, in deep mourning and shock."

The film is drenched in 9/11 imagery and rhetoric. From its title to its entire "after the fall" trajectory and tone, *25th Hour* makes it clear that, as novelist Don DeLillo (2007) has written in *The Falling Man*, "These are the days after" (138). Preparing for the last party with Monty, his two best friends, Francis and Jake, meet in Francis's downtown apartment, which overlooks Ground Zero. After some mordant banter about Francis's location, including Jake's nervous report of a recent *New York Times* article on the continuing bad air quality downtown (Francis: "Oh yeah? I read the *Post*"), their talk turns to Monty's future. Jake, the trust-fund, liberal Jewish private-school teacher, spins a fantasy about Monty's potential for a happy post-prison life. With steely-eyed intensity, Francis, the up-from-the-working-class Irish bond trader, sets Jake straight: "It's over after tonight." With this, the camera turns from the close shot of Jake and Francis and takes us out Francis's window – to a ghostly vision of a nighttime work crew at Ground Zero who seem to be arrayed in the form of a question mark.

The two pivotal scenes in the movie involve Monty's dad, a former firefighter who seems to have left the FDNY because of his alcoholism.

Now in recovery (at least for the moment), the sober James Brogan owns a bar in the Bronx that is, in typical post-9/11 fashion, festooned with firefighter photos and regalia. During a last supper with his father, Monty excuses himself to go to the bathroom, where he proceeds to stare into the mirror and lay a curse on New York. Reviving and revising a scene from his earlier film *Do the Right Thing* (1989) and the famous mirror scene of Martin Scorcese's *Taxi Driver* (1976), about a would-be assassin, Lee has Monty Brogan launch his own attack on New York: from the gay men of the Village, to the Italians of Bensonhurst, from Jewish diamond merchants to African American basketball players, from Wall Street cowboys like his buddy Francis, to his own father ("with his endless grief"), Monty says "Fuck you" to each in turn, and finally to "this whole city." But, in a politically charged climax to this incendiary scene, Lee again pulls the rug out. With a final mirror shot, the director has Monty finally say "Fuck you" to himself – with an admission that all of his problems are ultimately a product of his own bad actions. With this, Lee opens up his film into the realm of political allegory: as rapper Mr. Lif put it in his song "Home of the Brave" (2002), "they killed us because we've been killing them for years."

The dark vision dominates *25ᵗʰ Hour* but Lee does allow for a powerful utopian counternarrative, one that grants Monty's father a degree of dignity and parental power that he has lacked up until this point. Driving Monty to prison, James Brogan begins to tell Monty what is essentially a fantasy about what his future could be. "Give me the word," Monty's dad says, and he will get off the Henry Hudson Parkway, go over the George Washington Bridge, and head west with Monty. Digging deep into American mythologies about the West as a place of rebirth and reinvention, James Brogan offers a gift to Monty, a fairytale about his new life in a little desert town – where he will rename himself James after his dad, reunite with his New York girlfriend Naturelle Rivera, and raise a passel of beautiful brown children. "You live your life," James Brogan tells Monty, "the way it should have been."

James Brogan's story is incredibly powerful: I always have some students who leave viewings of *25ᵗʰ Hour* with the feeling that this all "could" really have happened in the movie. After spinning out this wonderful fantasy, though – a story virtually as old as white settlement on the American continent – Lee returns us to the car, where Monty is still Monty, weak and bruised from the beating he finally got Francis to lay on him the night before, on his way to jail. Monty is not James Fenimore

Cooper's Natty Bumppo, still on the hunt for a "trackless" forest, nor is he Huck Finn "lighting out for the territory." He is much more like the doomed Montgomery Clift for whom he was named ("poor bastard," his father remembers). Over the closing credits, instead of the towers of light again, we get Bruce Springsteen's dark song "The Fuse" from *The Rising*, Springsteen's own broadstroke attempt to construct a musical sampler of American responses to 9/11. With its opening image of a flag coming down at the courthouse through the remainder of the song's desperate and seemingly doomed search for physical human connection, "The Fuse" acts as punctuation on Spike Lee's anti-triumphalist rendering of New York realities after 9/11.

On some level, giving Springsteen's song this prominent place is a simple and elegant act of cross-marketing. While this book is concerned with investigating all manner of expressions, including street-level (or personal computer level) utterances and amateur photographs, it would be foolish to ignore the fact that by now there are well-established "stars of 9/11": Springsteen is one, for sure, as are country singers Toby Keith and the Dixie Chicks, film directors Steven Spielberg and Clint Eastwood (for his World War II exacta, *Flags of Our Fathers*, and *Letters from Iwo Jima*), actor Adam Sandler (for *Reign Over Me*, *I Now Pronounce You Chuck & Larry*, and *You Don't Mess with the Zohan*), and novelist Don DeLillo. By the time Lee's movie hit theaters Springsteen was already established as a major player on the 9/11 cultural scene – a 9/11 brand, in a sense. (Springsteen's 9/11 bona fides were established by his appearance at the start of the *Tribute to Heroes* telethon, and were deepened with the release of *The Rising* in 2002; they have remained more or less intact except for a brief moment in 2006 when he was rumored to have left Patti Scialfa, his wife and bandmate, for a 9/11 widow.)

25th Hour is framed by a haunting score composed by jazz artist Terence Blanchard and, unlike most Spike Lee movies, features very little music in the action of the film itself (outside of one important nightclub scene that features a remix of Grandmaster Flash's anti-cocaine song "White Lines"). "The Fuse," then, offers a hint – if we need it – that Lee wants his movie taken with Springsteen's work as a summarizing effort, an attempt to say "this is how we live and feel now." On an artistic plane this may fall a little flat; more than once Lee has ended a movie with a direct-address declaration that undercuts the complexity of what has come before. In *25th Hour* the appearance of Springsteen's song acts as a final reminder, and certainly a gratuitous one, that 9/11 is the explanation for the feelings of fragmentation and loss that anchor the movie. 9/11 is the 24th hour implied by the title: the 25th hour is what comes after, which Lee's film tells us looks a lot like prison. While it would be nice to understand the "afterwards" hinted at by *25th Hour* as a commentary on the surveillance culture that has been put in place as an official governmental response, Lee's conclusions are much more speculative and diffuse.

As the "answer to every question now," ritualized invocations of 9/11 sometimes make it seem as if the already narrowcast, corporatized possibilities of American cultural life have come under the control of a wizard with obsessive-compulsive disorder. 9/11 as a sort of magical-thinking response has shaped every imaginable cultural script from the centralized popular culture locales of Hollywood, Nashville, and New York City itself – to the amateur 9/11 animations of the internet (usually simple Flash productions). Animated computer games offer us one of the fullest glimpses into how quickly a certain kind of cultural unanimity – about Muslims, masculinity, and violence, for instance – developed in the wake of the 9/11 attacks. Here we find, among hundreds, if not thousands, of titles, "Osamagatchi," a play on the popular Tamagotchi handheld electronic "pets," a game that allows players to "maim and brutalize" their very own Osama character. Or "Cokehead 2," which encourages players to "fill Osama with enough cocaine to withstand nuclear holocaust." Web creations were preceded by what we might call pieces of "occasional art" found in New York city: fliers, as Leti Volpp (2003) has described, that depict Osama bin Laden being sodomized by the World Trade Center, with a caption that reads "You like skyscrapers, bitch?" (154).

Such hysterical artifacts were joined in the fall of 2001 by all manner of bumper stickers, t-shirts, clip art, and other elements of what Daniel Harris (2002), with a distressing level of elitist scorn, calls "the rhetoric of kitsch" (204). Harris dislikes the content of much of what he found as he surveyed the immediate post-9/11 terrain of American expressive life – the "car window decals ... featuring a lugubrious poodle with a glistening tear as large as a gum drop rolling mournfully down its cheek" along with "the overkill of ribbons and commemorative quilts, haloed seraphim perched on top of the burning towers and teddy bears in firefighter helmets waving flags" (203).

There are good reasons to be put off by what Harris refers to as the "emotional pornography" (214) of public displays of 9/11 mourning and community building, especially in the more market-driven and jingoistic articulations. Harris's dismay over the "morbid conviviality" of internet message boards in the immediate aftermath of the attacks is another matter entirely (218): you would think the man had never been to a wake or post-funeral gathering where food and drink are served and laughter is abundant. But it is the messenger that Harris wants to kill, and here he gives us good access to what might be the central fact of post-9/11 cultural life in the United States. Harris is put off above all by the internet and by what we have, with the development and popularity of wikis, blogs, YouTube, Facebook, MySpace, tagging, and so on, learned to call "Web 2.0." This tapestry of user-generated content has, to reduce the matter considerably, changed the internet from predominantly a one-way street into a very much more complicated weave of highways, side streets, and dead ends. In the domain of Web 2.0, "content provider" may still mean a record company or film studio, but it may just as well mean your old grampa or little sister.

More than one observer has noted that the "birth of the blog" coincided with 9/11. As one account summarizes, as "phone networks and big news struggled to cope with heavy traffic, many survivors and spectators turned to online journals to share feelings, get information or detail their whereabouts. It was raw, emotional and new – and many commentators now remember it as a key moment in the birth of the blog" (Andrews, 2006). Up until this moment, easy to use blog services were hard to find, and blogging was, according to Matthew Yeomans, "still very much the geek toy of the Slashdot set" (Andrews, 2006). Blogs became, in the aftermath of 9/11, a kind of wireless wire service, an undefined, anarchic first-responder news and opinion service. While the archaeology of Web 2.0 is outside of my concern here, and the relationship of 9/11 and 2.0 will no doubt remain cloudy for some time, a consensus has developed that the events of 9/11 contributed to the rapid development of Web 2.0 in the early twenty-first century.

Harris was writing just a bit too soon to see this all and no doubt all of us who dare to write about 9/11 need to be generous with each other as we together construct our history of the present. That said, there is something unseemly (and I think just plain wrong) about Harris's wholesale attack on these decentralized and communal 9/11 expressions as constituting at once an aesthetic of "jumble" and "the prefab" that ultimately operates as a kind of intellectual clip art (217). "As an experiment in democracy," he concludes, "the internet has failed." In Harris's reckoning the internet is the "grave of free speech" and only gives its users "freedom to repeat" (217).

The first and probably most obvious response to Harris's misguided attack on 9/11 expressive culture is to say "so what's wrong with repetition?" In literary criticism, film history, theater studies, musicology, and so on, scholars write often of "generic conventions," the endlessly repeated artistic strategies that define a form. It is a given for the most astute commentators on American popular and vernacular culture that repetition is more or less a neutral fact of artistic creation. What is more important to figure out is how repetition (or, what Amiri Baraka called years ago in reference to African American music, "the changing same") makes meaning.

Perhaps more important to get a handle on is how Harris's screed forces us to "embrace the chaos" (to borrow the title of a record released on September 11, 2001, by the West Coast rap/salsa group Ozomatli) of American expressive practices of the past five years or so. The everyday realities of Web 2.0 mean that the usual gatekeeping mechanisms that have defined American cultural life since World War II were being surpassed by a less organized and, at times, anarchic set of possibilities. Harris's critique reeks of high culture condescension of a type that we simply cannot afford if we want to understand the contours of American cultural life since the fall of 2001. While my own focus in this book will turn, at times, to the works of "high" literary artists and while it is certainly true that some of these writers have influence on how we think, feel, and act about 9/11, it would be impossible to get a true picture of how 9/11 has come to serve as an "answer to every question now" without looking at all the places it is appearing as an answer.

The 9/11 art under discussion here is, by and large, an anti-monumental art. This is not to say that we have no rich, complex, and challenging individual works created in response to 9/11: *"V" for Vendetta* and *25th Hour* are only two of many examples that I want to explore in these pages that manage to "use" the answer of 9/11 to open up all manner of fascinating inquiries. What I mean, simply, is that the most important 9/11 culture(s) might not be found in a freedom tower, an album by Bruce Springsteen or in a novel by John Updike (or any of the other big boys). The Web 2.0 givens that guide this book include that 9/11 art is being created daily, is revised constantly ("remix" or "mashup" might be the more up-to-date words), and reaches its audiences through myriad channels of image and information. Most important here, I think, is that we remain open to the possibility that the most powerful individual artistic endeavors in our 9/11 culture might gain their deepest resonances not in the more traditional high art frameworks (i.e. modernist architecture, the thematically unified musical composition, or the "big issue" novel) but in a more humble register and as part of the kind of shared effort that Web 2.0 exemplifies.

And clip art, after all, can be a force of good. In his introduction to David Rees's (2002) comic strip collection *Get Your War On* (the title itself a "repetition" that usefully revises "Get your freak on," "Get your game on," and so on), novelist Colson Whitehead reminds us that Rees's "master stroke," after all, in creating his web comic, was in deciding to represent his characters and settings only through manipulations of found clip art (iv). The immediacy, desperation, and hilarity of *Get Your War On* rely perhaps above all on the incendiary and innovative (and crude) language that fills its panels. But for readers of the strip – first on the web and then later in the book collection – the launching and definitive visual element is the appearance of clip art figures. These miserable and seemingly interchangeable office workers are *Dilbert*'s pissed off and alcoholic cousins; they are the heirs to an important subgenre of contemporary American film and television that focuses on the alienating challenges and indignities of white- and pink-collar office life. The visual repetition so anathema to Daniel Harris is put to sharp political use (see Figure 2), as Rees's characters blandly (and at times bizarrely) comment on the increasingly surrealistic nature of American political discourse after 9/11.

In this strip Rees uses not only his standard clip art repetitions, but also adds in some key hip hop phrases ("throw your hands in the air," "wave 'em like you just don't care!") to remind us that repetition is functional. In actual hip hop performance these phrases would likely appear in call-and-response pump-up-the-crowd contexts; borrowing them, repeating them, putting them in the mouths of his clip art clones, Rees makes us

Figure 2   David Rees transforms clip art into political art. Source: "Get Your War On," © 2008 by David Rees. Used with permission.

feel for these "representative citizens" – as Whitehead calls them – who "re-enact the same poses again and again, mouth the same platitudes and speculations over and over, without progress or relief" (iv).

To get a handle on 9/11 arts, in any useful fashion, means we have to approach it all as an economy of scale. Rachel Rubin (2003) has written of the challenges facing the scholar studying Asian American cyberzines, noting that "because of the sheer volume of zines, it's hard to make a case for the importance of any particular one; rather, analysts must read a large enough number of them to get a sense of general currents." The idiom of 9/11 is so vast and various that it would be foolish to operate with any pretense of comprehensiveness. There are certainly signal works of compelling artistic vision that will endure outside of the 9/11 context. Just as important as it is to make sense of these notable achievements, so too must we consider the occasional, the ephemeral, and the partial cultural expressions – be they rumors, jokes, confessions, or snapshots – that collectively form that terrain we call post-9/11. The sheer volume of digital archives, oral histories, photo collections, web comics, Flash animations, novels, and so on should serve as a check on anyone who, at this early date, aims for general pronouncements, taxonomies of creation, or logically unfolding chronologies. Hence my desire to introduce 9/11 culture through the series of sketches that follow – sketches that make no claim to completeness even within their own borders and certainly no claim to presenting a total vision when taken together. *Under Construction* is not just part of my title, but a motto, too.

And of course when I write "9/11 art" or "9/11 expression," it will almost always be clear from my contexts that I am really talking about work that journalist Mark Lawson (2002) says should be "date-stamped September 12." As Lawson notes, correctly I think, "Art directly about 9/11 is rarely going to work. Almost any piece will have too little tension and too much sentimentality to be anything other than a memorial ser-vice posing as art." The works I will be most concerned with here were made (usually) "in the shadow of events, rather than the glare."

The notion that 9/11 is the answer to every question now is another way of saying that this tragedy makes us confront what it means to live in an "after" time and to consider how every time we engage with the public sphere it is a post-9/11 world we meet. One of the most fascinating examples of living in this after time is the desire to "read" two major music releases of September 11, 2001, as themselves elements of 9/11 culture: Bob Dylan's *Love and Theft* and Jay-Z's *The Blueprint* (both titles borrowed, one from a book on blackface minstrelsy, one from an earlier hip hop album). Of course, neither record can be "logically" understood to be 9/11 art, any more than can any of the other hundreds of works released that day (Tuesday is the standard day for new music releases, just as Friday is when new movies hit the screen). But with both *Love and Theft* and *The Blueprint* we find two major New York critics making the case for taking these works as the first important pieces of 9/11 art. These two critics, Greg Tate (2001) and Armond White (2002), are operating within (and against) the dominant rhetoric of 9/11, a rhetoric that emphasizes heroism, selflessness, and national purpose. This instant jingoistic turn was represented quickly and fully by President George W. Bush, who described the passengers on United 93 thusly: "they said a prayer" and "drove the plane into the ground to serve something greater than themselves." (Critic J. Hoberman [2006] notes that this description more closely describes the terrorists than the passengers). In any case, when it came to reviewing Dylan's September 11 record a few weeks after its release Tate called attention to the "many prescient, portentous lyrics" unfolding over the course of *Love and Theft*, and then wondered, in an oft-quoted line, "What did Dylan know and when did he know it?" Citing numerous lines from *Love and Theft* that are, frankly, no more or less prescient and/or portentous than those on any other of Dylan's albums, Tate is not trying to offer a literal argument, but is launching an important analytical framework. Whatever Dylan meant by these songs up until midnight on September 10, and however we might have heard them up until that moment, the songs changed the minute the record dropped and the planes hit.

Armond White (2002) makes similar, wonderfully inflated claims for Jay-Z's *Blueprint*. First, White establishes that Jay-Z serves as a "citizen" as opposed to a "civilian." This means, he explains, that Jay-Z is a person "willing to fight for his ... people, country, planet" and in doing so "defines hiphop's highest ideas of how an artist earns privilege and esteem in the midst of the confusion most American's feel post-Sept. 11." White gives special mention to the song "Jigga That N*****" in which Jay-Z raps "if y'all go to war for me/I go to war wit' y'all," taking it as an unfashionable but necessary call for a new kind of patriotism. This is a willful but consequential misreading: of course, as White himself admits, there is "no way Jay-Z could have planned *The Blueprint* as a response to 9/11." Even so, like Greg Tate, Armond White is pointing to how the very fact of 9/11 makes it impossible to live with a critical stance that pretends to be outside of those attacks and the new world they created. White finishes with Jay-Z by writing simply "it stands up beautifully in the aftermath because he has found a way to make art out of America's complexity."

What Tate and White are both most intent on establishing is that we must come to grips with what it means to exist in the "aftermath." A guiding principle of this book is that we all are currently looking through a glass, darkly – and that glass, as the language of the King James Bible makes clear, is a faulty mirror, not a window. Each time we take 9/11 as the answer to a major cultural question, we are admitting that it has the most awesome reflecting power. However imperfectly our image comes back to us in this glass, the most important thing that is happening each time we invoke 9/11 as an answer to our question is that we are admitting that 9/11 is too high to get over, too wide to get around.

"Post-9/11" indexes a profound rupture in time and space. It is clear that the events of 9/11 shape not only our understanding of nearly every-thing in the political and cultural lives of Americans since that date, but that those events also shape our understanding of much of what came before. I mean this not only (or mostly) in the sense of those inquiries that all seem to be titled "The Road to 9/11," earnest and necessary investiga-tions into how the attacks themselves could possibly have happened. What I am more concerned with is how that day has also changed, at least for now, how we understand the cultural life of the United States in the years leading up to 9/11. There is an "Amazing Grace" quality to much of what I am thinking of here: once we were blind and now we see. Once we loved irony and took refuge in that distancing strategy; now we are earnest and authentic. Once we fragmented into our various political and social identities; now we stand united. Once we loved movies where tall buildings exploded or burned to the ground. Now we don't like those so much. And then again, *now* we do.

Plenty of people are exhibiting 9/11 fatigue, not surprisingly. Under the headline "9/11 is Over" *New York Times* columnist Thomas Friedman made a plea in the fall of 2007 to move beyond 9/11, especially when it comes to evaluating presidential candidates. In glossing a satirical piece in *The Onion* that joked about Rudy Giuliani announcing his run for "president of 9/11," Friedman concludes – with a strange bit of national-istic fervor – that the United States is not "about 9/11": "Al Qaeda is about 9/11. We are about 9/12, we are about the Fourth of July ..." But simply wishing that the United States is not "about 9/11" cannot make it so.

While the web-based and surprisingly influential activist group might call itself MoveOn, this does not guarantee that most people have or even want to.

There are some wispy indications in the cultural sphere that the historical period we have been calling post-9/11 might have an expiration date, but it is important not to look for the usual sorts of historical closure prematurely. In her book *Legacy of Conquest*, Western historian Patricia Nelson Limerick (1987) grapples with a question that has bedeviled American historians for over a century: how do we know when westward expansion really ended (i.e. "when did the frontier close")? After surveying the dominant explanations that have been offered over the years, Limerick offers up her own sensible notion: the frontier was closed when tourism about the West became a major force in the states that had previously been understood as frontier areas. It will not, of course, be tourism that marks the end of the post-9/11 era, of course, because we have plenty of evidence that tourism to "9/11" began as the attacks were still in progress; there is a picture in *The September 11 Photo Project* collection, in fact, of tourists on a sightseeing bus taking pictures of the World Trade Center site just after the attacks. But Limerick's paradigm is useful because it tells us something about that moment when a certain distance from the primary historical activity in question has been achieved.

The boys-telling-a-nasty-joke-to-each-other film *The Aristocrats* offers an interesting vision of how post-9/11 might end. In this supremely narcissistic film (countless comedians take their turn one-upping each other in telling their version of an old dirty joke) the filmmakers give us a glimpse of manic comic Gilbert Gottfried doing a routine at a Friar's Club roast of Hugh Hefner on September 29, 2001. The film has built to this moment, letting us know that after all the renderings of rape, incest, pedophilia, and the most amazing exchanges of bodily fluid, this is going to be the truly transgressive moment. Director Paul Provenza drapes an almost mythological aura around this performance and lets us finally see Gottfried. In his moment, what Gottfried does is tell a joke whose punchline is that he has to leave the show early to "catch a plane to L.A." Unfortunately, he recounts, he could not get a direct flight and his plane will have to stop at the Empire State Building. The joke is met with boos and shouts of "too soon"; Gottfried proceeds to tell what might be the filthiest version of the "aristocrats" joke yet shown in the movie. (Of course nobody in the film seems worried about whether it is too soon to be holding a celebration of *Playboy* founder Hugh Hefner ... Recall too that the Friar's Club roast is a notoriously raw affair – in 1993 it was host to Ted Danson appearing in blackface.)

Part of the burden of this book is to figure out just what post-9/11 means. By 2005, when *The Aristocrats* was released, the filmmakers were clearly no longer worried about breaking any post-9/11 rules. In an animated sequence, the boys from television's *South Park* listen to Cartman tell a version of the joke, with the requisite feces, semen, and intrauterine abuse. But then Cartman, in the voice of the father of the entertaining family at the heart of the joke, announces "Now for our impersonation of the victims of 9/11," which is followed by Cartman describing the family, covered in "shit, piss, and cum" and screaming in faux-hysteria "the building's coming down." While numerous film critics, bloggers, and the like commented on Gottfried's supposedly transgressive act of 2001, there is no indication that anyone thought it was too soon in 2005 to depict the family featured in the filthy *Aristocrats'* joke as finding their ultimate degradation as victims of 9/11. This is, to be sure, a modest moment in the cultural history of post-9/11 that I am interested in, but a telling one: with its usual take-no-prisoners-and-offend-all-constituencies approach, this *South Park* moment works to remove the aura of sanctification created by the "missing" posters that formed, as Pete Hamill has written, "an immense collage" of the city (Goodman and Fahnestock, 2002: 28), the *America: A Tribute to Heroes* telethon, and the almost universally loved *New York Times* "Portraits of Grief."

Joining the *South Park* eruption in *The Aristocrats* was a seemingly innocuous song released that same year by the rock group Bon Jovi, and then almost immediately reissued by Jon Bon Jovi and country singer Jennifer Nettles, called "Who Says You Can't Go Home." Into a song that gleefully strings together as many lyrical (and musical) pop music clichés as can fit into its rhythmic structure, Bon Jovi offers the line "I hijacked a rainbow and crashed into a pot of gold." The song went to number one on the country charts; fans were clearly far enough from the trauma of 9/11 to either not notice or not mind that this key line uses the all-too-familiar image of hijack-and-crash in the service of a generic and ephemeral narrative of coming home. It is, if I can put what might be too fine a point on the matter, a *post*-post-9/11 song. On some level it assumes that a certain resonance will be achieved by operating out of the 9/11 playbook, while also demonstrating a confidence that using 9/11 as an answer can now safely be "repurposed" for non-9/11 cultural work – base scatology in *The Aristocrats*, bland sentimentality here.

More daring yet is the opening credit sequence for the television series *Mad Men*, which debuted in the fall of 2007. This cable show, about the American advertising business in the 1960s, begins each week with an animated representation of a suited office worker tumbling down the front of the skyscraper he has been working in. While the reference to the deaths of World Trade Center workers on 9/11 (and 1929 stock market crash jumpers) could not be more clear, the show and its credits were met with near-universal acclaim. This credit sequence itself has received a great deal of positive comment, mostly for how it captures some important elements of the graphic arts of the 1960s and how it invokes a couple of Alfred Hitchcock movies. But no one seems much bothered by the fact that this plummeting ad man is a double of the "falling man" of 9/11 (more on that image in Chapter 4); by the fall of 2007, what might have seemed like an edgy provocation a few years earlier now just seemed clever. The rhetoric of Rudolph Giuliani's run for the Republican nomination for president of the United States that same fall makes it clear that we have not fully transitioned into a post-post-9/11 time. But insofar as 9/11 remains the "answer to every question now" it is no longer completely clear what the answer *means*.

Another way of saying that, of course, is that rather than providing a readymade answer, 9/11 is morphing, profitably, into a generative question. Two short story writers, Sherman Alexie and Judy Budnitz, have proposed this in full and breathtaking ways. In her 2005 story "Preparedness," Budnitz imagines a lockdown America, in which the president attempts to use the threat of apocalypse as a tool of social control. On "the most beautiful day anyone could remember" the president organizes a crisis drill, during which people are supposed to go to protective shelters. But the people do not listen: acting as if, indeed, "the end had come," the people reach out to each other – they touch, make love ("in phone booths, on sofas, on the hoods of cars, up against trees and walls"), and sing ("tunelessly, abrasively, whole-heartedly"). Apparently, "more than anything else," singing "was one thing that people secretly longed to do but were normally afraid to" (251–3). Here, in allegorical fashion, Budnitz imagines that the apocalyptic crisis, rather than forcing the American public into compulsory and ritualized behaviors, actually functions as liberation – the keys to the kingdom of creativity. Mapping Web 2.0 interactivity onto the "real-world" of city streets, Budnitz encourages her readers to imagine the American people united in life-affirming responses to the potential trauma of invasion and the ongoing injuries of government surveillance.

Imagining 9/11 as an open question rather than as a readymade answer is taken to an even more extreme level in Sherman Alexie's 2003 short story "Can I Get a Witness?" The story borrows an African American church refrain for its title as a simple and profound way of asking "Does ANY body agree with me?" Alexie sets his story in the Pacific Northwest in the aftermath of an attack that leaves its main character, an unnamed Native American woman, dazed and wandering the streets of Seattle. She is taken care of by an emotionally distant video-game designer who admits to her that just before 9/11 he was working on a "first-person shooter" game that allows players to attack a mall, an Ivy League college or the World Trade Center. In a disturbing rant, the injured woman suggests to her caretaker that she has thought hard about the 9/11 attacks and the aura of innocence that surrounds its victims: "You know," she says, "I don't think everybody who died in the towers was innocent." She goes on to note that the "towers were filled with bankers and stockbrokers and lawyers. How honest do you think they were?" (89).

As shocking as this is, Alexie was certainly not the first to have reservations about the growing secular religion of total American innocence. Cultural geographer David Harvey (2002), in an essay published a year before Alexie's story saw print, argued that the *New York Times* "Portraits of Grief" were serving as an important ideological tool, with their "local emphasis upon loss and grief" that drew from and supported "the idea of innocence." The overall effect of these obituaries, according to Harvey, made it "impossible to raise a critical voice as to what role bond traders and others" in the towers "might have had in the creation and perpetuation of social inequality" (59). Prosecuting a much more particular gripe, cultural critic Marshall Berman (2002) objected to the "lives of the saints" approach of the "Portraits," admitting that he felt he "would throw up" if he "had to hear about one more Little League coach. (Didn't they know how many of those parent coaches are pure poison?)" (6).

Sherman Alexie takes the protest much further than Harvey or Berman, mostly by using the relative freedom of the fictional form to personalize the challenge to the widely held belief in shared innocence. His main character operates from a proposition that inspires much of what will follow in this book simply by suggesting to her befuddled companion that maybe September 11 "means things that nobody has thought of yet" (89). With this very basic insight (which turns 9/11 from an answer to every question into a question with countless answers), Alexie's "madwoman" – who, like so many fictional madwomen, has important truths to tell – overturns the applecart of 9/11 memorialization.

Alexie's bleak fictional tale has at least one real-world echo: a contributor to *Salon.com's* "Forbidden Thoughts" feature that ran approximately a year after 9/11. This "Name Withheld" writer remembers: "My father was one of those people who was supposed to be in the city that day but didn't go in that morning due to a freak coincidence." With breathtaking abruptness, the next line of this narrative is "I hate him." The writer goes on to admit, "I wish he'd died in the attacks, because then memorializing him would have been easy. I wouldn't have ever had to hate him again because he would have been one of the people lost in 9/11. As we waited to get in touch with him, I prayed we'd never find him. No one knows this" (Cave, 2002). Joined with Alexie's literary evocation of "improper" 9/11 thoughts, this *Salon* writer helps us begin to see that much of what we will have to confront as 9/11 culture operates well outside of the obligatory documentary and quasi-documentary offerings that have at times dominated 9/11 discourse (think of the near-universal praise for the rather foursquare film *United 93*), but which have not been able to completely corner the market on 9/11 expression.

And it is a market, of course. My students at Babson College in Massachusetts are business students, bright and savvy, but even they resist the notion that the week after 9/11 there must have been countless Americans employed in the entertainment and publishing industries who worked hard to start thinking about how they (or their clients) were to access the new realities of "post-9/11." Author Ken Kalfus has recounted fielding calls from editors in the first week after 9/11 who were saying, "Can you write something about this?" (Giese, 2006). In viewing *America: A Tribute to Heroes*, a celebrity telethon that aired about a week and a half after the attacks, it is at times difficult to move students beyond the old "my Uncle has a barn, let's put on a show" notion of spontaneous performance that *Tribute* is selling. Even with the motley collection of folks in the phone bank ("Look, it's Goldie Hawn. And Cuba Gooding, Jr. Oh, there's Jack Nicholson"), even with the seemingly obvious demographic slant of the musical acts (in the direction of baby boomers with the most ready cash), and the incredibly obvious moments of product tie-in (Will Smith appearing with Muhammad Ali as a speaker just a few months before Smith's *Ali* movie would hit the screen), there is a powerful claim that would influence much post-9/11 art in the telethon that instructs audiences to receive it as natural, authentic, heartfelt, and without any motive outside of the eulogistic and patriotic.

Even if we resist the gruesome vision of Alexie's short story, it is crucial for us to study not only all the ways that 9/11 has become the answer to every question now, but also how it has begun to function as a generative and beguiling question. Keeping our eyes on 9/11 questions and answers allows for an inquiry that makes no claims to the encyclopedic but that does require a wide net and a careful eye. Taking this broad approach will allow all of us, I hope, to find 9/11 culture on our movie, television, and computer screens, in our books and blogs, on our t-shirts and cars, and in our daily speech. That daily speech, in the form of 9/11 rumors, forms the basis of the first investigation here, a primer on how 9/11 gave rise to stories that we told each other – mostly for the pleasure of the telling and the community-building that such telling enables.

CH/1
Rumors

In an essay about 9/11, American novelist Don DeLillo explained in 2001 that opposing the dominant narrative that had been created in the past months, the coercive, "official" language that had been teaching us how to think, feel, and even speak, there was also an emergent "counternarrative, a shadow history of false memories and imagined loss." Not stopping there, DeLillo went on to note that the most important vehicle for counternarrative is the internet, "shaped in part by rumor, fantasy and mystical reverberation." Nobody needs me to uncover the elements of the "official version" that formed the first wave of the American cultural responses to 9/11. For those of us living in the United States, even outside of New York City, these constituents of the "official version" were as immediate as the music and graphics accompanying major network and cable news reports, each of which traveled as a very particular brand – hooked with theme music, font choices, and a snappy motto ("America Under Attack" belonged to CNN). Before long these corporate-sponsored 9/11 tags were to be joined by presidential and mayoral speeches (and other moments of pontification), mainsteam media punditry, print media imagery, and editorializing.

Joining, and at times resisting, these powerful and efficient attempts to erect a virtual tower of rhetoric to replace the actual ones that had been knocked down, was a disorganized and yet forceful array of claims that held that somehow the "official version" was either incomplete, a partial cover-up, or a purposeful lie. There are too many rumors that circulated in the months immediately following 9/11 to do anything like a complete inventory; nor would such a listing be particularly useful for our purposes here. Pioneering work on this front has been done by Snopes.com and other online urban legend websites and they offer a great glimpse into U.S.-based rumors. What I want to offer here is a brisk run-through of three major forms of rumor that flourished in the post-9/11 era. First came what folklorists call "wedge-driving" rumors – bits of fantasy that are meant to separate out a particular group for punishment, be it physical abuse, social ostracism, or cultural boycott. The second type of rumor I want to investigate is the corporate-sponsored rumor. The most famous of these is the Clear Channel rumor that developed in the weeks after the 9/11 attacks, and whose basic form held that some management-level person at Clear Channel had created a list of songs that were not to be played (i.e. they were to be censored) out of sensitivity to listeners in the painful days after the attacks. The Clear Channel story is not usually treated as a rumor, but I want to (re)introduce it here as another species of rumor – a corporate strategy to control consciousness (and product) in the wake of the attacks.

Finally, I will turn to the whole set of rumors that would, over time, congeal into what we now refer to as the "9/11 truth" movement. Many of these rumors are rooted in the simple doubt (or profound disbelief) that *this* could have happened *here*. A number of novels written in the wake of 9/11, most notably Philip Roth's *The Plot Against America* (2004), took this cultural impulse and mapped it onto an earlier histori- cal era, in this case the time of World War II. Taking off from the widely held "common sense" that the American aviation hero Charles Lindbergh was a Nazi sympathizer, Roth develops an entire fiction around the notion that the future of the United States would have been materially changed had Lindbergh been elected president in the 1940 election.

It is important to study the content of 9/11 rumors: truth-hunting in rumors has its place, to be sure, and the good folks at Snopes.com have become a major cultural force by debunking the content of the most egre- gious rumors that have circulated in recent years. Before the internet age, scholars in many fields admired the popularizing work of Jan Harold Brunvand published in books such as *The Choking Doberman* and *The Vanishing Hitchhiker*; Brunvand again and again demonstrated that what I'm calling "rumors" and what he convincingly introduced as "urban legends" into the cultural lexicon have real force, reveal major truths about power relations at a given moment, and embed important informa- tion about contemporary anxieties, desires, and relationships.

The content of this or that rumor is rarely the whole story. In fact, what we might think of as the "job" of a rumor is not its content, but rather its trajectory. What matters most is who the rumor travels from and to, and how in making its journeys it accomplishes some important cultural work that may not be done by any other means. In her 2002 book *Fast Girls*, for instance, journalist Emily White studies the webs of communication supporting the myth of the "high school slut." White is able to demonstrate that early physical development does seem a dire indicator of future persecution by the "slut" rumor. But more significant in the findings of *Fast Girls* is how dedicated so many high school boys, and some girls, are to the "myth" of the slut. Telling the slut rumor in all its variants ("the whole football team," etc.) forms a primary role in clique development, White finds, and serves a very important disciplining function of any high school girl who might dare to step out of the preset molds that are meant to determine her social positioning. The obsessive telling, more than its particular content, is what is most functional here. Likewise with the rumors that Patricia Turner tracks in her book *I Heard It Through the Grapevine* (1993), which explore the bonding function of rumors that have traveled around various African American communities.

* * *

The "wedge-driving" rumors that developed in the immediate wake of the 9/11 attacks were virtually all fairly predictable. Scholar Janet Langlois (2005) has carefully tracked one of these rumors, which has been named "Celebrating Arabs." Langlois studied Arabs at a Middle Eastern restaurant in the Detroit, Michigan area, where they represent a large minority. These Arabs allegedly cheered the 9/11 attacks. In fine Brunvandian fashion, Langlois finds evidence of this rumor first at one remove; in other words, like Brunvand, with his wonderful FOAF acronym that he often uses (for "Friend of a Friend"), Langlois can only get as close to the source of this rumor as a "My son-in-law" email. This rumor has cousins on the West Coast, where a driver for Budweiser alleges to have seen "Arabs" in a store near Bakersfield cheering the Twin Tower deaths. To much acclaim, this spectral driver pledges at that moment that this store – these people – will no longer be drinking his good Budweiser beer. On the East Coast, the location is a Dunkin' Donuts in Cedar Grove, New Jersey, where its employees were similarly seen to be applauding the attacks. Working the same vein was the rumor/not a rumor about CNN supposedly showing "old" footage of Palestinian children dancing in response to the attacks. In classic "lore cycle" fashion (to borrow a phrase from W. T. Lhamon [2000]) this rumor was ultimately debunked – it seems the footage was fresh – but not before an auxiliary rumor developed suggesting that the children only danced after Israeli soldiers came by and gave them candy in exchange for dancing.

Even *Time* magazine, within a few weeks of the attacks, recognized that these "dancing Palestinians" and "celebrating Arabs" stories seemed at heart to be important "wedge-driving" rumors: *Time*'s writer, summarizing generations of complex work done by folklorists, anthropologists, and other scholars, saw these wedge-driving rumors as one of three major categories in play – along with wish-fulfillment rumors and "bogey" (or fear-mongering) rumors (Tyrangiel, 2001). What is perhaps most interesting about wedge-driving rumors, at least in the context of 9/11, is that more than simply creating a social mechanism for identifying a "them" who exists outside the circle of proper American citizenship, they simultaneously work as a bonding device for groups that may not otherwise have very powerful social glue keeping them together.

To put a finer point on this: in the "celebrating Arabs" of Detroit outbreak, it seems clear from the research of Janet Langlois that Jewish Americans were major transmitters of the emails that were the prime vehicle of transmission. In classic FOAF fashion, Langlois finds the first articulation of this rumor in an email dated September 12, 2001, which establishes its claims to validity through a report from "my son-in-law the Doctor" who heard about the "celebrating Arabs" of The Sheik restaurant from a nurse who worked with him at Henry Ford hospital and went to The Sheik on the 11th to pick up lunch. After this classic urban legend set-up, with its necessary two-handshakes-away format, the writer of the email calls on her recipient to boycott The Sheik. The Detroit area is home to a relatively large Jewish American population, and a bigger-still Arab American population. However much Osama bin Laden and his followers may or may not care about the Israeli–Palestinian conflict, the wedge-driving rumors on the American scene make it clear that Americans knew right away that somehow the 9/11 attacks were related to conflict in the Middle East.

What I am most concerned with for now, however, is how fabricating, transmitting, and acting on such wedge-driving rumors allowed the Jews of the greater Detroit area to be Jews together. It is interesting to note that, in some diffuse cultural way, going to The Sheik restaurant before 9/11 was – in Detroit – part of a vague but definitive cultural repertoire that we might call "acting Jewish." Just as eating Chinese food has become widely recognized as an identifiably Jewish American activity – from its early twentieth-century canonization as "safe *treyf*" (i.e. relatively acceptable non-Kosher food) to its decades-long function as a punchline in stand-up comedy routines and sitcoms – so too, it appears that eating at The Sheik was a Jewish thing to do before 9/11. According to the owner, Dean Hachem (who launched a lawsuit for slander after the rumor traveled and hurt his business), his clientele was somewhere around 80 percent Jewish before 9/11.

In her wonderful research on the "celebrating Arabs" rumor Janet Langlois has tracked the origins of the rumor to a particular sisterhood organization of a Detroit-area synagogue. From here it is clear that the "celebrating Arabs" rumor was very much a Jewish affair; while the rumor was powerful enough to gain the attention of plenty of people outside of the Jewish community, gaining coverage in the *Wall Street Journal*, for instance, it was initially an occasion for an intense in-group discussion (in emails, in the Jewish press, and so on) about the proper way to relate to this particular Arab American and his business. As with so many rumors that developed in the hours after the hijackings, the "celebrating Arabs" rumor functioned, perhaps above any other concern, as an opportunity to say in some fairly direct way: "Here is our new circle of 'we.' "

Of course those new circles of "we" were just as commonly drawn to put Jews, and even more frequently Israelis, on the outside. Rumors about Jews range from the still murky story of "celebrating Israelis" (actually "dancing Israelis") spotted in New Jersey just after the attack, to the more widely circulated rumor that 4,000 Jews or Israelis stayed home from work at the Twin Towers on 9/11. Besides the obvious questions about the methodology underpinning this particular mythology (is there a phone tree the Jews have for such occasions?) what is most consequential in the circulation of this rumor is, first, the confusion of Jews and Israelis, and, next, the idea – which would seed many of the larger paranoid visions of the 9/11 attacks that would develop in the coming months and years – that a shadowy alliance of Jews around the world control just about everything. New Jersey writer Amiri Baraka takes great pains in his long poem "Somebody Blew Up America" (2001) to articulate this rumor claim in a way that "Jewish" and "Israeli" cannot be confused:

> Who knew the World Trade Center was gonna get bombed
> Who told 4000 Israeli workers at the Twin Towers
> > To stay home that day
> Why did Sharon stay away

Versus:

> Who put the Jews in ovens
> and who helped them do it
> Who said "America First"
> and ok'd the yellow stars

Repeating the story that the Israeli Prime Minister cancelled a planned visit to New York, Baraka, who struggled to find a third-world revolutionary Marxist stance in the late 1960s that would not be hamstrung by accusations of anti-Semitism, tries here to underscore the important difference between "Israeli" and "Jew." This is a poem, obviously, and not a rumor. But one thing I want to emphasize here is that the rumor cycles of 9/11 were (and are) multimedia: joining the usual person-to-person transmissions that always form the heart of such cultural activity were numerous less predictable contributions – poems, songs, works of visual art, and so on.

Unlike the contributors to the "celebrating Arabs" thread, Baraka was not able to control very effectively the circulating message, and was particularly unable to secure the borders of the circle of "we" that he is drawing in this part of his poem. His inclusion of the "absent Israelis" legend is certainly intended to draw attention to a legible history of United States government interference in Middle East affairs and the ways that an acknowledgment of that involvement might help Americans better understand the geopolitics framing the attacks; Baraka's repeated "Who/Who/Who" is plainly meant to challenge the "Why do they hate us?/They hate our freedoms" refrain which became a kind of collective public poetry in its own right in the weeks following 9/11. But rumor culture is decentered, irrational, audience-driven, and (usually) ahistorical. In the case of "Somebody Blew Up America," Baraka's attempt to incorporate, strategically, the "absent Israelis" rumor as part of a larger anti-imperialist and anti-racist critique was no match for the joined forces of politicians, mainstream media, and advocacy groups. From the New Jersey General Assembly (which abolished the position of state poet laureate that Baraka held) to the Anti-Defamation League, the response was swift and decisive. The ADL was particularly intent on "calling the question" and in numerous press releases, open letters, and the like, the organization rendered Baraka's use of "Israeli" as synonymous with "Jewish." With its single-minded focus, the ADL powerfully took the reins of the "absent Israelis" rumor from Baraka and rode it as if it were their customary horse of anti-Semitism. (See for instance http://www.adl. org/anti_semitism/baraka_main.asp)

In a fascinating process of wedge/counter-wedge, the ADL (with help from mainstream media outlets and key political figures) guaranteed that the "absent Israelis" rumor would come to fullest life – and become the easiest target – instead as an "absent Jews" rumor. Post-9/11 rumors about Israelis and about Jews are multivalent, sometimes in direct competition with each other, and it is often difficult for reasonable people to give them serious attention. (Type "NYC" into a Microsoft Word document. Now change the font to Wingdings. ✺✿✆ See! It's death by Jews and a thumbs-up! Or is it death *to* Jews and thumbs-up?) What I want to call attention to here is how the rumor culture of the post-9/11 United States acted as a site of dynamic conversation about the relationship of the attacks to the place of Jewish and Arab Americans in the United States, about the relationship of the United States government to Middle East politics, and about the perceived difference between Jews and Israelis. It should be clear from the morphing of "absent Israelis" into "absent Jews" that the clay of post-9/11 rumor gets shaped by many hands. While it is essential that we reveal all the anti-Semitism at play in post-9/11 rumor mongering (as filmmaker Marc Levin, for instance, has done in his useful film *Protocols of Zion*, which traces the historical roots of one of the most pernicious contemporary anti-Semitic 9/11 rumors), it is also important to get a handle, in each 9/11 rumor situation, on who all the significant stakeholders are.

The Anti-Defamation League did not *start* the "absent Israelis" or "absent Jews" rumors, but they did, ultimately, supervise its proliferation. The ADL's intervention in the life-cycle of this wedge-driving rumor was powerful enough to enlist support in the form of an official denunciation of the rumor from the U.S. Department of State in a document that says Jews died in the Twin Towers in numbers that were almost exactly proportional to their numbers in the New York City area at the time ("The 4,000 Jews Rumor," 2005). This press release also goes on to give "Portraits of Grief" style information about 76 of these Jews who worked for Cantor Fitzgerald or Marsh & McLennan, coached soccer or baseball, and had memorial services held in their honor at synagogues and Jewish centers around the metropolitan area. I elaborate all of this not in an attempt to enter the logic of the rumor's content, but to sketch out how, on the post-9/11 landscape of rumors, sometimes the real headline can be found not in the originating tale, but rather in the organized responses to them.

The "celebrating Arabs" tale has another major wedge-driving function that has nothing to do with Jews or Israelis. The Sheik cycle was joined by other "celebrating Arabs" rumors that serve a major disciplining purpose in the commercial arena, as with the widely circulated story featuring a Budweiser delivery man who observed two Arab employees of a convenience store in a town north of Bakersfield, California, "whooping and hollering" as they watched the attacks unfold on television. As the most common variant of the rumor puts it, this Budweiser driver reported what he saw to his boss, who pledged that there would be no more Budweiser delivered to this store. As I have suggested about many 9/11 rumors, this one does not even exactly "work" as a logical expression of racism. The boycott being promoted here is a shaky proposition ("We'll show them! We won't let them sell our beer anymore!"), but the larger point cannot be missed. A large subset of the rumor culture of 9/11 promoted economic violence against Arab Americans (or people who "look Middle Eastern" – which often meant that South Asians got caught in the web) as an adjunct to the military violence that was being promoted in Afghanistan and later Iraq.

It does not seem far-fetched to tie these consumer-oriented rumors of 9/11 to official instructions given by George W. Bush and his deputies, now widely lampooned and criticized, that told Americans to go shopping as the best response to the terrorists. To be fair, I am not certain that Bush ever actually said the words "go shop" to the American people, but the actual content of his post-9/11 speeches is no match for how Americans have processed those orations in collective memory. Bush *did* ask for "continued participation and confidence in the American economy" and urged Americans to "enjoy America's great destination spots" with the added suggestion that it might be a good time to "Get down to Disney World in Florida" ("At O'Hare," 2001). Bush did opine that one objective of "the terrorists" was to frighten our "nation to the point where we don't ... conduct business, where people don't shop. That's their intention" ("Bush Gives Update," 2001). During his 2007 campaign for the presidency, Republican John McCain, for one, seized on such pronouncements in an attempt to create distance from Bush: "I believe that the big mistake that our leadership of our nation made after 9-11 is we told people to go shopping and we told them to take a trip" when a call to military service should have been issued instead ("McCain," 2007).

But long before McCain or the countless stand-up comics got around to making hay of President Bush's post-9/11 pronouncements, a few rumors had already been put into play as guerrilla commentary on the "go shopping" directives. The "Malloween" rumor of October 2001 (a cousin to the "Grateful Terrorist" tales that actually predate 9/11), for instance, instructed its recipients to stay away from American malls on Halloween because terror attacks would be focused there on that day. This rumor *always* involved a FOAF who has a former boyfriend from Afghanistan who tells her to stay away from the mall on Halloween, and it came from everywhere – Baltimore, "my friend Jill," the offices of Sprint. It is clearly a multifunctional rumor; it at once humanized Afghanis (all those Afghani Muslim men taking such care of their ex-girlfriends!) in absurd fashion and reminded Americans that, formal proclamations notwithstanding, it was definitely not safe to go shopping.

The rumor strategically places the danger not only in the space that functions as the new American town square but also in a crucial time: the day of revelry that is Halloween, when we and our children "pretend" to be scary and scared, and when strangers with candy become trusted friends. In the wake of the 9/11 assault and the anthrax attacks that followed that fall, the Malloween rumor erupted as a symptom of American unease about the simple and everyday ritual of shopping. On September 11 itself Americans responded with a surge in shopping: according to Jennifer Scanlon (2005), Wal-Mart sold 116,000 flags on that day, up 110,000 on the same day in the previous year. But once this flurry of activity subsided, numbers fell way off. Mall traffic, for instance, fell by 6.8 percent, in Scanlon's estimation, during the months of September and October (175, 177). The Malloween rumor, then, acted as a kind of surrealistic annotation of this depressed consumer behavior. It reminded us that more than anything else, the confused logic of so many post-9/11 rumors can be explained by remembering that their central cultural work was to articulate confusion itself. So many of the 9/11 rumors make no sense because their social function was to articulate mystification. In this case, Malloween was at once pro- and anti-Muslim, with its careful demarcation of good ex-boyfriend and bad terrorists who were going to attack the mall, and at once consumerist and anti-consumerist: we *want* to go shopping, we just *can't*.

The "Candyman" rumor (as Snopes.com has named it) served similar purposes with, perhaps, a sharper anti-Arab and anti-Muslim point on it. In this October 2001 rumor cycle, parents in New Jersey were warned not to let their children go trick-or-treating that Halloween because a "gentleman of middle eastern descent" (sic) was reported to have bought large quantities of candy at a North Jersey store. Variants of the rumor inflate the amount of cash this man is alleged to have spent, but in every case the rumor seemed to suggest that Middle Eastern terrorists would be dosing Halloween candy with anthrax. Of course, as Snopes.com and other debunking websites have explained, this rumor built on the decades-old fear that Halloween candy, or the dreaded unwrapped apples of my youth, might have poison or razor blades in them. (Perhaps the Tylenol-tampering murders of 1982 were also lurking in the collective unconscious.) In the time of 9/11, however, the much more focused disciplining intent of this rumor cannot be missed. To begin, the rumor utilized a conspicuous vagueness with regard to what marks the dangerous candy-buyer as "other": the North Jersey context, with its concentration of South Asian immigrants, makes it clear that the one purpose of the Candyman rumor was to create a circle of we that excluded a huge number of people who might or might not be Arab and might or might not be Muslim, but certainly *were* non-Latino brown people.

Moreover, the Candyman rumor also reminded "us" to distrust (or boycott) immigrant and ethnic entrepreneurs, who rely heavily on being able to buy in bulk from "wholesale clubs" to distribute goods to smaller retailers or to use in their own neighborhood-oriented stores. Joining with the delicious experience of imagining children in peril, this rumor also allowed its participants to pretend that "Middle Eastern looking" business people were a puzzling and brand-new disruption of the proper workings of the American economy. What were they doing with all that cash? And all that *candy?* What explanation could there be, other than anthrax-loaded goodies for Halloween? The distribution of this rumor, then, acted as a meaningful display of ignorance about how contemporary retail culture *works*. The hands-on, community- and cash-based nature of the real transaction that formed the basis of this rumor was presented as a puzzle and a call for heightened surveillance by the American people who facilitated it. If President Bush could not control the rumor culture fully enough to get it to bolster his calls to go shopping, perhaps "the folks" of rumor nation were at least willing to use their power to support his post-9/11 anti-immigrant and pro-surveillance initiatives.

For all of the ways that the wedge-driving rumors had important social and collective jobs to do, perhaps their ultimate meaning can be found in how they satisfied individual narcissism. These rumors, whatever else their content communicated about the dangerous possibilities of living in the United States in the fall of 2001, always encouraged the people reading, forwarding, or discussing them to stitch themselves into the developing story of 9/11. Scholar Marshall Berman (2002: 1–2) explains that he has written of "wrecks and ruins and early deaths" and that his first thought after learning of the attacks on television, was "Oh my God, it's like my book!" He catches himself, and thinks, "What's wrong with me? Parts of buildings and parts of bodies are flying though the air … and I put my ideas and me in the foreground?" Soon, however, Berman recovers from his self-blame by noticing that his own narcissism is a typical response to the attacks; as he puts it, the people he observes on television and on the streets of New York are also "making enormous mythical constructions that would make the whole horrific event revolve around them."

The wedge-driving rumors relied on an elaborate construction of a first-person narrative that was anchored by a habitual skeptic who has just this moment been convinced. This identity position offered "average" citizens (that is, the decisive majority of us who were not "heroes" on 9/11 or after) a place to get into the story, a relatively undemanding way to be a part of the national relief effort. In the next chapter I will discuss the celebrity telethon that aired on September 21. Among its many "performances," this show offered a number of shots of its celebrity phone bank, letting the audience see Whoopi Goldberg, Tom Cruise, Brad Pitt, and others answering calls, showing us that they had found a way to "do something," as Tom Hanks promised they would, in his opening remarks (which echoed a passenger from Flight 93). Repeating a rumor isn't much, of course, but it did serve as a gateway to the emerging American confederation of victims.

Much of what I'm calling "9/11 culture" is, in fact, constituted by the labors of historians, fiction writers, journalists, musical artists, and so on trying to make the tragedy available to the widest possible public as their own story. At times, as with the massive 9/11 oral history projects that have been launched by a variety of institutions, these efforts seem organic, necessary in fact for the development of a trustworthy national record of the event and its aftermath. But the wedge-driving rumors, along with numerous other components of 9/11 culture, used the illusion of care and community-building to satisfy much more self-absorbed goals. The "Forbidden Thoughts" published by *Salon.com* on the first anniversary of 9/11, with their facile "aren't we all daring" tone, fits this paradigm, as does Nina Davenport's 2004 documentary *Parallel Lines*. In *Parallel*

Lines the filmmaker drives across the country from Los Angeles to New York, asking "average" citizens how they were affected by 9/11 and reveals (inadvertently, I think), that most of her subjects are frying much different fish. It is only with a push that Davenport can get most of the Americans she meets to somehow talk themselves into a relationship with the national tragedy and justify her project, which is ultimately about her own painful reentry to New York City after being stranded on the West Coast. For many Americans, living in a time when 9/11 was turning into the answer to every question – an FBI agent in Ken Kalfus's 2006 novel *A Disorder Peculiar to the Country* says simply "It's all 9/11 all the time" (197) – it sometimes seemed compulsory to find a personal access point to the catastrophe. The FOAF constitution of rumors offered a perfect two-handshakes-away distance from 9/11 to feel at once connected to this huge story and still relatively safe.

While the wedge-driving rumors of 9/11 were sustained by mainstream media outlets, they mostly circulated in the relative freedom of peer-to-peer transmission. But one of the most popular rumors deployed in the immediate days following 9/11 was invented, and thoroughly controlled, by Clear Channel Communications, a powerful media conglomerate that exerts major social power through its ownership of radio stations, its concert promotions, and its control of advertising venues. The basic outline of this story is well known. Media industry magazines reported on September 14 that Clear Channel Communications had released a list of "banned songs" that should not be played on their radio stations (over a thousand of them) in the United States, out of sensitivity to their distraught listeners (Nuzum, 2004). The banned list is a bizarre and at times hilarious compendium of songs by bands from AC/DC to The Zombies (more on the songs themselves momentarily). What I am most interested in establishing here is that Clear Channel understood almost immediately after the attacks that they could exploit the machinery of the rumor to reinforce their position as a major agent of corporate control in the United States and beyond. This corporate control would be instrumentalized in a number of ways in the years following 9/11 and ultimately could be best understood in the larger context of Clear Channel's ties to George W. Bush and a militaristic political agenda.

A number of the major internet rumor-debunking websites (e.g. Snopes. com, urbanlegends.com) have simple accounts of the Clear Channel story that identify as "false" the claim that Clear Channel circulated a list of banned songs in the wake of 9/11. These accounts follow closely the party line developed by Clear Channel itself that the banned songs list was a "hoax." But Eric Nuzum, in his meticulous research, demonstrates clearly that it was Clear Channel's disavowal that was the real hoax. In what Nuzum calls a "savvy statement" released by Clear Channel on September 18, the media giant, which by some accounts controls 60 percent of rock music programming in the country, insisted that "Clear Channel Radio ha[d] not banned any songs from any of its radio stations." Taking refuge in semantics (as Nuzum points out, Clear Channel "didn't order anyone to ban any songs") the company also did not "deny that a list of 'lyrically questionable' songs was created, edited by management, redistributed by management, and then acted upon by its employees." Corporate censorship gets much of its power by establishing organizational structures and administrative strategies that together act as a firewall between the highest management and local practice. Such bureaucratic distance makes it possible for the corporation to protest, on the one hand, that Clear Channel "believes that radio is a local medium" while also creating an incredibly powerful, vertically integrated monopoly on musical radio broadcast in the United States. Since the Telecommunications Act of 1996 removed hurdles facing media conglomerates looking to increase their local holdings, Clear Channel has become more and more able to "program" American musical life.

One indication of Clear Channel's power in the United States market is how successful it was in selling this act of corporate censorship as a grassroots and decentered effort. The best measure of this is how willing the mainstream media was to report on the Clear Channel effort as if it were operating on the same level of peer-to-peer rumor-passing as Malloween, the "celebrating Arabs," or any of the other wedge-driving tales. In promoting this vision of the story, Clear Channel, amazingly, co-opted the very spirit of peer-to-peer interaction (p2p) – music file-sharing, most notably – that corporate conglomerates had been, over the past few years, bemoaning as the death knell for the music industry. The *Guardian* of London was typical in its report:

> You may have got the email and have, incredulously, scanned the list of what US radio has deemed inappropriate in the wake of last week's terrorist attacks. But yesterday Clear Channel Communications, the US's biggest radio station chain, has denied that they released a list of banned songs. Spokesperson Pam Taylor told Hollywood.com: "It is a rumor. We never banned any songs from airing on our radio stations." ("Banned Songlist," 2001)

The "banned song" list got its widest circulation, then, as a disavowed rumor. But this purposeful closing of the barn door after the horse had bolted must be seen as part of the corporate strategy: Clear Channel was clearly one of the first corporate/cultural agents to get out of the gate after 9/11 with a strategy for brand positioning. What I am explaining as Clear Channel's management of the rumor network is, of course, what half a decade later we might more accurately label "viral marketing." The *Aqua Teen Hunger Force* "hoax" of January 2007 is perhaps the most infamous instance of viral marketing – a technique that uses existing social networks, rather than traditional advertising venues, to market brands, events, products, and so on. In the *Aqua Teen* case, Boston-area artists were employed by Turner Broadcasting System to place electronic light boards strategically around the city to promote the forthcoming *Aqua Teen* movie. Although hired by a major media company, Peter Berdovsky and Sean Stevens did not market the movie using traditional, centrally placed advertisements, but relied on word-of-mouth at the street level to promote their images.

Capitalizing on not only email, but also on the growing interactivity of Web 2.0, Clear Channel was instructing the American public that the first wave of cultural activity to get ready for after the attacks was on the level of cultural belt-tightening: in this frightening new post-9/11 world, Americans would have to sacrifice some treasures (even those we might not miss, like John Parr's when-was-it-last-played-in-the-United-States-anyway "St. Elmo's Fire") as part of the larger effort of fighting terrorism. The Clear Channel "rumor" acted, then, as a kind of dress rehearsal for the assault of the PATRIOT Act, to be signed into law just over a month later. Again, I am not arguing that this was a heavy-handed act of corporate censorship. As Eric Nuzum explains, it did not take a statement of official doctrine for local radio station owners to get the message that they should follow the dictates of the banned song list. Many program directors admitted that in the wake of the circulated instructions, "they did indeed remove songs from broadcast because of the list or its suggested sense of restraint."

The list itself is ridiculous, except when it is scary. It mostly imagines a fragile American public, which might endure great pain if it were to hear a song with "Fire" or "Heaven" or "Hell" in the title. It is only a parlor game to pick your favorite list absurdity – is it Shelly Fabares' "Johnny Angel"? Or J. Frank Wilson's "Last Kiss"? And, hey, why isn't "Tell Laura I Love Her" here? – but a much more serious matter to consider just what

Clear Channel was trying to accomplish with these "suggestions." There *are* hints of something more significant in the list itself: with the inclusion of John Lennon's "Imagine" (which Neil Young would soon sing at the celebrity telethon on September 21) and "All Rage Against the Machine," the banned song list reveals itself to be concerned with ideology as well as sensitivity.

Carrying much greater weight than the list itself is the declaration it makes that in the post-9/11 world, Clear Channel would take off the mask of corporate neutrality and work as an agent in support of the Bush military program. Others (Krugman, 2003; Boehlert, 2004) have explained how Clear Channel's post-1996 consolidation has allowed the company, with its deep historical ties to George W. Bush, to promote a conservative agenda. (Top executives at Clear Channel, as Paul Krugman has explained, were intimately involved with Bush during his Texas years as major supporters of the Republican Party there; Clear Channel Vice Chairman Tom Hicks also bought the Texas Rangers from Bush.) Supporting the work of the rumor of the "banned songs" list were pro-war rallies sponsored by "local radio stations" (all owned by Clear Channel), and corporate suppression of the Dixie Chicks and radio host Howard Stern (who was suspended by Clear Channel after years of getting away with all he got away with). Clear Channel drew a line in the sand almost immediately after 9/11: if there was to be a political front and a military front in the newly declared "war on terror" so too would there be a cultural front. The "banned song" rumor served an important function in this post-9/11 America – like so many of the other rumors I have been discussing here it may not have been exactly "true," but it gained its power as a litmus test of patriotic feeling rather than as an appeal to pure rationality. As with the wedge-driving rumors, the Clear Channel rumor offered many Americans the chance to join the putative fight against terrorism through their consumption practices. Remove Everclear's "Santa Monica" (1995) from your playlist (presumably because of how the song's narrator implores his beloved to move West with him, and go swimming, and "watch the world die" – i.e. watch the sunset), or get rid of Lynyrd Skynyrd's "Tuesday's Gone" (1973) (because 9/11 was a Tuesday?) about a character whose girlfriend, Tuesday, has just broken up with him, and, Shazam, you are fighting for the good guys.

* * *

It is a kind of magical thinking, of course, that Clear Channel attempted to stimulate with its complicated "banned song" rumor. Exploiting therapeutic keywords that would be familiar to its captive listeners ("healing," "local sensitivities"), Clear Channel ventured a friendly take-over of the American cultural marketplace. Two major countervailing forces undercut these efforts by Clear Channel to control consciousness through the airwaves and one came from Clear Channel itself: the realities of Clear Channel's own market interests made it impractical for the company to stay on message in any consistent way. Organizing anti-Dixie Chick hysteria through radio station censorship after Natalie Maines' infamous early 2003 anti-Bush statement ("Just so you know, we're ashamed the President of the United States is from Texas") is one thing, but Clear Channel did not want to risk losing the Dixie Chicks as a client for the concert-promoting division of the company as the group launched a major tour.

The other, and ultimately more significant, counterforce acting as a check on centralized corporate censorship came with the "9/11 truth" movement, rooted in the new possibilities of Web 2.0 that were growing exponentially and which were tangled up inextricably with 9/11 culture. The origins and evolution of these challenges to the "official story" of 9/11 are outside my scope. I do want to explore how the collective of dissenters who generally travel under the banner of "9/11 truth," but constitute dozens of real and virtual groups and individual actors, have turned rumor into a vital challenge to the control exerted by the U.S. government and mainstream media interests (e.g. Clear Channel) over the flow of 9/11 information. The opposition that began as scattered rumor quickly evolved into "fifty people a day … singing" as Arlo Guthrie, in his "Alice's Restaurant Massacre," described an earlier generation of war protesters.

Scattered rumors about each attack site developed within days:

- The Twin Towers were taken down not by the planes that hit them, but by explosives placed at their base.
- United 93 did not crash in Pennsylvania, but was shot down.
- The Pentagon was not hit by planes, but missiles.

The larger story/rumor framing each of these particular arguments is that the United States government, or at least key members of it, either planned themselves or had inside knowledge about the attacks. Debunking efforts have been more or less immaterial. The 9/11 Commission report issued in 2004, for instance, only added more fuel to the "9/11 truth" fire by offering up more details that the "truth community" found laughable: how did those passengers on United 93 get their cellphones to work on board? Within a few years of the attack, the 9/11 truth community formed a conspicuous subset of anti-Bush protesters; at an anti-war rally on the Boston Common in fall of 2007, for instance, members of what was once a diffuse "rumor community" now staked a seemingly unchallenged claim in the larger peace movement, handing out literature (see Figure 3) alongside the immigration rights activists and Iraq Veterans Against the War.

The 9/11 truth rumors are perhaps the hardest of all to deny the logic of. What I mean is that (in my small inventory of student responses to 9/11 rumors – some 300 students now), these truth rumors are the ones most likely to "capture" young people. When I give an assignment about rumors to my 9/11 culture classes, these are the ones that students have the hardest time defining as rumors, even in their earliest, most rudimentary form, and these are the ones that students have the most difficulty framing in the context of transmission and impact: they are desperate, instead, to prove each (or all) of the truth rumors true (or false). In April of 2006, when I taught a "sample" class to 50 or so prospective students and their parents visiting my college, I invited them to initiate a discussion on 9/11 rumors by first writing down what they recalled to be the most dominant rumor in the United States in the first months after that Tuesday. Much discussion ensued about what I "counted" as a rumor, and every single question from the crowd had to do with an individual internet message they received that we now understand to fall under the 9/11 truth rubric. This is another way of saying that the claims of the 9/11 truth movement have lived well beyond the usual rumor duration and taken on a second life as a well-articulated political belief system. In the weeks following the initial attacks, however, these stories about the hijackings and crash sites traveled many of the same routes taken by any of the major wedge-driving rumors.

There are a number of explanations, I think, for the transformation of 9/11 truth rumors from isolated protest into a major social force. The first appeal, as more than a few commentators have suggested, is that the bundle of 9/11 truth rumors take the chaos of that day and map an intelligent design onto it. On a psychological level, then, as film critic Jonathan Rosenbaum (2006a) has argued in reviewing the film *United 93*, in the 9/11 truth rumors "*someone* at least is in control. The inept air-defense command actually got it together to scramble a jet and bring down a

The Independent Thinker's
9/11 FACT SHEET

What occurred on September 11th, 2001 is a matter of facts, physics and unprecedented violations of national protocol by American officials themselves. Here are 10 points to consider. There are hundreds more.

1. No steel-framed building before or since 9/11 has ever collapsed due to fire.

2. No official agency (FAA, FBI, or the airlines) has ever released a list of the 9/11 passengers. But within hours, the FBI released a list of the hijackers.

3. Multiple air-defense drills were planned for the morning of 9/11. These exercises left only two fighter jets available to protect the entire Northeastern United States.

4. Building 7, a 47-story skyscraper and part of the World Trade Center complex, was not struck by a plane but collapsed in 6.5 seconds at 5:20 p.m. on September 11th, in the exact manner of a controlled demolition.

5. There was no visible airplane debris where Flight 93 supposedly crashed in Pennsylvania – only a smoking hole in the ground, much like a bomb crater.

6. Office fires burn at low temperatures of 600-800 dF. Jet fuel is an ordinary hydrocarbon; its maximal burning temperature is 1200 dF in open air. Steel melts at 2750 dF. Neither jet fuel nor the burning contents of the buildings could cause the towers' steel structure to buckle or fail.

7. Tests have shown that cell-phone calls cannot be made at altitudes over 4000 to 8000 feet, as cell towers are located on the ground. Commercial airliners fly at 30,000 feet and above. No passenger could have successfully placed a call for help by cell phone from an airborne plane on 9/11, as reported.

8. 9/11 was immediately declared an "act of war" by President Bush. The rubble from the Twin Towers' collapse was carted away and the steel sold and shipped overseas without examination.

9. Enormous profits were made by insiders on plummeting stock prices of the two airlines involved in 9/11 – American and United. Federal law protects their identities.

10. Accepting victims' compensation barred 9/11 families from further discovery through litigation.

Figure 3 Promoting "truth" at an antiwar rally

plane that was set to commit mass murder" ("Hijacking"). Rosenbaum goes on, with a wider focus, to suggest that in the broader-scale rumors (often dismissed with the label "conspiracy theory") there is "One Big Conspiracy of the Illuminati, and Skull and Bones, the Elders of Zion, and the Bush Administration exercised its Total Control of History." The facile dismissal of the 9/11 truth rumors is shared by many, and is not far off from the conclusions offered by Trey Parker and Matt Stone in their *South Park* episode "Mystery of the Urinal Deuce" (2006) which suggests that the president and his minions are actually the masterminds behind all the major 9/11 truth rumors: controlling the conspiracy theories is the ultimate demonstration of the administration's power. What Rosenbaum and the *South Park* makers refuse to acknowledge (or purposely erase) is the fact that President Bush and other key players in his administration *were* lying to the American people in order to prosecute the case against Iraq; signing on to the position that the "official story" was concealing much turns out to have been pretty reasonable.

The one-dimensional debunkers satisfied the same simplifying impulses that they accuse the 9/11 truth rumors of speaking to and their assessments cannot account for the energetic acts of public refusal that have helped convert individual 9/11 truth rumors into the oppositional movement it has become. All of the major post-9/11 rumors relied heavily on Web 2.0 and their transmission is inconceivable without the growth of YouTube, Google video, internet message boards, and political blogging and wikis. Some estimates suggest that *Loose Change*, a documentary that has become something of a calling card for the 9/11 truth movement, has been viewed around 10 million times on the internet – with countless additional viewings facilitated by other p2p modalities – burned DVDs, and the like (one man handing out a 9/11 truth DVD at the fall 2007 anti-war rally in Boston kept up a steady chant of "make lots of copies").

I want us to understand the 9/11 truth rumors that were passed, developed, and codified in the months and years after September 11, 2001, as a major "open source" initiative. In this light, as I have been suggesting, the collection of 9/11 truth rumors must be regarded as a key grassroots rebellion, as a revolt not only against governmental control over 9/11 inquiry but also as a critique of the centralized control of American media held by corporate actors such as Clear Channel. "Open source" originally referred to an explicit set of principles elaborated in the late 1990s, concerning the design and circulation of computer software; the contemporary civil disobedience of open source has, as a central goal, the dissolution of the too-intimate ties between government and commercial interests that are embedded in laws having to do with intellectual property. The ultimate aim of this collective effort is enhancing innovation and broadening access to new technology and content.

It has become useful in recent days to think about the implications of the open source concept outside of the domain of software development and exchange. The open source challenge of the 9/11 truth movement is built into its decentralized and non-discriminatory workings. While it cannot, of course, satisfy the software-specific provisions of the original open source doctrines, the 9/11 truth movement shares many of the ideals of collective creation, constant modification, and non-discrimination that nurtured the development of Linux and Firefox on the one hand, and Wikipedia on the other. The peer-to-peer character of the 9/11 truth rumors relies in part on existing associations (of scientists and political activists, for instance) but also developed from the exponential growth of a variety of new social networks. From the "friend of a friend" formulation so central to Jan Harold Brunvand's work, we see "friend" becoming a verb in the post-9/11 world. Through the whole range of Web 2.0 possibilities – including Friendster, Live Journal, Facebook, and MySpace – "friending" has become a new language of connection, and one that has anchored the 9/11 truth movement and helped it transform from rumor to doctrine.

The rumors that coalesced into 9/11 truth mean what they mean, of course, but they also function as an occasion to mobilize around distrust of the federal government. In this light, it is important to notice that the largely white leadership of such groups as 911truth.org have been joined in their work by an important cluster of hip hop artists. The rappers, including Afro-Peruvian artist Immortal Technique, and African Americans Paris, Jadakiss, and the Lost Children of Babylon, have used a variety of 9/11 truth elements to carry much broader arguments about imperialism, race, and the control of corporate media. In doing so, they have opened conversations with young Americans who might not otherwise have immediate access to the kind of cultural analysis they are promoting. They have also joined the long list of American popular artists who have "used" 9/11 as an opportunity to expand their own marketing reach.

The most sustained musical activism has come from Immortal Technique and Paris. Paris, in particular, has used not only his music (in particular his 2003 release *Sonic Jihad*, with its cover image of an airplane – United 93? – about to hit the White House and its inner sleeve photo of Paris with his mouth duct-taped), but his "Guerrilla Funk" website, interviews, and other media to solidify his position as a major African American protest voice. In interviews, Paris insists that in addition to their music, rap activists must use the internet to reach fans: speaking to *Political Affairs* ("Paris Gets a Bad Rap," 2003) Paris argues that "there's such a concerted attempt to clamp down on dissent and on alternative points of view that it's necessary for us to turn to the Internet. The Internet is the only thing that exists now that remains uncensored." Paris's website (guerrillafunk.com/paris) uses the relative freedom of the internet to treat his listeners as citizens. With its suggested reading list, an incredibly rich archive of political and cultural essays, its qualified support for p2p file sharing, and fascinating information on financial planning ("Guerrilla Funk Wealth Builder" – drawn from the work Paris did for years as a stockbroker), Guerilla Funk becomes a platform for a rich and thoughtful protest.

The website, the *Sonic Jihad* record, and the Paris-narrated documentary *Aftermath: Unanswered Questions from 9/11*, launch a concerted assault on the official story of 9/11. The song "What Would You Do" in particular summarizes the strong current of distrust of the federal government that runs all through the 9/11 truth rumors: "Don't forget they made us slaves, gave us AIDS and raped us/Another Bush season mean another war for profit/All in secret so the public never think to stop it/ The Illuminati triple 6 all connected." Once Paris cites the Illuminati it is tempting to dismiss this all as conspiracy theory; popular allegations about a shadowy world government and its control of *everything* (including imagery on American money), is often barely a handshake away from one kind of hate speech or another. But renaming an argument "conspiracy theory" is always used as shorthand to dismiss not only a particular utterance, but really the very right of the speaker to be heard. On the website Paris wisely takes the conspiracy theory charge head on:

Understand the label "conspiracy theory" is a tactic that the media often invokes to immediately discredit voices of dissent and people who seek truth. The tactic of creating manufactured enemies for personal gain has been around for as long as there have been conflicts. Of course there's no concrete proof of a conspiracy – the media would never allow that – but rather an abundance of evidence that points to a conspiracy on behalf of

US interests. Know that there's no concrete proof of the involvement of any other country either. The first thing that you must do is ask yourself, over and over again, the following question: "Who benefits?"

Paris's own song, with its reference to the idea that AIDS was deliberately inflicted on African Americans by the U.S. government, reveals how deeply Paris is invested in a race-based protest that links homegrown oppression with overseas imperialism.

"What Would You Do" leaves little doubt that Paris is speaking *as* an African American, and using the platform of 9/11 truth rumor to launch an anti-racist analysis. "Now ask yourself who's the people with the most to gain (Bush)/'fore 9/11 motherfuckas couldn't stand his name ... Now even niggas waving flags like they lost they mind." The song continues: "The oldest trick in the book is MAKE an enemy/Of phony evil so the government can do its dirt/And take away ya freedom lock and load, beat and search/Ain't nothin' changed but more colored people locked in prison./These pigs still beat us, but it seem we forgettin'./But I remember 'fore September how these devils do it/Fuck Giuliani, ask Diallo how he doin'." As a popular intellectual, Paris does crucial work here. He is, no doubt, committed to the 9/11 truth cause. But mobilizing these truths (or rumors, depending on your point of view) is also how he opens a window of opportunity, a window through which he wants to shine a light on the continued injuries inflicted by state-sponsored racism in the United States, including the murder of African immigrant Amadou Diallo by New York City police officers in 1999. While Arab Americans would, of course, be the focus of much post-9/11 persecution, Paris here puts 9/11 into a legible history of Black–white relations in the United States. Drawing on a long rhetorical tradition that stretches back at least to Frederick Douglass's 1852 speech "What to the Slave is the Fourth of July?" Paris demands that we recognize the ways that African Americans have been denied (or must, at times, deny themselves) the seductive pleasures of patriotism.

Two other rap acts have given a similar level of sustained attention to the "rumors" that have morphed into "9/11 truth." Immortal Technique has become something of a poster boy for the movement. His record *Revolutionary, Vol. 2*, released in 2003, established Immortal Technique as a notable "truthie" (as opponents of the movement often refer to the faithful); the song "The Cause of Death" is often cited as an important contribution on 9/11 truth websites. Working unlikely phrases like

"Wolfowitz doctrine" into his rhymes without missing a beat, Immortal Technique joins the chorus of people suggesting that the towers were purposely imploded: "you act like America wouldn't destroy two buildings/... I was watching the Towers and though I wasn't the closest/I saw them crumble to the Earth like they was full of explosives." Immortal Technique goes on to anticipate the criticism that this theory projects too much power onto Bush, assuring "Conservatives" that "I don't think Bush did it, 'cuz he isn't that smart."

In various versions of a 2005 song titled, simply, "Bin Laden," Immortal Technique and his collaborators (including Chuck D, KRS-ONE, and Mos Def) performed a complex racialized reading of 9/11. The refrain of the song, "Bin Laden didn't knock down the projects/It was you nigga," is punctuated by a line from a 2004 hit, "Why," by rapper Jadakiss, that suggests Bush was responsible for knocking down the Twin Towers. What "Bin Laden" achieves is a complex stitching together of the familiar 9/11 truth claim that the attacks were an inside job, with a devastating reminder of how the U.S. government has imploded public housing sites, beginning with the Pruett-Igoe projects in St Louis in 1972, and carrying on through the entire hip hop era. In a classic bait-and-switch, Immortal Technique uses a rumor ("Bush knocked down the towers") to tell a history – of how "urban renewal" became "urban blight" – that had been hiding in plain sight.

The song prosecutes its race-based case even more fully, explaining that the interpretations of Iraqi insurgency as loyalty to Saddam are bogus:

> I'll show you why it's totally wrong
> Cuz if another country invaded the hood tonight
> It'd be warfare through Harlem, and Washington Heights
> I wouldn't be fightin' for Bush or White America's dream
> I'd be fightin' for my people's survival and self-esteem.

Responding to the seemingly compulsory requirements of "United We Stand," Immortal Technique promotes a vision of race unity that refuses the widespread calls for a militaristic nationalism.

The most extended rap challenge to the dominant narratives of 9/11 came with the release of *The 911 Report: The Ultimate Conspiracy* (first issued in 2005) by the very underground Philadelphia hip hop group The Lost Children of Babylon (LCOB). LCOB includes followers of

Nuwaubian spiritual leader Malachi Z. York. In addition to the mystical dogma of York, the group also show traces in its lyrics of the influence of the Five Percent Movement, an offshoot of the Nation of Islam that was a major force in hip hop in the late 1980s and 1990s. LCOB takes 9/11 rumors almost to the level of abstract mathematics: following the chain of logic that threads through their song "Conspiracy Theory," listeners have to follow an obscure history that includes the Rothschild banking family, the Trilateral Commission, the relationship between the symbology on the back of American dollar bills and pentagrams. *911 Report* is narrated from multiple subject positions (the hijackers themselves, President Bush, an Al-Qaeda operative, and so on) and with varying affect. Evincing sympathy for all victims of 9/11 in the context of an extended critique of the Bush administration, the ultimate goal of *911 Report* is to establish a position from which non-Christian African Americans – "Muslims" for lack of a more precise word – can enter debates surrounding the attacks and their aftermath. As LCOB member Richard Raw put it in an interview, *911 Report* is meant on one level to be taken as the soundtrack to Michael Moore's documentary *Fahrenheit 9/11*, because "the fuck didn't want to put no real hip-hop shit on there!!!" ("Lost Children of Babylon Interview," 2006)

For all the rhymes and beats offered by Paris, Immortal Technique, and The Lost Children of Babylon, it took a mere seven words offered up by mainstream rapper Jadakiss in the summer of 2004 to bring the inside-job rumor to a mass audience. With his song "Why," a major hit in the summer of 2004 (the album it appeared on, *Kiss of Death*, debuted at number 1 on the Billboard charts), Jadakiss added much fuel to the fire of 9/11 truth rumors. In a long line of questions that begin "Why" (and give the song its title), Jadakiss asks "Why did Bush knock down the towers?" In the initial press run-up that accompanied this release, Jadakiss cultivated the controversy, and spoke clearly as an African American and an entrepreneur. On the first score, Jadakiss insisted that the inclusion of this line grew from his feeling that George Bush "had something to do" with the attacks: "That's why I put it in there like that. A lot of my people felt that he had something to do with it" (Heim, 2004). Again, it is clear that repeating a 9/11 rumor is not simply an act of protest, but also contains within it a separate strand of African American protest against post-9/11 attempts to erase race identification in the interest of national unity.

But Jadakiss was also operating as a savvy businessperson, and was quite willing to explain how delighted he was with the controversy surrounding his 9/11 truth moment. As he told *Billboard* on July 9, 2004, "They're censoring me all over the place, and that's good ... That means it's reaching out to everybody" (Hall, 2004). Having stoked the media machine so successfully, with the predictable outcry from right-wing bloggers and talk show hosts, Jadakiss took his promotion of the song to the next level, telling interviewers that the line was "obviously" meant to be "a metaphor" (Soults, 2004). Unlike Bruce Springsteen, who situated his 9/11 record *The Rising* as an organic, populist, and inevitable response to the attacks, Jadakiss admits how he manipulated the market to build acceptance for his own 9/11 release. Jadakiss's masterful management of "Why" and its critical seven words is a wonderful example of the central role played by rumor in American culture after 9/11, and the fascinating way that grassroots cultural efforts have worked in tandem with more centrally located social forces. Rumors were cultural first responders – one of the important cultural forms to grapple with the changes wrought by 9/11 immediately after the attacks. In the first week after 9/11, as the initial 9/11 rumors were in development, the American entertainment industry was also figuring out how its own first responders should enter the picture. *America: A Tribute to Heroes* was the answer that came from Hollywood, Nashville, and New York.

CH/2
Telethon

The immediate cultural response to 9/11 was centered, not surprisingly, around news programs. With new brands ("America Under Attack"), logos, and theme music – heavy on the kettle-drums – ABC, NBC, CBS, FOX, and CNN were first out of the gate in packaging the event for the American public and viewers around the world. It did not take long for other major players in the entertainment industry to enter the breach, and conversations about how the tragedy should be understood in the context of popular culture began almost immediately. The major elements of consensus that developed relatively quickly were that the attacks were going to wean Americans (and quickly at that) from their taste for violence in the movies and from their taste for irony in any of the popular arts.

Discussions about popular culture violence began immediately and seem to have been fed not only by the basic truth that September 11 was a day of terrible carnage, but by the notion that the mode of attack was somehow inextricable from visual codes developed by Hollywood. Cultural critic Slavoj Žižek (2001) was one of first to present this analysis: "[T]he shots we saw of the collapsing towers could not but remind us of the most breathtaking scenes in the catastrophe big productions ... just recall the series of movies from *Escape from New York* to *Independence Day*. The unthinkable which happened was thus the object of fantasy: in a way, America got what it fantasized about, and this was the greatest surprise." Film director Robert Altman was to summarize this interpretive stance about a month after the attacks, with a more accusatory tone. According to Altman, the "movies set the pattern, and these people have copied the movies. Nobody would have thought to commit an atrocity like that unless they'd seen it in a movie. How dare we continue to show this kind of mass destruction in movies. I just believe we created this atmosphere and taught them how to do it" (Roten, 2002). Numerous commentators rushed in during the first weeks after 9/11 to insist that Americans would now be shaken out of their inertia, would refuse to pay to see violent movies, and would demand some new kind of entertainment. Widely publicized reports circulated about movie projects that were being shelved, reedited, or held back from release (perhaps most famously Arnold Schwarzenegger's *Collateral Damage*) in order to account for the new media realities of the post-9/11 world.

Looking back at reports on the attacks it is striking to see how completely the media coverage was saturated with references to the movies. Tom Englehardt (2006) has written of how often print and television journalists "compared the events to Hollywood action movies" or made reference to particular disaster films, and how common it was to find people-on-the-street interviews peppered with similar citations. What is most important in all of this 9/11-as-film talk is the reflexive and obsessive insistence that no cultural sense could be made of the attacks until they were "derealized" and put into the familiar fictional contexts that Hollywood is in the business of constructing. To put this another way, and to say something fairly obvious, some of the major purveyors of media culture in the United States rushed onto the post-attack scene and in a predictably self-aggrandizing act told American audiences: "Stay tuned and we'll tell you what to feel." In mainstream media, television producers were less likely than popular musicians or filmmakers to enter this thicket; perhaps because of the more obvious commercial nature of network television (i.e. there are advertisements every few minutes) it was difficult to maintain the aura of sanctity that surrounded other early popular culture attempts to memorialize the victims of the attack. When television did enter the post-9/11 marketplace it did so cautiously, with special framing (as with the telethon and *The West Wing*'s special 9/11 episode, both of which were presented as existing outside television's usual ad-driven format). Such efforts were meant to guard against charges of exploitation. The real job of television, as Marita Sturken (2007) has smartly observed, was to signal when it was time for Americans to get back to normal. Noting that television networks lost millions of dollars in advertising revenue because of their initial advertising-free coverage of the attacks, it was crucial to return to regular programming – with ads: "The reappearance of television commercials," Sturken writes, "marked the end of the state of emergency."

By the first weekend after the attack Americans were well schooled in the new "realities." Among the most powerful instructions citizens received was that irony would no longer have any place in their cultural lives. This announcement came from talking head Roger Rosenblatt, on the PBS *News Hour* program, in a rough draft for an essay he was to publish a week or so later in *Time* magazine. Asked what had really changed in the few days since 9/11, Rosenblatt (2001) suggested that "One change we have is that this will mark the end of the age of irony. For 30 years, just about as long as the twin towers were up, we have been operating under an attitude that things were not to be believed in, that nothing was quite to be taken seriously and that nothing was real. Nothing could have been more real than the savage zealots who hit the twin towers and the Pentagon and who caused the plane to go down in Pennsylvania. So one change certainly will be that the smirk on American intelligent life, the idea of giggling and thinking that nothing was serious, that's certainly going to change." Rosenblatt's "new seriousness" prediction was echoed around the land and quickly rose to the status of doctrine.

Talk of this new thoughtfulness was accompanied by action. "We're going to try to do something," Tom Hanks solemnly intoned early on in the telethon *America: A Tribute to Heroes*, which was broadcast on over 30 stations and seen by some 60 million people on September 21. The show's direct aim – "to raise spirits and, we hope, a great deal of money," as Hanks put it in the first celebrity talking spot of the night – seems to have succeeded at least on the second front. According to most accounts, *Tribute* brought in somewhere in the range of 150–200 million dollars for the September 11 Telethon Fund, administered by the United Way; the United Way itself says the telethon's take was 128 million dollars.

The telethon was directed by Joel Gallen, whose major credits before that night mostly had to do with industry celebrations of itself: The MTV Movie Awards, the Academy Award Preshow, a Rock and Roll Hall of Fame Induction Ceremony. (This was to become a kind of niche for Gallen over the following few years, and he went on to direct the Hurricane Katrina telethon and a special called *CNN Heroes*, "honoring ordinary people who do extraordinary things.") The choice of Gallen represented an apt harmonizing of director and material: in many ways *Tribute* felt more like a tribute to entertainment industry largesse, a display of how well our celebrities were taking up the task of instructing the rest of us how to act in this newly ordered universe.

Major fundraisers featuring rock music performances had a 30-year history by that point, a history that began with 1971's Concert for Bangladesh, a Madison Square Garden show (and later film) that ex-Beatle George Harrison organized to call attention to that country's war and famine-related devastation. Since then popular musicians have regularly banded together in mega-events in support of Amnesty International, American farmers, and victims of famine in Ethiopia, to name just a few. *Tribute* was at once more homogeneous and strangely hybrid than most of these other fundraisers. The uniformity came with matters of style, stage sets, song choice, and how the musicians and speakers generally went about their business. But the show had more than one fish to fry and its attempts to multitask led to some interesting juxtapositions and omissions, as well as many revelations of just how crassly the forces of marketing were at work in its creation.

It is always interesting to try to get students to piece together how *these* celebrities ended up on *these* stages at that moment. It is clear to them that certainly it could not have been just chance that brought George Clooney, Neil Young, and Wyclef Jean, Goldie Hawn, Clint Eastwood, and Alicia Keys onto the roster. But what could it have been? When I suggest in class that perhaps agents in New York, Hollywood, and Nashville may have been burning up the phone lines and high-speed cables during the week of planning for the telethon, I am usually met with a steady chorus of catcalls; that said, the young people who discussed the telethon on the fraternity- and sorority-based greekchat.com site had no problem suggesting that Céline Dion's presence must mean she was "getting ready to drop another recording". Without worrying over the exact details of the telethon's planning (though it would not be hard, I imagine, to trace the influence of the powerful Creative Artists Agency, for instance, on its shape) it is more important to observe that *Tribute* represented a major expression of entertainment industry, baby-boomer muscle. Supporting Gallen's directorial work were a number of hugely influential writers, including key political figures such as Reagan speechwriter Peggy Noonan (who claims credit for Tom Cruise and Julia Roberts' lines) and Ann Lewis, a communications aide to Bill Clinton. Perhaps most emblematic of the demographic heart of the program were scriptwriters Marshall Herskovitz and Edward Zwick, the team responsible for bringing *thirtysomething* (to some, the nadir of boomer narcissism) to television in the late 1980s and early 1990s. For all of its big-tent, non-partisan and commercial-free character, *Tribute* operated very much as an active participant in the marketplace of goods and ideas. The show not only acted as a summary of boomer style, affect, and political stance but also helped establish a grammar and vocabulary for the 9/11 art that was to follow in its wake.

The show did feature some non-baby boomers, with special places reserved in the musical lineup for post-boomers, and a few key presenter roles saved for Greatest Generation representatives (i.e. people who were of an age to have lived through World War II). Including artists born after 1964 seems, above all, to have been inspired by a desire to achieve some semblance of gender parity, along with a less energetic attempt to include non-white celebrities. The bulk of the rock-era performers were men, as were the presenters (Tom Hanks, George Clooney, and Jim Carrey) who appear in the crucial early slots. The show closed with a Canadian (Céline Dion singing "God Bless America" – see, we have allies!) and a few pre-boomer father figures.

The last two couplings in *Tribute* did pull back somewhat from the baby-boomer demographic that defined the show. First was 58-year-old Robert De Niro introducing 59-year-old Paul Simon, constituting a final "New York exacta" for the program. De Niro's New York-based movie credits, particularly his run of Martin Scorcese-directed films in the 1970s (*Mean Streets*, *Godfather II*, *Taxi Driver*, *New York, New York*), established him as an icon of "white ethnic" New York life. At the telethon, De Niro wore his familiar "I'm in pain, I see the cosmic unfairness that defines the universe, and yet I'm resolute" face and was given lines to read that quoted from Franklin Delano Roosevelt's "Four Freedoms" speech, delivered in 1941, the year that Paul Simon was born. Until that instant, *Tribute* had been defined by a direct appeal to the tastes and wallets of baby boomers. Robert De Niro, invoking the "Greatest Generation," accessed a deeper history than the show had heretofore admitted and in doing so appealed to a nostalgic sense of unity that (allegedly) characterized the United States during the World War II era.

De Niro's moment on *Tribute* drew on his cultural capital as a white ethnic hero (mostly, but not only, playing Italian American characters) that made him an accessible representative of the firefighters, police officers, and other rescue workers who perished in large numbers on the 11th, and who were the most available emblems of heroism in the wake of the attacks. De Niro's introduction of Paul Simon, another artist closely associated with New York (from his various New York-themed songs released on Simon and Garfunkel albums before their split in 1970, through their reunion concert in Central Park in 1981), helped establish the actor as a primary "voice" of 9/11. Six months later De Niro was to serve as narrator for the Naudet brothers' documentary *9/11*, broadcast in March of 2002. More egregiously, the actor went on to "star" in a television ad directed by Martin Scorcese for American Express, that is drenched in 9/11 language and imagery. Beginning with a title card ("A Love Letter to a City") that is framed by a mournful Philip Glass score, the advertisement strings together a set of "My" phrases – "My East Side ... My private side" – and climaxes with "My heartbreak" and a shot of the altered New York skyline. The payoff in the ad, of course: "My card is American Express." De Niro's star image – perhaps defined by his portrayal of boxer Jake LaMotta in Scorcese's *Raging Bull* (1980) – made him the perfect carrier of a quickly developing rhetoric about American masculine resilience in the days after 9/11.

Following Paul Simon's rendition of "Bridge Over Troubled Water," Clint Eastwood introduced the Willie Nelson-led celebrity chorus who sang "America, the Beautiful" (with only Nelson making it very success-fully into the second verse). Eastwood, looking uncomfortable and badly mangling his call-to-war remarks, was most memorable for wearing a hitched-up blazer that suggested that he was, perhaps, packing heat. Even so, Eastwood did the work of organizing the American public to under-stand 9/11 as the "twenty-first century's day of infamy." "Oh, they left us wounded," Eastwood said, "but renewed in strength." With broad strokes, the script for Eastwood had him very carefully framing the 9/11 attacks as an act of war: "in the conflict that's come upon us," Eastwood argued, today's Americans would be as resolute as their parents and grandparents had been in earlier wars. Finally, his insistence that instead of "300 million victims" the terrorist attack would instead create "300 million heroes" was a crucial act of redefinition: in essence Eastwood was drawing attention away from the rescue workers most commonly named as the heroes of the day and instead instructed his audience to consider what sacrifices they would make for the cause, vague as that might have been on September 21. Susan Faludi (2007) has observed that both the simultaneous reconstruction of the heroic male and the insist-ence that both 9/11 happened to "all of us" have been central to nation-alistic narratives of post-9/11 vengeance. Talking tough and drawing more from his "Dirty Harry" persona than his taciturn Western charac-ters, Eastwood's position in *Tribute* acted as a tryout, of sorts, for his later role as director of the Greatest Generation, with his pair of 2006 World War II movies (*Flags of Our Fathers* and *Letters from Iwo Jima*).

Tribute's creators did give dramatic pride of place to a few Greatest Generation figures, no doubt as a reassuring attempt to invoke masculine power, continuity, and resolve. Although Eastwood's twitchy "I'm going to shoot somebody" affect was more reminiscent of Mel Gibson's borderline psycho Riggs of the *Lethal Weapon* series than of Eastwood's own taking-care-of-business Dirty Harry, and Willie Nelson's glassy-eyed, show-closing sing-along suggested that America's elders had begun self-medicating in response to the attacks, Joel Gallen and his writers were unmistakably interested in scripting a show that emphasized a legible American history of just war in response to surprise attack. With the film of *Pearl Harbor* only a few months old, it is only puzzling that Ben Affleck was not part of the *Tribute* proceedings. Cuba Gooding, Jr (who did appear in *Pearl Harbor*) was on hand, as part of the phone bank and finale chorus, perhaps to remind viewers of the simple math of revenge that brought the United States into World War II.

Mostly, the historical resonances and personnel choices in *Tribute* are boomer reference points, and not Greatest Generation ones. I want to be clear about my demographic argument here: this was an exercise in cultural triumphalism by white, *male* baby boomers. If we study the birthdates of the primary male musical performers (taking one leader per group and adding in the special guest Goo Goo Doll who appeared with Limp Bizkit), we discover that the average birth year is 1956. In the admittedly smaller cohort of female performers, the mean year of birth is 1970. There was no major female musical performer on *Tribute* born before 1960 – no Aretha Franklin, no Dolly Parton, no Bonnie Raitt. This was television after all, and women who were authorized to appear on the telethon had to pass some very stringent (if unspoken) entrance requirements having to do with age and physical appearance. While more than a few of the male artists could operate comfortably outside of American beauty norms (i.e. they could look old, sloppy, and/or ugly – e.g. Willie Nelson, Neil Young, and Tom Petty), the women who appeared were unlined, streamlined, and dressed fine.

Strangely, but perhaps not surprising giving the demographic tilt of the performers (and assumed audience of callers), the heart of *Tribute* came with evocations of the Vietnam-era and Civil Rights music. What is striking is how *Tribute* anchored itself in the once countercultural sounds of Vietnam War protest and the singing Civil Rights movement and converted them into domesticated vehicles of unity. With two notable exceptions that I will discuss, the telethon operated from the premise that its viewers would take its Black-and-white-together orientation as a comforting translation of racial unity into national unity. Strikingly absent from the picture, of course, were any of the complexities of identity (i.e. Arab American or South Asian Muslims) that would be of pressing concern in the days after 9/11.

How many gospel choirs there were! The show opened with Bruce Springsteen's retrofitted "My City of Ruins," originally written in 2000 about Asbury Park, New Jersey, a city that looms large in Springsteen's career and mythology. (At a later 9/11 benefit, Springsteen introduced "My City of Ruins" by saying – with a clear Woody Guthrie inflection – "I wrote this song for Asbury Park, but songs are good for whoever needs them.") Springsteen's first album, *Greetings from Asbury Park, New Jersey*, was released in 1973, just 3 years after race riots had put an exclamation point on Asbury's steady decline of the previous few decades. "My City of Ruins" is organized around a melody line that evokes Curtis Mayfield's 1964 song "People Get Ready," a hit for his group the Impressions, and a mainstay of the mid-sixties Civil Rights movement songbook. If the Civil Rights subtext of "People Get Ready" was not immediately available to all audience members, none could miss the visual cues offered by Springsteen's backup singers. While Springsteen's regular bands of the 1970s, 1980s, and early 1990s had always featured at least one African American member (most consistently saxophonist Clarence Clemons), his *Tribute* choir included not only Clemons, but two other African American singers as well, joining regular bandmates Steve Van Zandt, Patti Scialfa, and Soozie Tyrell.

Musicologists Kip Pegley and Susan Fast (2007) have suggested that the presence of gospel choirs (or smaller scale allusions to them) supported the *Tribute*'s appeal to a unified American community, and this seems true as far as it goes. But the harmony represented on the telethon was, as I have suggested, almost exclusively a Black and white affair. While the lineup of presenters included some very token efforts to represent the actual demographics of the United States (Jimmy Smits for Latinos, Lucy Liu for all Asians – and she was there to talk about how un-American it is to be prejudiced!), the musical roster featured mainly white and African American acts, with Mariah Carey as the sole exemplar of a mixed heritage that confounds the more usual binary system of racial classification in the United States.

The big-tent "gospel" sounds generally came from behind white performers. It is not saying much to notice that these non-African American secular artists – Bruce Springsteen, Sheryl Crow, Enrique Iglesias, and Faith Hill – turned to African American backup singers and gospel-influenced arrangements to signify seriousness of purpose in this time of grief. This move draws perhaps most directly from a few key 1980s songs, notably Foreigner's 1984 hit "I Want to Know What Love Is" and Madonna's "Like a Prayer" (1989), whose inclusion of gospel choirs on record and in videos functioned as a marker of sincerity, depth, and intensity.

More than 30 years ago, Asian American writers Frank Chin and Jeffrey Paul Chan (1972) wrote an essay about what they called "racist love." Joining the more obvious workings of "racist hate" (the direct oppression of non-whites through enslavement, policing, legislation, and so on) is the powerful force of racist love, which, in their formulation, is defined as a set of cultural practices of representation that lock people of color in the United States into narrowly defined roles. Without suggesting that the creators of *Tribute* were consciously drawing on very old stereotypes of African Americans as more emotional or "better" at grieving than white people, there is a clear enough effect produced by all those gospel singers and sounds. Most of these white performers do not regularly draw from gospel traditions in their music (nor do they usually have gospel singers on the payroll) and *Tribute* couldn't avoid communicating the sense that African Americans were being drafted in that moment to intensify the expressions of mourning that served as the organizing principle of the program. The obvious visual element provided by African American singers was underscored by musical moments that drew from gospel traditions – most notably Paul Simon's "Bridge Over Troubled Water" (which borrows its title from a gospel song by the Swan Silvertones) and the Hallelujah-vocals of U2's "Walk On."

The racial unity (Black–white unity, that is) of *Tribute* was communicated not only through the presence of gospel sounds, but also through the notable integration of various bands that do not usually feature African American musicians. *Tribute* invested in a watery version of American multiculturalism that is familiar to anyone who has attended a musical performance at an American grade school in the past decade or so: we are all flowers in one garden, our varied colors shine. The telethon offered us up not only Lucy Liu and Jimmy Smits, but also Ray Romano telling a story about a Christian and a Jew, and Cameron Diaz reminding us that women were heroes on that day too (schoolteachers at Ground Zero who did not abandon their charges). The telethon also offered up a perfunctory video interlude that the later DVD release depressingly but aptly called "Muslim Kids." This short piece was a species of cultural performance often accessed during celebrations of Martin Luther King, Jr's birthday in January – the "Dr King would want us all to play together" approach. As a writer at one webzine put it during a live chat held parallel to the telethon: "Nice segment on the Muslim-American kids. this is very effective. we suck that we have to tell ourselves not to pick on Muslim kids. we so utterly suck" ("Chat Room Review," 2001).

Outside of this vignette, which featured at least one *very* agitated "Muslim kid" who recounts the schoolyard persecution he had already suffered, the telethon offered up only one other extended Muslim tale, and this one was delivered by Muhammad Ali. Will Smith, whose *Ali* biopic – surprise! – was due out three months later, introduced the boxer as "the most famous person in the world," a great hero, and a Muslim. From there the job of Smith was to reassure the telethon audience that it was "hate, not religion" that motivated the September 11 attacks. Ali, whose Parkinson's disease had left him visibly shaking and barely audible, supported Smith's words and, in an attempt at humor, said he wished he could have stopped the hijackers with his own hands.

Cultural commentators love to play the game "When did the 1960s really end?" One popular answer includes the free Altamont music festival in 1969, organized by the Rolling Stones, which climaxed with the fatal stabbing of a young African American man by the Hells' Angels, who were working as security guards for the concert. Or Richard Nixon's resignation in 1974 – the "end of our long national nightmare," as incoming President Gerald Ford put it. Perhaps it was when the last Americans left Saigon in 1975. More fanciful, yet still resonant, is the case made for when The Beatles' song "Revolution" was used in a 1985 Nike advertisement. This is just a parlor game, of course, but not a pointless one; it serves as a way to mark off generational change, shifting historical paradigms, and so on. So here I nominate Muhammad Ali's performance as comforting Muslim daddy as a reasonable entry in the "end of the sixties" sweepstakes. During a press conference just a few days before the telethon (on September 17), President Bush responded to a reporter's question about whether he wanted Osama bin Laden dead by saying "There's an old poster out west, as I recall, that said, 'Wanted: Dead or Alive'" (Harnden, 2001). Naming bin Laden as Muslim Public Enemy No. 1 was no surprise to the assembled journalists or Americans watching at home; it is, however, worth remembering that from the time of Muhammad Ali's public announcement of his conversion to Islam in 1964, perhaps until 1974 when Palestinian leader Yasser Arafat eclipsed him on the enemy list with his "olive branch and gun" speech at the United Nations, it would have been the boxer's face up on that poster.

Ali's conversion to Islam – to the African American group the Nation of Islam, that is – was nothing short of a scandal in 1964. Widely vilified and feared for his association with Malcolm X, Ali's 1960s career as a Muslim marked him as a "bad Black man" to countless American spectators. His ethical refusal to enter the military in 1967 solidified his public image as radical, dangerous, and un-American. Ali's association with the Nation of Islam, with its separatist and Black-centered ideology, rendered Ali a flashpoint for a great deal of white resentment by the end of the decade. In this light, his appearance as a calming voice at the telethon stands as a remarkable transformation. Of course there had been much build-up: through the 1970s and 1980s, not only did Ali move away from the Nation of Islam and toward a more orthodox version of the religion, but he also carefully tended his image as boxing's wise old ambassador.

The most important thing to notice about Ali's presence at the telethon is probably also the most obvious thing. He was not only the most famous man in the world, and the most famous Muslim in America, but he was also the *only* Muslim (good guy) that any substantial number of American viewers would recognize – save perhaps another athlete or two and Nation of Islam Minister Louis Farrakhan. This should give us pause. For all of the talk of respect and diversity that ran through *Tribute* one truth it could not hide was that very few Muslims or Arab Americans had made any particular headway into mainstream American consciousness. Another parlor game: if Ali had not been available that night, who else could have spoken for Islam? Kareem Abdul-Jabbar? Rapper Q-Tip? Disgraced boxer Mike Tyson? (A final parlor game: if the creators of the show had wanted a recognizable Arab American – Muslim or not – who could they have called? Ralph Nader? Disc jockey Casey Kasem, familiar only once he had spoken? Actor Tony Shalhoub? Paula Abdul, post-chart success and pre-*American Idol*, but with her nice Arab-sounding last name and Jewish parents?)

If Muhammad Ali did not exist, it would have been necessary for the producers of *Tribute* to invent him. He served double-duty here, affirming that his people (times two) would "close ranks" with white Americans after the attacks. In July 1918 African American leader W. E. B. Du Bois called on African Americans to wholeheartedly join the American effort in World War I. "Let us not hesitate," Du Bois wrote. "Let us, while this war lasts, forget our special grievances and close our ranks shoulder to shoulder with our own white fellow citizens and the allied nations that are fighting for democracy" (Du Bois, 2004: 505). Ali's brief appearance at the telethon made no such explicit statement as Du Bois, but if the business of telethons is to collect pledges, then the pledge made by Ali, with an important assist from Will Smith (who was to be the subject of rumors in early 2002 that *he* had converted to Islam), was that African Americans and American Muslims were completely and uncritically supporting American responses to 9/11.

Tribute was so successfully able to orchestrate scenes of harmony that even seemingly modest instances of dissent cut very deep. Cover versions of two songs from the early 1970s – John Lennon's "Imagine" (1971) and Donny Hathaway's "Someday We'll All Be Free" (1973) – carried the first hints of dissent. Appearing back-to-back on the program, Neil Young and newbie Alicia Keys (her first album had been released only three months earlier) broke at least somewhat from the simple scripts of solidarity and human fellowship that the show promoted. Neil Young, clad in cowboy hat and fierce sideburns, not only performed the Lennon song, but arranged it as if it were a missing London Symphony Orchestra number from his own 1972 *Harvest* album. "Imagine" is essentially a catalog of provocations and it stands alone on the telethon for its insistence that an embrace of *no* religion, rather than an embrace of *all* religions, might provide the surest path to peace. "Imagine" veered off-message with its anti-religion challenge, and added anti-nationalism and anti-materialism to boot. (In a neat twist, Young changed Lennon's "Imagine no possessions/I wonder if you can" to "I wonder if *I* can.") The universal kinship at the heart of "Imagine" ran counter, in its own relatively non-confrontational way, to the patriotic, commercial, and religious pressures of the first days and weeks after 9/11.

Alicia Keys' resistance to the prime directives of the occasion was, perhaps, less conspicuous than that of Neil Young, but still striking. Keys dug more deeply into the pop songbook than Young, choosing to sing Donny Hathaway's "Someday We'll All be Free." Hathaway was an important soul artist of the 1970s best known for his 1972 duet with Roberta Flack, "Where is the Love?" "Someday" was never a significant charting song in its own time, but its broad message of Black pride ("manly pride" in the original, here changed by Keys to "womanly pride") has resonated with audiences for decades and was given an important second life in a version by Aretha Franklin that ran over the end credits of Spike Lee's Malcolm X film in 1992. Performing alone at the piano, Keys mined as much gospel, both vocally and instrumentally, as she could from Hathaway's understated song. Without introducing any overt protest material into the telethon, Keys was, at the very least, able to invite audiences to reconsider the "we" at the heart of this song and, by extension, to consider critically its relationship to the "we" being promoted by *Tribute*. Returning to a 1970s song associated, however vaguely, with the African American liberation struggle was one way to defy the rush to national consensus that had already been "weaponized" by September 21.

The true tear in the fabric of this program came a bit later in the night, just after New York-associated Conan O'Brien and Sarah Jessica Parker finished a spoken ode to the city and the camera found Haitian-American rapper Wyclef Jean. Clad in a stars-and-stripes jacket, Jean spoke "one-two" into the microphone, and began to play a simple guitar figure just after his drummer laid down a martial "one-two, one-two-three" beat. Then Jean started to sing: "Old pirates yes they rob I/sold I to the merchant ships." With this introduction of Bob Marley's "Redemption Song" – the last song on the last studio album that the international reggae superstar released in his lifetime (1980) – Wyclef Jean demonstrated with breathtaking power that it might be possible actually to *say something* meaningful in response to the "attack on America."

In a rant published early in 2002, cultural critic Greil Marcus made this broad assault on the entire telethon:

> At the austere September benefit concert *America: A Tribute to Heroes*, Bruce Springsteen offered his song "My City of Ruins" – and, really, you could answer its chorus of "Come on, rise up! Come on, rise up!" with, "Shut up, God dammit! Give me time to despair! Give me time to hate!" Did the song, written two years ago for the residents of Asbury Park, New Jersey, need to be sung in this utterly different context? Wouldn't it have been more powerful, more shocking – more of an affirmation of the terrorist attacks not as a "dose of reality," as Susan Sontag described them, but as a rent in reality – for an artist as eloquent and honest as Springsteen to step forward and attest that for the moment he had nothing to say?

With two sung lines of six words each, Wyclef Jean stopped the show and attested that he had something very particular to say. By introducing the history of slavery into the *Tribute* proceedings, Jean interrupted the evening's programming and offered a rejoinder to the rapidly developing rhetoric of national blamelessness and Black–white unity that was so central to American responses to 9/11. If "Redemption Song" had been in danger over the past 20 years of being co-opted by dominant media forces, like so many Bob Marley songs, as a fable of universal fellowship, Jean's dramatic performance of it on September 21 recovered its radical heart. Rooting his 9/11 response in a foundational moment of racial violence, Wyclef Jean was able to offer a powerful "minority report." His choice of "Redemption Song" and his insistence on performing as if a live audience were there with him ("New York City! Won't you help me sing …") made it more difficult to take easy comfort in the myth of American unity that the telethon promoted so energetically.

Just about four years later, in early September of 2005, rapper Kanye West was famously to go "off script" during a nationally televised Hurricane Katrina telethon. Speaking of how race shaped federal responses to this tragedy, West put a sharp point on the matter with his simple declaration that "George Bush doesn't care about Black people." In September of 2001 Wyclef Jean "spoke" with much less clarity and caused nothing like the national outcry that greeted West's remarks. *Tribute* was not aimed so simply, as Tom Hanks suggested, at raising spirits and money: it was also part of an effort – loosely organized but quite real – to persuade Americans to get their war on. The attack on Afghanistan began just a bit over two weeks after the telethon. Jean acted here like one of the "precogs" from Steven Spielberg's *Minority Report* – his first of three major 9/11 movies – who have a preternatural ability to foretell a crime that has not yet happened. Putting race and imperialism at the heart of the matter, Wyclef Jean's "Redemption Song" was an early indication that American cultural responses to 9/11 would escape the one-dimensional reassurances that characterized this telethon, this first communal effort to define how "we" felt.

CH/3
Snapshots

At the Country Music Awards held on November 7, 2001, superstar Alan Jackson debuted his 9/11 song, "Where Were You (When the World Stopped Turning)." Radio programmers had it on the air by the next morning and it topped the country music charts for 5 weeks starting in late December. The song's title was Jackson's vehicle for carrying a series of rhetorical snapshots – prescriptions, really, for what Americans should have been doing as the planes hit, and then just after. The imagined "you" of Jackson's song is a teacher of "innocent children," who calls Mom, turns off the violent movie on the television in favor of *I Love Lucy*, in which a running gag finds Lucy cringing in fear as though her husband Ricky is about to hit her, and most important, dusts off the Bible, presumably to read the verse from First Corinthians that Jackson paraphrases in the chorus ("Faith, hope, and love are some good things He gave us"). Using a method that parallels the procession of sincere stars that constituted *America: A Tribute to Heroes*, Jackson's song enlists the putative neutrality of the catalog form to smuggle in some very potent arguments about art and politics.

We can now see that Jackson's song was part of a larger wave that developed in the first few months following 9/11, a "snapshot culture" that promoted the anthology of accidental or naive artistic statement as the purest response to the attacks. If we are to understand how 9/11/2001 stands as an important date in American cultural history (and not only its political or military history), then one task is to explore how "first responders" in the world of the popular arts made claims – explicit and otherwise – about how they could best do their work now. It was to take some time before many individual artists had full-length 9/11 works to offer up to the American marketplace and the 9/11 compilation acted as a stopgap of sorts, a way to fill the cultural void where all that irony and violence used to be. 9/11 was not the first time the "accidental footage" came to stand at the center of Americans' collective memory of a major tragic event: think of how impossible it is to conjure up the assassination of John F. Kennedy without the presence of the Zapruder film, for instance.

The photograph itself quickly took a central place among the 9/11 arts, and claimed its status as the most valuable form of democratic cultural expression in the months after the attacks. It has become commonplace to note that September 11, 2001, is the most photographed day in history: more specifically, many note that the time between the second plane hitting and the towers collapsing represents the most photographed "event" in human history. Marita Sturken (2007) argues that "photographs seem to have played a dominant role in the response to 9/11, far more than the television images ... [T]he photograph seems to aid in mediating and negotiating a sense of loss" (186).

Some cultural critics have posited that the very idea of hitting the Twin Towers *must* have been planned with visual impact in mind. Just 5 days after the attack, Neal Gabler (2001), a historian of Hollywood, wrote in the *New York Times* that the hijackers were "creating not just terror; they were creating images." Gabler continued in this vein, going on to note that when "the first plane hit the World Trade Center, presumably there would be no camera ready. So the terrorists provided a second attack at a decent interval that they knew would be captured on film or video, and then repeated from many different angles – a montage of death and destruction. It was terrorism with the audience in mind."

The tragic attacks on the World Trade Center (and the Pentagon to a lesser extent, and United 93, as it turned out, not so much at all) were experienced by most in the "audience" as endlessly reproduced images and not direct experience. A dominant interpretive stance invented immediately after the attacks, and itself endlessly reproduced, is that the events of the day were somehow "like" a movie in their production and reception. This "film" script was usually articulated with some despair, as what appeared to be an apolitical observation, but one that harbored within it a quite shocking appraisal of contemporary American culture. Every time some person-on-the-street or well-positioned cultural commentator argued that the 9/11 attacks were "like" a Hollywood movie, they were also admitting (or arguing) that this terror that had reached

U.S. shores was not so "foreign" after all – that somehow it was connected to the corrupt, centralized activity of moviemaking in America. Claire Kahane (2003) has argued that "the actual reality before our eyes was almost immediately transformed into and by the virtual reality of Hollywood." Kahane goes on to suggest that "our response to 9/11 made disturbingly clear how much our perceptual experience as well as our psychic life is filtered and managed through films we have seen" (107).

One significant response to the developing anxiety that film was some-how *too* powerful a force in shaping the American people's experience of 9/11 was a quick and decisive enshrinement of photography as the people's art. There have been notable – and officially sanctioned – attempts in American history to establish "the people" as the most important *subjects* of the camera: the portfolios of the photographers employed by the New Deal's Farm Security Administration and the Office of War Information during the Great Depression offer ample documentation of this impulse. But 9/11 brought with it a newer idea that the crucial images, those that would contribute the most to the historical record and the affective inventory of 9/11 culture, would not only be of the people but also by the people for the people. We have at least some anecdotal evidence that many in downtown New York felt the call to take pictures as the planes hit. The manager of a Duane Reade drugstore near the World Trade Center reported selling somewhere between 60 and 100 cameras within an hour of the planes hitting (Heller, 2005: 8).

One explanation for why photography became so important on 9/11 is straightforward enough. In the years leading up to 2001 digital camera sales were increasing dramatically; revenue from digital camera sales in the United States surpassed that from film cameras for the first time in 2000. Digital cameras brought with them many opportunities, including internet sharing and archiving, that were not easily accessible to most film camera users. Now able to produce images comparable to film cameras, digital cameras quickly became part of the nascent Web 2.0 culture of peer-to-peer exchange, and its generative assumptions of user-generated content. (A few years later, with the Asian tsunami of 2004 and the London bombing of 7/7/2005, the digital camera itself was to be eclipsed by the cell phone camera, with its stunning ability to document and transmit almost instantaneously.)

The push for photography as 9/11's art may have come first with the heartbreaking missing posters that blanketed New York, some put up as early as the afternoon of September 11. As Marshall Sella (2001) has written, these posters were organized around snapshots, pictures chosen by family members of the missing to reflect "the happiest images they could find, that one perfect moment lived out one final time before the end of things. So the missing people stood smiling in wedding pictures; they were poised above birthday cakes, with babies and puppies and at graduations." The posters' images were, first and foremost, instrumental; they were put up as visual aids for rescue, and then, dreadfully, for recovery of human remains. Soon, though, these missing posters, born of panic and grief, became a city-wide work of art. The task of these unplanned snapshot memorials was soon transformed, and their activity was now therapeutic, rather than directive. "Mounted together on a hundred walls," Marshall Berman wrote in 2002, "these men and women had a stronger collective identity after death than they ever had in life. And they created a collective identity for us, one we didn't want but couldn't shed: survivors, the survivors of mainland America's first great air raid" (4). Since Rodney King's beating by Los Angeles police officers was captured on video in 1991 by an onlooker, Americans had been well aware that they needed to be camera-ready – in order to testify, to help make sure that justice would be served.

But the photographic work of 9/11 obviously had much more motivating it than any simple police-blotter, documentary impulse. The curators and archivists who have done the most work to gather the 9/11 images suggest that faced with the horror of September 11, New Yorkers grabbed their cameras in order to participate more fully in the democracy that had seemingly just come under attack. Three major photo collection sites are framed by declarations that the anthology of images is the best possible expression of the people in this moment of terror and pain. According to *Here is New York*, *The September 11 Digital Archive*, and *The September 11 Photo Project*, taking photographs on 9/11 is what democracy looked like. Each of these curatorial efforts also makes fairly direct claims that this is what 9/11 art looks like, and this is what the telling of 9/11 history looks like. By the time of the London bombing and Asian tsunami the most important news agencies were elbowing in on this social activity and trying to recruit amateur photographers and filmmakers to provide content for their feeds. The co-optation of this visual imagery by commercial interests was not in play at the time of 9/11 though, and these efforts were protected, with few exceptions, from corporate raiders.

Taking snapshots on 9/11 and then passing them on (like sharing rumors, but more distinguished) was a way for "average" Americans to enter the picture. The organizer of the large *Here is New York* archive puts it this way:

> Photography was the perfect medium to express what happened on 9.11, since it is democratic by its very nature and infinitely reproducible. The tragedy at Ground Zero struck all New Yorkers equally, leaving none of us immune to shock or grief. Although the disaster was the lead story in every newspaper in the world, and searing footage of the planes destroying the towers was running on television 24 hours a day, to New Yorkers this wasn't a news story: it was an unabsorbable nightmare. In order to come to grips with all of this imagery which was haunting us, it was essential, we thought, to reclaim it from the media and stare at it without flinching. (Shulan, 2004)

Michael Shulan's assertion for *Here is New York* is that all the photographs on his site act as a kind of spontaneous media criticism, that more or less immediately after the attacks New Yorkers rose up and said a loud "No" to the centralized corporate media that was in the best position to dominate the telling of the story of the attacks.

Cultural responses to the 9/11 attacks have alternated between commercially exploitative efforts and grassroots expressions. Dana Heller has asked how we might begin to "understand the selling of 9/11 as both a cynical manipulation of consumers engineered by powerful corporate and political interests and a potentially liberating and authentic expression of the people's creative energies in the face of profound grief, genuine love of country, and sudden fear of national as well as global instability" (5). The guardians of 9/11 photography have worked in a sustained way to claim cultural pride of place for their artistic goods – often with an implied comparison of photography to the debased spectacles of Hollywood and the ad-driven products of the television industry.

Michael Feldschuh (2002), of *The September 11 Photo Project*, explains that the photography collection he organized (not "curated," he, like the other photo-promoters, is quick to add) was a natural outgrowth of grief. In fact, he insists, the photography collections evolved from the public shrines that sprouted in various spots around the city, capturing the "emotional authenticity" that "lay in the open nature of what was occurring." Feldschuh goes on to comment that no limits were put on the gallery space where his exhibit first appeared before traveling: "no one curated what was given; no one judged certain objects or statements better than others" (viii). Shulan writes almost identically of *Here is New York*: "It has not been edited to showcase the 'best' or the 'strongest' images, but to give the most coherent sense of the whole." *The September 11 Photo Project* and *Here is New York* anthologies claim to best represent the needs and desires of New Yorkers at a time of extreme crisis. In many ways the "snapshot" collections built on the success of the NAMES Project AIDS Memorial Quilt, begun in 1987 and described as the largest contemporary community-based art project in the world.

The daunting multiplicity of photographs collected in these two archives (as well as in *The September 11 Digital Archive*) is the central fact of their social existence. About 20 years ago, Alan Trachtenberg (1988) wrote splendidly about the photography solicited and collated by the FSA-OWI, arguing that the very system of organizing them – "the file" – "deserves to be recognized as one of the prime cultural artifacts of the New Deal" (45). Similarly, we might say that the 9/11 digital archive – the anything-goes, all are-welcome-at-the-table approach of the major online 9/11 photo sites – has already become an important political and artistic mode in the years since the tragedy. Uncurated, omnibus, and non-professional (mostly), these collections of 9/11 photographs have a tale to tell through their very abundance. The "immensity of the here and now," as Paul West titled his 9/11 novel, called into being a similarly outsized photographic response, and a few New Yorkers took it on themselves to collect and preserve that largeness, brandishing it as a talisman to ward off further destruction.

The introduction to the *Here is New York* book notes that it contains nearly 1,000 of the more than 5,000 pictures that some 3,000 photographers submitted to the exhibition. *Here is New York* has by now amassed one of the largest photographic archives in world history devoted to a single event. But whereas after other events of this magnitude one striking picture has sometimes come to symbolize what happened, the "one picture" that will probably symbolize the World Trade Center tragedy will be all of these pictures.

This post-9/11 visual abundance draws, in an implicit way, from a major strand of American transcendentalist thinking of the nineteenth century – the line that runs from Ralph Waldo Emerson to Walt Whitman and connecting Emerson's "transparent eye-ball" (*Nature*, 1836) to Whitman's "I am large, I contain multitudes" (*Leaves of Grass*, 1855). Each photograph has its own individual "I" behind it, holding "Leicas and digital Nikons," "homemade pinhole cameras and little plastic gizmos that schoolchildren wear on their wrists" (*Here is New York*).

What unifies them, according to Shulan, is that they are being presented in unmediated fashion:

> If one photograph tells *a* story, thousands of photographs tell not only thousands of stories but also perhaps begin to tell *the* story if they are allowed to speak for themselves, to each other, and to the viewer directly, unframed either by glass, metal or wood, or by preconception or editorial comment. In the political sphere it is this principle, after all, which America's Founding Fathers advanced when they developed the notion of democracy – that wisdom lies not in the vision and will of any one individual, or small group of individuals, but in the collective vision of us all.

On the *Here is New York* website, that multitude of pictures is organized by subject and, not so surprisingly, one of the most heavily populated categories (after "Memorials" and "Flags") is "Onlookers." As with the process of sharing rumors that could possibly involve ourselves, one important social function of taking photographs during and after the 9/11 attacks was to make 9/11 be about as many of us, at once, as possible. In the 1950s and then again in the early 1970s there was a popular television show called *You Are There* which allowed viewers an entry point into some historical event or other. With the advent of digital cameras and uploading capabilities, onsite photographers were able, within minutes, to create miniature versions of *You Are There,* and the quantity of pictures offered of "regular folks" on the street presented something of a balm, a reminder that most of us were still here. While the photographic anthologies have the occasional shot of a dust- or blood-covered refugee from the towers, and even more rarely of a person who jumped from the towers, by and large they are made up of "onlookers" – those of us left to make and collect images, posters, and histories.

The photo projects and digital anthologies promote the notion that on 9/11 and in the days after, all Americans had equal access to creating photographic imagery and that every piece of visual art created was equal to the next. This "democratic" positioning is ultimately an argument *against* photography as an art at all. As Feldschuh writes in his introduction to *The September 11 Photo Project* "we would not treat the contributions as relics or artifacts, but rather as their creators had intended, as objects for direct display for all to see" (ix). Writing of the photograph, historian Lawrence Levine (1988) has argued that it is "beguiling" because it seems "to be the quintessential objective document." Levine warns us, however, that these images "are also the products of human intelligence, like all other sources historians utilize" and must "be read with the same care and thoughtfulness we have learned to apply to written sources" (23).

Levine is writing here about professional New Deal photographers. The flood of photographs taken in the aftermath of the 9/11 attacks and then almost instantaneously circulated were mostly by amateurs, however, and this has made it difficult to take measure of photography's two main functions, as Alan Trachtenberg has noted, of "utility and aesthetics" (1988, 50). This is significant cultural work that the photographic anthologies and other digital archives accomplish: positing photographic realism as the most "authentic" (Shulan's word) way to respond to the horrors of 9/11, the collectors help establish the documentary as an especially privileged form of post-9/11 expression. These early efforts bore fruit not only in their own reception (the popular tours that the photo exhibits launched, the hardcover books, and so on) but also in establishing the critical vocabulary for praising artistic offerings as disparate as the Naudet brothers' 9/11 television documentary (2002), Bruce Springsteen's 2002 record *The Rising*, the *New York Times* "Portraits of Grief" (2001), and Paul Greengrass's film *United 93* (2006).

The power of photographs is difficult to gainsay. Promoted as "snapshots" by "average" Americans, the 9/11 archive has developed a forceful ability to function as natural outpouring, collective effort – in short, as the "genius of the people." Of course every single 9/11 image we have is the product of a very subjective selection process, varying levels of technical skill and training, desire to upload and access to a good internet connection, and just plain luck. In sociological terms, who was likely to have been out on the streets of New York taking these pictures? What relative freedoms might they have enjoyed that put them in that place, in that moment? Of all the pictures I have studied that were taken in the hours after the attacks, I have yet to see, just for instance, one of (or by) a caregiver putting a toddler down for a nap after fleeing the playground. (That focus on New York City's domestic realities would fall largely to fiction writers, such as Helen Schulman, who, in her *A Day at the Beach* [2007]), would show her main character spending much time worrying over the snacking and sleeping patterns of her young son.)

It is a simple point I am trying to make: for the thousands of images we have been privileged to see after and about the attacks of 9/11, there are innumerable others that have gone uncollected – or that have been actively censored – and therefore don't "count" as 9/11 art. Perhaps the most notorious "disappeared" image of 9/11 was the proposed cover for *Party Music*, an album by the Oakland-based rap group The Coup (see it at http://gothamist.com/2008/01/29/nyc_album_art_t_4.php) that was ultimately released November 6. In the original design, rapper Boots Riley was shown using a remote control device to blow up the Twin Towers. This cover, widely circulated on the internet, was replaced, after much record company pressure, with a more benign image of a Molotov cocktail.

When we face the claims made by dedicated culture workers like Michael Feldschuh, Michael Shulan, and the creators of *The September 11 Digital Archive*, it is important that we respond not only with gratitude for the hard work they have done, but also with some critical distance: as Alan Trachtenberg has written of the New Deal "files" of FSA photographs, we too are responsible for studying the archives themselves, their layout, their content, their implicit and explicit claims, in order to make sure that we know how to evaluate properly their declarations of authenticity and completeness.

A simple tour through *Here is New York*'s taxonomy of pictures reveals how much *may* have been left out of this collecting effort. There is no category, after all, for looters – although William Langewiesche (2002) and others have documented serious episodes of such exploitation, perhaps even by firefighters. Nor do we have, really, any documentary evidence of the category we might call "people behaving badly in a moment of crisis." The *Here is New York* exhibit says right up front that it means to capture "not only grief, and shock, and courage, but a beauty that is at once infernal and profoundly uplifting." These collected photographs speak, according to the organizers, "not with one voice, but with one purpose, saying that to make sense of this terrifying new phase in our history we must break down the barriers that divide us." The photographic anthologies have a tale to tell, and it is a narrative of an uncomplicated "we," pulling together during this time of unprecedented hurt, anxiety, and fear.

The digital archives are noteworthy for what they *did* capture but also for what they didn't get. Art Spiegelman (2004) explains how he felt compelled to draw one image as the centerpiece of his *In the Shadow of No Towers* because nobody else caught it: "The pivotal image from my 9/11 morning – one that didn't get photographed or videotaped into public memory but still remains burned onto the inside of my eyelids several years later – was the image of the looming north tower's glowing bones just before it vaporized" (n.p.). Forced to trust Spiegelman's admittedly "subjective" art, we are confronted in one dramatic way with the limitations of one snapshot or 5,000: their phenomenal core is their phenomenal curse. Also interesting in this respect is the work of two major novelists, Don DeLillo and Ken Kalfus, both of whom feature main characters in their 9/11 novels who are troubled by the fact that they can find themselves in no pictures taken that day, despite having successfully fled from the towers. We have so gratefully embraced the abundant *presence* framed by the countless snapshots taken on 9/11 that it has taken fiction writers to remind us to think about all of the unexamined absences.

The photo archives do interesting work through their insistence that all snapshots are created equal. *Here is New York*, as I have noted, actually invokes the Founding Fathers, in order to remind us that "wisdom lies not in the vision and will of any one individual, or small group of individuals, but in the collective vision of us all." These are nice words, as far as promoting a vague and probably meaningless "democratic vision" goes, but what is also troubling here is the premise that there is no difference between the 500th shot we look at of the North Tower burning and a completely unique composition that actually communicates something new to the viewer. Even the most cursory look through any of the digital archives exposes a wide range of photographic skill, intentionality, and narrative arc. A picture of two toddlers, arm in arm on a wall in Brooklyn, looking across the water to Manhattan, filed by *Here in New York* under the rubric "Missing," is an obvious attempt to stitch these two children into a story that may or may not be theirs.

Snapshots can do all sorts of work, and at least some photographers were able to create more critical imagery in the immediate aftermath of the attacks. *The September 11 Photo Project* includes a picture (136–7) of a Grey Line sightseeing bus that is stopped, with a crowd around it, all looking toward the burning towers. The tourists on the bus, acting like good tourists, have begun to rise – realizing no doubt that they are in the midst of what might be the single greatest photo opportunity in Grey Line history. What we have, then, is a picture of 9/11 picture-taking, an amazing on-the-fly meditation on how quickly the wounded towers (not yet Ground Zero) were becoming a tourist attraction.

Such striking images serve as a reminder that the unprecedented visual power of the two planes hitting the World Trade Center made it very difficult to turn our gaze away from the actual site of destruction in order to see more, more of New York, more of the rest of the world. And while the amateur photographers who provide most of the images in the digital archives often have much to say – on both documentary and aesthetic grounds – it is also worth reminding ourselves that more than a few of the photographs included in the digital archives are, no doubt, the work of trained artists.

In *The September 11 Photo Project*, for instance, we find an amazing picture of "innocent" college tennis players, practicing on the astoundingly green courts of NYU. They are innocent because they – in the picture's framing – are in a valley, surrounded by buildings, with the Twin Towers visible to us, but not them. The Twin Towers have exploded, we see, and the tennis players don't know it. If the Gray Line snapshot is the artfully constructed work of the "just after," here we find a photographic ballet of the "just before." Intensifying the photographer's effect are the billboards that loom in the near distance: one for Christina Perrin's fashion line seems to show a veiled Muslim woman; another shows what appears to be a broken watch.

Similar in effect is Matt Weber's stunning photo (see Figure 4) of a toddler kneeling at play in a New York park while its mother tends to another child: all are heartbreakingly oblivious to what we see in the background – the Twin Towers on fire. Snapshots are not always the simple products of luck we take them to be. These few images I have chosen to discuss in more detail are not necessarily the "best" 9/11 photographs, though Matt Weber's is certainly in the top tier. They do, however, challenge the "democracy of photographs" directives that define the encyclopedic impulse. In that hour of most intense stress, it is not surprising that professional artists might have been able to represent grief in richer and more complex ways than the rest of us could manage.

The "democracy of photographs" approach to creating post-9/11 art was soon co-opted and homogenized by a powerful corporate actor, in this case the *New York Times*, with its "Portraits of Grief." Borrowing and building upon the rhetoric of the grassroots "snapshot" movement that appeared as soon as the planes hit the towers, the *Times* at once deployed the language of the "accidental" (with emphasis on the anecdote, the serendipitously discovered characteristic, the ephemeral moment that tells it all) while at the same time developing a highly formalized template for memorializing the dead of 9/11. Feminist critic Nancy K. Miller (2003) has suggested convincingly

Figure 4 Matt Weber's photograph of the just before. Source: © Matt Weber

that the "Portraits" were meant to capture the energy of the missing flyers that covered the city in the days after the attack. Miller contends that while "the flyers varied widely in size, style, and presentation ... The newsprint portraits were of necessity uniform" (114). This is technically true, but it might be more apt to say that the *Times* was invested in uniformity, in creating a *Times* "brand" to put on these memorial statements, a brand defined by a sleight-of-hand that turned "snapshot" into "portrait."

The "Portraits" have been incredibly meaningful to a huge number of readers, including Bruce Springsteen who says part of his impetus in creating *The Rising* came with his realization that so many people that the *Times* sketched were described as diehard fans of his music. I do not mean to interfere with all the ways that the *Times* "Portraits" were cathartic or healing for their many readers, but I do want to note that the "newspaper of record" was also incredibly efficient as it cornered the market in remembrance. Cultural geographer Kenneth Foote (2003) has written very persuasively about the four major types of memorialization that have generally followed great tragedies on the American landscape: sanctification, designation, rectification, and obliteration (7). Foote is writing about the actual physical sites of destruction and violence, but his work is relevant to the "Portraits" as well. The two middle terms of his scheme, designation and rectification, refer to social processes that acknowledge a calamity has taken place, but offer relatively low-impact responses. "Designation" simply means that a marker of some kind is erected that communicates "this happened"; rectification involves transforming the site of suffering into a useful new form. Obliteration describes a cultural attempt to erase all traces of the terrible event. It is obliteration's opposite term, "sanctification," that the *Times* was promoting by creating a template that could turn the "snapshot" of each victim of 9/11 into a "sacred" text. As Foote writes, sanctification always involves setting the "sacred place" apart from the surrounding landscape. By turning "snapshots" into "portraits" and printing them in a special section, the *Times* did just that: eschewing the standard obituary form and location, the *Times* instead built on the spontaneous biographies that first appeared on the missing posters, and turned them into a ritualized expression of reverence.

The first Sunday that the *Times* printed these life stories, they ran under the headline "Snapshots of Their Lives, Told With the Pain of Those Who Loved Them" (September 16). A month into the series, the *Times* ran an editorial congratulating itself for the achievements of "Portraits of Grief" and again emphasized that "each profile is only a snapshot, a single still frame lifted from the unrecountable complexity of a lived life" ("Among the Missing," October 14). Nancy Miller (2003: 115) suggests that the *Times*' obsessive focus on the "visual" in its own descriptions of the "Portraits" series is a symptom of the newspaper's inability to rely on its usual textual form; it was as if the paper "found itself at a loss for words, words suddenly seeming inadequate to the task" at hand. But I think it might be more useful to think of the *Times* operating from strength, rather than deficit. With its army of writers and researchers, and its access (through reputation and infrastructure) to interviews with victims' families, friends, and co-workers, the *Times* was the first major cultural actor to take note of the "snapshot culture" sprouting up all around it, and rationalize it – to reproduce it in a representational economy of scale. These were not really "snapshots" after all, as the title tells us: these were "portraits" and just as most portraiture follows the rules of its time and place, so did the *Times* editors and staff very quickly develop a set of guidelines for these sketches. As with the Clear Channel controversy, the *New York Times*' standardization of the snapshots being taken and shared all over the United States made it clear that a corporate 9/11 culture was born almost simultaneously with the collapse of the towers.

* * *

The release of the Abu Ghraib torture photographs in 2004, of course, made it impossible for Americans to continue promoting snapshots or collections of photographs as the "people's art." This horrific photo album, leaked from a prison in Iraq, removed the aura of innocence from the activity of picture-taking. Additionally, the enshrinement of collective art as a tool of national healing was gradually revealed to be a stopgap strategy, a way to bide time while solo artists prepared their own singular works.

While a few "omnibus" efforts still came to public attention after 2001 – the compilations of memorial fundraising CDs such as the *Village Voice*'s *Love Songs for New York: Wish You Were Here* and the folkie *Vigil* collection, the 11 filmmakers who contributed to *11'9"01* (all 2002), and a few others – from around the summer of 2002 onward, the pieces of 9/11 art that were to have the greatest impact left behind the snapshot culture that was so compelling during that first fall. As individual American artists began trying to make sense of the towers coming down on 9/11 they frequently turned to images of rising and falling, and struggled to develop representations – some spiritual, some cartoonish, some documentary – that would seem meaningful to an American public that had watched films of those tall, tall, buildings crumbling more times than most would care to admit.

CH/4
Rising

Since 2002 American artists have been struggling with how to represent the central visual reality of 9/11: falling. With constant visual reminders of the crumbling of the two towers, the American mediascape was dominated for months by what came to seem like an endless loop of rerun imagery. The already limited cultural and political vocabulary of American news programs was narrowed even further by the attacks; the moment of each tower collapsing became, in the fall of 2001, the *ne plus ultra* of the "highlight" film. A number of cultural agreements were quickly made about what "we" were willing to watch and what should be ruled out of bounds. Complete accord was reached, as far as I can tell, around the idea that it was culturally acceptable to view the crumbling of the World Trade Center over and over again. The fact that we were watching the devastating creation of a mass grave was rarely articulated: it was years later that novelist Ken Kalfus was to write, with a sort of perplexity, that you "had to make an effort to keep before you the thought that thousands of people were losing their lives at precisely this moment" (2006: 3).

And while, of course, there was no film of the struggle aboard United 93, there was instant unanimity around the notion that its defiant passengers were freedom fighters. In the days and weeks after the attacks, invocations of United 93 joined footage of the towers falling as the top items on America's new menu of options. United 93, in fact, quickly came to serve as what film critic Jonathan Rosenbaum (2006a) called 9/11's treasure. Rosenbaum rightly described the constant citations of Flight 93 as forming the heart of the tale of "redemptive uplift" that always serves as the "official religion of the media": "There must be a silver lining; it's always darkest before the dawn; the human spirit will triumph over evil; there must be a pony."

Since there were no actual pictures of this "pony" to trot out – none of the compelling visual material that bolstered media narratives of heroes and victims in the World Trade Center – the United 93 narrative depended on next-of-kin reports. Media reports of final, heartbreaking cell phone calls to loved ones turned family members into surrogate heroes. President Bush took every opportunity to describe the calls, framing the United 93 passengers as the first post-9/11 Americans to enlist in the army fighting terror. "They learned the plane was going to be used as a weapon," Bush said again and again, with only the slightest change in a word here and there, and "they got on their telephones. They were told the true story. Many of them told their loved ones goodbye. They said they loved them" (Rall, 2006). (Of course 9/11 truth activists do not accept this pony; many claim that cell phones do not work at that altitude and make this argument a centerpiece of their case.)

Lisa Beamer, the widow of passenger Todd Beamer, was perhaps the most willing survivor: as Susan Faludi (2007) has written of Beamer, she was the 9/11 widow who "seemed to fit the role better" than any other (97). Beamer was introduced by President Bush during a nationally televised address to Congress on September 20, and became one of the most significant embodiments of redemption on the post-9/11 landscape. A media savvy stay-at-home mother and an evangelical Christian, Beamer was 5 months pregnant with her third child at the time of her husband's death. Perhaps as much as anyone in the year following 9/11, Beamer served as a crucial sign of life after the fall. Beamer published a memoir in under a year, and during that time was joined by others of the Flight 93 relatives to create a tableau of recovery.

The consensus about what to "watch" after 9/11 (i.e. the towers coming down and United 93 relatives standing up for photo opportunities) contained subsidiary agreements about what *not* to watch as well. The attack on the Pentagon received little prime-time attention, perhaps because there simply was not the amount of quality footage that New York produced. Additionally, because of the Pentagon's sprawling, horizontal-plane architecture, it was hard to figure out just what to focus on there. The relative dearth of Pentagon visuals also grows, no doubt, from its status as a visible marker of America's military power; this meant that the people who died inside were not completely available to the media as "innocent victims."

More striking is the almost complete media blackout when it came to presenting images of the dozens, and perhaps hundreds, of people who leapt (or fell) to their deaths from the World Trade Center. In the vernacular, these victims of the 9/11 attacks have come to be known as "jumpers," although the New York City Medical Examiner's office made a real point of classifying them otherwise: because these people were forced out of the buildings, they were not, officially speaking, categorized in the same way as outright suicides. Distinct but overlapping currents of respect, shame, and squeamishness came together here and the outcome was that most mainstream media – after publishing or broadcasting an image or two – refused to offer up any other footage of bodies falling from the Twin Towers.

Tom Junod, writing in *Esquire* two years later (2003), summarizes this phenomenon well: "In the most photographed and videotaped day in the history of the world, the images of people jumping were the only images that became, by consensus, taboo." To Junod, the "sight of the jumpers" was a reckoning with reality that, in his evaluation, American audiences were not prepared for. This vision, he suggests, "provided a corrective to those who insisted on saying that what they were witnessing was 'like a movie,' for this was an ending as unimaginable as it was unbearable." Photographs and film clips of people in the air were (and are) accessible to anyone with an internet connection, but the centralized media outlets, both print and broadcast, quickly stopped offering any visual reminders of this awful reality. The main character of William Gibson's *Pattern Recognition* (2003) admits her own process of self-censorship; Gibson writes of Cayce Pollard, "she will know she must have seen people jumping, falling," but "there will be no memory of it" (137). And, of course, the much-discussed Clear Channel list of banned songs had a number of "falling" songs on it.

In the first few years after the attacks virtually no major cultural figured dared to represent the falling bodies of 9/11. The Naudet brothers, who were shadowing a probationary firefighter for a film project on that day, did include the sound of bodies crashing in their televised documentary that aired in March 2002; but Jules Naudet has said that for all of the footage they serendipitously captured that day, they have no images of people dying because a kind of "auto-censorship" had set in (O'Carroll, 2002). Mexican director Alejandro González Iñárritu did make the "jumpers" the centerpiece of his contribution to the omnibus film *11'9"01*, which brought together 11 short films each lasting 11 minutes,

9 seconds and 1 frame. In an anthology that ranges from the soberly literal (Ken Loach on the overthrow of Chile's government on September 11, 1973) to the maudlin (Ernest Borgnine muttering small talk at the wall in Sean Penn's entry) to the unintentionally hilarious (Shohei Imamura's allegory of post-war Japan – with snakes!), Alejandro González Iñárritu offers up a horrific sound-and-vision montage. Acting more like an early hip hop DJ demonstrating skills than a narrative film director, González Iñárritu samples the sounds of the day, including screams from the street, baffled newscasters, the second plane hitting the tower, and phone calls from United 93 and inside the towers. For 3½ minutes or so, the screen is black. The very first image we see is of a body in freefall: the shock is that of the repressed returning. The remaining minutes of González Iñárritu's short film make the falling bodies the heart of the story – a challenge to all who had been taking refuge in aestheticizing and heroizing the dead of 9/11.

There has been little public debate on why we must work to suppress images of desperate people plunging toward their deaths – simple respect for the dead and their families and friends, and concern over how such terrifying footage might affect our children are the most obvious answers. Choosing suppression of this imagery is not the only available path to take, of course; in historical memory, the Triangle Shirtwaist Fire of 1911 is emblematized by the image of young women leaping to their deaths from the fiery sweatshop. What is worthy of our attention is how some well-placed American artists not only turned away from the heartrending reality of the "fallen" and instead used the raw materials of 9/11's tragedy to create fables of redemption and resurrection. Numerous examples of this tendency could be tracked across the cultural landscape, but it will probably suffice to take a look at a widely praised rock and roll record, a complex work of literary fiction, and an exceedingly strange children's movie.

* * *

No other work of 9/11 popular art has been met with the full-on media embrace that surrounded Bruce Springsteen's *The Rising*. The record was released during the summer of 2002, about 6 weeks before the first anniversary of 9/11 and was carefully positioned by Springsteen and his people as a major memorial. In countless print and broadcast interviews Springsteen spoke eloquently (or shrewdly, depending on how you look at it) about how he felt called to do this work of remembrance, inspired first by a fan who yelled "Hey, Bruce, we need you" at him out of a car window at the Jersey Shore. (Kevin Guilfoile [2002] has satirized this whole media onslaught, which included an appearance on the *Today* show by the guy who yelled "we need you," in a wicked but apt article. Guilfoile writes, "If you're not familiar with The Guy Who Yelled 'We Need You!' At Bruce Springsteen Last September, then the Sony Records publicity department has failed you.") *The Rising* record and the marketing campaign that accompanied its release reminds us of Dana Heller's suggestion that if we want to evaluate post-9/11 art properly we have to gauge how it balances cynical commercialization with sincere expression of grief and longing.

The critical reception of *The Rising* as a piece of 9/11 art was inextricably linked to its promotion by Springsteen and a willing media as a marker of his own resurrection. Springsteen had not really mattered as a major cultural figure since the mid-1980s, when "Bruce," in his *Born in the U.S.A.* (1984) days, could rival Michael, Prince, and Madonna as a single-named popular music icon. In the 17 years following his phenomenal run of 1984–5, his loyal fans stayed loyal and he still sold out arena shows, but his work simply did not help create or capture the zeitgeist in any significant ways.

But in the weeks following its release, *The Rising* was greeted with headlines that all seemed to say "Reborn in the U.S.A." or "Springsteen Rising." Virtually every feature article and review covered the same ground: Bruce, we need you; Bruce finding inspiration in the *New York Times* "Portraits of Grief"; the calls he placed to 9/11 widows to hear more about their husbands (most of whom were Springsteen fans); the fact that Springsteen's home county lost more people in the towers than any other in New Jersey; and finally, the rediscovery of his "rock" voice in this moment of crisis after years of not having a clear sense of mission. Springsteen was ubiquitous in the weeks after *The Rising* was released, marketed by Sony, in the words of one grumpy columnist, as if he were "a Hollywood blockbuster." This was the first time Springsteen had made a full-out rock and roll record with his E Street Band since 1984, which gave the entire event the aura of rebirth. If Rudolph Giuliani had successfully marketed himself as "America's mayor" after his performance on 9/11, Springsteen here staked a claim as America's rock and roller. With a marketing campaign organized around a rhetoric of resurrection, Springsteen enacted what his record thematized.

Numerous reviewers suggested that *The Rising*'s use of recurring words and phrases was one of its strengths. A. O. Scott (2002), for one, understood the repetition as being psychologically operative – doing "part of the work of grief." Springsteen had experimented with strategic repetition earlier in his career, most notably on his acoustic record *Nebraska* (1982) which revolves around two repeated lines: "debts no honest man can pay" and "deliver me from nowhere." Here the repetition is more diffuse, with words like kiss, lips, sun, and hope deployed across the record to conjure up a conflation of personal and, at times, erotic feelings on the one hand, with communal and national ones on the other.

"Rise" and "rising" appear in 8 of 15 songs on this record. (A year later the art-Klezmer band The Klezmatics were to release a record called *Rise Up!* and their title usage had a much more clearly leftist politics behind it.) From the apocalyptic "dark sun's on the rise" in the opening track ("Lonesome Day") to the final song's incantatory, if non-specific, "Come on, rise up!" *The Rising* uses these words in a variety of moods, but in three record-defining songs ("Mary's Place," "The Rising," and "My City of Ruins") they establish resurrection as a dominant motif. All three of these songs became fixtures on the concert tour that supported *The Rising*, with "Mary's Place" turned into a 10-minute-plus showstopper. "Mary's Place" has only a glancing "rise" moment ("My heart's dark but it's rising") but is more significant for how it turns to music itself as a redemptive force in the wake of 9/11. With a horn arrangement meant to evoke the 1960s soul music that was so important to Springsteen's own early recordings, and direct citations to Sam Cooke's "Meet Me at Mary's Place" and "Havin' a Party" (as well as an incorporation of Major Lance's "Monkey Time" in the concert version), the song insists that the communal experience of music be embraced as a healing force after the fall.

In other words, "Mary's Place" is an argument in favor of what Springsteen himself is doing on *The Rising*. It is no coincidence that it puts the singer's "heart" where the "son" stood in "Lonesome Day." The towers themselves are graphically reborn on the compact disc itself, which is printed with Bruce Springsteen's name and the record's title forming one tower and the track listing forming the other. One student of mine noted that Springsteen's name "crashes" into "The Rising" at just about the level that the planes hit the towers; certainly this was just a bad choice on the part of a graphic designer, but it is in keeping with the overall marketing of Springsteen and this record as somehow organic to 9/11. The CD booklet, for instance, features the lyrics for "The Fuse" on what looks to be a falling piece of paper – one of the central visual emblems of the day.

Jon Pareles, writing in the *New York Times* (2002), more or less suggested that Springsteen had himself invented the people who died on 9/11. "The office workers, firefighters, police and air travelers who died on Sept. 11," Pareles commented, "were the stuff of Springsteen songs: people who became heroes by just doing their jobs." *The Rising* encourages this reading in many ways, but perhaps most strikingly in its lyrical return to "Mary" – a character who led off Springsteen's breakthrough *Born to Run* album (in 1975) and appeared again as the main character of *The River*'s title song 5 years later. (Other Mary characters appear in numerous songs over his career, but this triptych is the thread I want to follow.) In "Thunder Road," Mary is about 18, just graduated from high school; in "The River," she is 5 years down the road, pregnant, and then stuck in a loveless marriage.

"The Rising" finds Mary in middle age, the widow of a firefighter, tending her garden. The song is narrated by the dead firefighter, placing it in the great tradition of told-from-beyond-the-grave American artworks that includes "Long Black Veil," first popularized by Lefty Frizzell, and Neil Young's "Powderfinger" in song, the film *Sunset Boulevard*, Thornton Wilder's play *Our Town*, and countless short stories and novels, including the recent bestseller, *The Lovely Bones*, by Alice Sebold. It is a simple song, about a firefighter who keeps climbing the stairs, though it means certain death. Springsteen spoke in interviews about this central image: "I'd read in the paper, some of the people coming down talked about the emergency workers who were ascending. And you know that – that image to me was just what – what I ... felt left with ... the idea of those guys going up the stairs, up the stairs, ascending, ascending" (Yates, 2005: 12). Springsteen turns the camera *away* from the realities of the descent of planes, towers, and bodies that defined the day, and constructs instead a poetics of redemption organized around images of rising.

On *The Rising*, Springsteen first focuses on this ascent in "Into the Fire" ("love and duty called you someplace higher"), but it is in "The Rising" that the climbing of the stairs takes on its fullest historical and religious resonance. The narrator has gone off to work wearing "the cross" of his calling and doggedly climbs the stairs with his gear, "a sixty pound stone," on his back. As the building collapses, the firefighter describes his descent: "on wheels of fire I come rollin' down here." With this reference to Daniel 7:9 (in which Daniel recounts a dream he has of end times), Springsteen at once invites his listeners to think of terror and apocalypse, but also accesses a popular rumor that passed in the weeks after the attacks which insisted that somebody – a rescue worker in many versions – "surfed" safely down one of the towers, perhaps using a piece of wood as a boogie board, as it collapsed. The song pivots around its repetition of "Come on up for the rising" and the narrator's framing of his post-death vision as a "dream of life" – a neat shorthand for the resurrection, borrowed perhaps from the extended sequence of Jesus on the cross in Martin Scorcese's *Last Temptation of Christ* (1988).

In any event, Springsteen's insistent focus on rising surely shaped the visual imagination of Oliver Stone, who directed *World Trade Center* (2006). In this film the two trapped rescue workers look constantly to an opening above their heads, often suffused with heavenly light. At one crucial moment the younger of the two has a vision that includes Jesus offering him a water bottle. Ultimately the two men will ascend through the opening that has been discovered by a determined Marine.

Joined with the "Come on rise up" that ends "My City of Ruins" (and the whole record), "The Rising" serves as a quasi-religious meditation on what comes *after*. Springsteen is purposefully short on details on *The Rising*; for all of his "Portraits of Grief" reading and his love of their details, he opted for the generic and categorical as a strategy. Making room for the scale of this event also meant taking refuge in an available language of easy redemption, rather than struggling toward an earned or subjective fulfillment. It is worth noting that Springsteen's next E Street Band work, *Magic* (2007), was to chronicle the post-Iraq disillusionment experienced by those who were forced to learn – as the title of a song by Springsteen acolytes The Hold Steady puts it – "How a Resurrection Really Feels."

* * *

Jonathan Safran Foer's 2005 novel *Extremely Loud and Incredibly Close* ends with a visual trick that might be called "How a Resurrection Really Looks." Foer is more upfront than Springsteen about his need to leave the documentary behind, in favor of a more fantastical approach. Foer's book admits and embraces its mythical impulses; while the novel incorporates moments of historical realism, its overall feel is of a fable. *Extremely Loud and Incredibly Close* is told by a child, Oskar Schell, a 9-year-old New Yorker whose father died on 9/11. His basic motivation in the novel is to find out just how his father died, so that he can stop inventing scenarios in his head. There were, Oskar says, "so many different ways to die, and I just need to know which was his" (256). In perfect fable-fashion (specific action in the service of a more generalized mission), Oskar spends the time of the novel searching for the owner of a lock that will match a key he has found in his father's belongings.

The gift that *Extremely Loud and Incredibly Close* grants, through the use of pastiche and its savant-child narration, is liberation from the narrow channel of "uplift" that has confined so much 9/11 art. Foer's Oskar is scared and sad, but also angry and vulgar; he is never pious, however, and the book avoids the empty bromides that sometimes weaken Springsteen's effort. *Extremely Loud and Incredibly Close* is full of stories (and songs, and jokes) that Oskar's dad told him. The most important of these is the allegory of New York's sixth borough that Oskar's father tells him on September 10. In his Dad's story there used to be a sixth borough, an island separated from Manhattan by a narrow body of water. Once a year, the world's greatest jumper used to leap from Manhattan to the sixth borough: "For those few moments that the jumper was in the air, every New Yorker felt capable of flight" (218). Here, "jumper" equals sucess and safety.

Foer's insertion of the sixth borough story late in the novel is a way to insist that inventive fable might be one of the most powerful artistic responses to 9/11 – at the very least a side road leading around the clogged highway featuring "heroes and helpers," as one book of children's art put it. That book of children's art of 9/11 includes a wonderful drawing made together by two boys, Paul and Julian, that they have labeled "Dinosaurs rebuild the twin towers" (Goodman & Fahnestock, 2002: 118). It is, as anyone who has ever experienced the transcendent literal-ness of 7- and 8-year-olds might have predicted, a picture of dinosaurs rebuilding the Twin Towers. The two young artists must have noticed, of course, that dinosaurs look like the giant mobile building cranes that were populating Ground Zero. But more important, I think, is how the two used dinosaurs to tap into shared mythologies of power and security.

Dinosaurs already exist for kids – for boys mostly – as signs of benign monstrosity. They are huge and potentially dangerous, but mostly they just slowly lumber around the land until, finally, they give way to us. Unwilling to draw on such existing mythological structures – Oskar is an "inventor" after all – Foer's lead character instead draws on personal memories of his father (in the sense of the stories his father always told him) as well as new mythologies of his father (in the sense of those stories Oskar is actively creating in his year-long search for answers). Oskar is trying to turn his father into a dinosaur, a presence at once immense yet extinct. To do this, as the book ends, Oskar imagines ripping his book of memories open and reorganizing the pages from front to back, thereby reversing time. His father would come down from the top of the tower, back out of the subway, and into his home, back into the night before the worst day: "He would have told me the story of the Sixth Borough, from the voice in the can at the end to the beginning, from 'I love you' to 'Once upon a time …'" Finally, as the narrative ends, Oskar offers the payoff of the fantasy: "We would have been safe" (326).

But there is one more invention to present, a flipbook that Oskar has created out of pictures of the falling man. Putting the pictures in reverse order allows Oskar to reframe the "falling man" as the "flying man." After all the high literary tricks in *Extremely Loud and Incredibly Close*, Foer finishes with a return to one of the most unreconstructed forms of kid culture. Here Foer gives the flipbook a life of its own, a dream at the end of his novel which says that before Oskar can fully face the reality of his father's death head on, he might have to create skeins of metaphor and allegory that will give him a handle on the enormity of his loss. But the flipbook is an angry flipbook too: it says that our present reality is beyond unsatisfactory, that Oskar's father has betrayed the promise of his stories, the promise that there would always be more. Here the book's ending reminds me of Frank O'Hara's "Poem (Lana Turner Has Collapsed)" which ends like this:

> I have been to lots of parties
> and acted perfectly disgraceful
> but I never actually collapsed
> oh Lana Turner we love you get up

The loving pique that makes the poem so affecting also infuses Foer's finish. Oskar knows he cannot reverse the story, nor stop time. But he can begin to honor his own inventions, his own language, and trust that his own fables are the ones that will guide him now, and that he will not have to rely on the fractured fairy tales told to him by his therapist or anybody else.

Released 5 months after Foer's novel, the movie *Chicken Little* is actually meant *for* children, and it reached lots of them. The top-grossing G-rated movie of the year, *Chicken Little* was also the fourteenth top earner of all films by the end of the year and by the fall of 2006 this Chicken Little would appear as a float in the Macy's Thanksgiving Day Parade. The movie is strange, not least because it turns Chicken Little into a boy. (Yes, chickens can be male, but the original Chicken Little was female, and most cultural imagery surrounding chickens in the United States has been gendered as female. The whole point of the fable, in fact, rests on the notion that this fowl is a hysterical female.) Zach Braff's Chicken Little is a kind of milquetoast, a little boy unable to please his macho father, who is trying to figure out how to raise this motherless child.

The sky is falling, of course, but no one believes Chicken Little. Chicken Little is dismissed as a feminized lunatic and quickly parodied in a movie-within-the-movie that is called *Crazy Little Chicken*. In the year that follows, however, Chicken Little achieves his mini-masculinity by having success in a baseball game and kissing up on Abby Mallard (as the compulsory heterosexuality is foisted on even the smallest and most obviously pre-pubescent Disney characters). Ultimately he and his friends discover an alien baby that has been inadvertently left behind when its parents came to earth searching for acorns. The parents think this is a kidnapping and begin laying waste to Oakey Oaks. Soon, though, Chicken Little and his friends are able to clear up the confusion (but not before some *War of the Worlds*-style tripod-damage) and the aliens recover their child.

Before *Chicken Little* ends, the "aliens," realizing their mistake, undo all the damage they have done. The most striking image of the movie comes when the tall buildings that have been knocked down in that attack magically grow back up from the ground to the sky. This is the kind of consequence-free narrative that troubles so many parents and why so many activists have worked together to address concerns raised by violent video games. When violence has no visible cost it begins to instruct children that violence actually is not real, that it operates in some protected sphere of social interaction. Foer's book (which is for adults after all) still bothers to announce that we have entered the realm of fantasy and that we are to understand Oskar's inventions as crucial to *his* subjectivity but nobody else's. *Chicken Little* undoes that cultural logic and plunks the viewer in a world where the sky continues to fall, if only so that we can see the buildings destroyed and rematerialized.

Chicken Little is a hybrid production: it tells children, "Oh, there's no bad guys, that was just a mistake." But this is too little and too late for that. For all the newscasts and talk radio that America's children have been exposed to, there is no doubt that they know what "evildoers" means, and maybe even who the "Islamofascists" are. The fear on the parents' faces when the "alien attack" comes, the not-funny-enough references to *War of the Worlds*, and the overall sense that the father has no power in this scenario all work to undo whatever comfort the movie means to give to its audiences. Perhaps most significant is how the movie self-consciously describes the year that follows Chicken Little's ultimate heroism. One year after the event, there is a book, website, board game, bumpersticker, commemorative plate. Of course, in "real life," at the time of *Chicken Little*, the towers of light might have raised beams and spirits, but the towers themselves had not risen. They remain fallen, shipped off as scrap metal to points far from New York City in India and China.

The rhetorics of rising (and even flying) dominated this first generation of 9/11 art; only Steven Spielberg, in his 2005 film *War of the Worlds*, demurred – constructing rising (of alien tripods, from underground) as danger. Even Frédéric Beigbeder (2004) ends his dark and bitter novel *Windows on the World* with this description of a man jumping out of the titular restaurant with his two kids: "For a split second, I really believed we were flying" (290). Flying was to be popular for a while after 9/11. In a tongue-in-cheek short story titled "Pitching September 11," Lev Grossman (2002) proposed a handful of fictionalized ideas for 9/11 movies. One plot outline shows a Dominican elevator operator trapped and finally deciding to jump from the 83rd floor: "Instead of falling he hovers in midair, then rockets upward. The trauma of the attack, and of his impending certain death, has awakened latent superpowers he never knew he had. Soon, others in similar straits join him hovering above collapsing buildings ready to soar away together in formation to take vengeance on evil everywhere." As an aside, Grossman wonders if John Lequizamo would be right for the part and whether this could be *X-Men 3* (124–7).

As it turns out, that third installment of the *X-Men* (2006) series features a character named Angel who has wings (here an allegory for being gay) and must decide whether to have them removed or not. After an early self-mutilating effort, Angel keeps his wings and later uses his power of flight to save his own father. There have been a few attempts to respond to these dominant fantasies of rising and flying. Marvel Comics produced three tribute books in the wake of the attacks. One of these, *Heroes*, says something interesting on the back cover of the book about the characters we will meet inside: "They can't stick to walls. They can't summon thunder. They can't fly. They're just HEROES." (Nyberg, 2003: 179)

＊＊＊

Ultimately American audiences would have to face the reality of falling bodies, but before many found the nerve to write of or create such imagery about falling, a cluster of activity developed that promoted falling paper as the ultimate emblem of the tragedy of the day. While journalist William

Langewiesche (2002) focused mainly on the functional role of paper on that day, on how the immensity of paper in the towers fed the fires, even he could not avoid a metaphorical flight: "all the white paperwork floated down on the city as if in mockery of the dead" (6). The falling paper of 9/11 is often given a supernatural, or at least non-human, quality. For novelist Lynne Sharon Schwartz (2005) the "sky rained paper" (46). For Jess Walter, in his novel *The Zero* (2006), it looked like this: "they burst into the sky, every bird in creation, angry and agitated, awakened by the same primary thought, erupting in a white feathered cloudburst, anxious and graceful … it wasn't a flock of birds at all – it was paper. Burning scraps of paper" (2).

A number of filmmakers have made use of the falling paper motif as well, from Oliver Stone to, surprisingly, Kasi Lemmons, in her film *Talk to Me* (2007). *Talk to Me* is a biopic about Petey Greene, a Washington, D.C. disc jockey who gained fame in the late 1960s. When it comes time to represent the D.C. riot that ensued as news of the assassination of Martin Luther King, Jr., in 1968, spread, the film evokes a visual short-hand of destruction by showing a veritable rainstorm of falling paper. It is an odd back-formation: the usual movie coding of "riot" almost always relies on visuals of storekeepers trying to protect their shops as large objects go hurtling through the plate glass. Lemmons' movie offers one piece of evidence for how powerful 9/11 imagery has become. The falling paper of 9/11 now seems like a convenient way to capture visually an earlier moment of crisis.

* * *

A few years out from 9/11, the bodies would begin to fall more steadily in popular art. Singer Kimya Dawson rejected official attempts to represent New York as a healthy place to be in her song "Anthrax" (2004). Here, Dawson insisted that "the air is filled with computers and carpets/skin and bones and telephones and file cabinets/coke machines, firemen, landing gear and cement/they say that it's okay but i say don't breathe in." Novelist Ken Kalfus was even more relentless in his desire to focus attention on the "jumpers." Early in his novel *A Disorder Peculiar to the Country* (2006) Kalfus's narrator contemplates "a woman in a navy business suit, possibly a suit that could be described in regard to its cut and weave, and possibly even its likely provenance if you knew about such things, thumped hard less than twenty feet away, and bounced and burst" (16).

Later in this novel, which is about the dissolution of the marriage of Joyce and Marshall Harriman in the months after 9/11, we see their children jumping happily from the porch at a country house where their mother has taken them for a family wedding. Again and again they jump and holler and whoop it up. But then Viola is in the grass, writhing in pain, tattling on her brother: "The World Trade Center was on fire and we had to jump off together! But he let go of my hand!" (114) Soberly, she summarizes for her mother, "We were playing 9/11" (115).

Jess Walter also released his 9/11 novel, *The Zero*, in 2006. In it, one rescue worker is amazed at how many people will ask him "what the bodies sounded like when they hit the sidewalk." He tells them to "clap their hands as hard as they can, so hard that it really hurts. Then they clap, and I say: No. Harder than that. And they clap again, and I say, No, really fuggin' hard. And then they clap so hard their faces get all twisted up, and I say, No, really hard! And then, when their hands are red and sore, they say, 'So that's ... what it sounded like?' And I say, 'No. It didn't sound like that at all'" (85). Oliver Stone's *World Trade Center*, also from 2006, allowed filmgoers to hear the sound of a falling body's impact. By the fifth anniversary of 9/11, American artists and audiences seem to have agreed that the major taboos that structured immediate responses to the attacks had now been lifted.

One result was a new focus on falling. In the literary world's equivalent of the rapture that greeted Bruce Springsteen's *The Rising*, the bells were rung in the spring of 2007 for Don DeLillo's 9/11 novel *The Falling Man* (2007). DeLillo had been writing about terror and spectacle for much of his impressive career as a novelist, but did not, as it turned out, have that much to bring to this particular table. He did, however, put the falling man at the center of his novel – in this case, a performance artist version of the actual falling man of 9/11. While DeLillo claims not to have heard of him during his writing, it is at least worth noting that an actual performance artist named Kerry Skarbakka received quite a bit of press in 2005 for "installations" during which he would leap from buildings and cliffs and so on. In DeLillo's novel, when Lianne sees the "falling man" she quickly understands that he is meant to bring back "those stark moments in the burning towers when people fell or were forced to jump" (33). Lianne, unfortunately, cannot know everything we readers know, and is not able to "read" the dangling/falling man as a representation of her husband who has been similarly trapped in space ever since escaping from one of the burning towers on 9/11. If she could have known this, perhaps she could have saved him from the dark pits of high stakes poker he ends up in.

Figure 5 Eric Fischl's "Tumbling Woman." Source: © by Eric Fischl, photograph by Ralph Gibson

Of course by the time the novelists got around to the falling man, journalist Tom Junod had already published his long piece in *Esquire* (2003) on the actual person in the famous picture by Richard Drew. Part detective story, part meditation on what we want to see in the wake of 9/11, Junod's piece (now also a video documentary) opened the door to numerous novelists and visual artists interested in testing the "jumper" taboo. A year earlier, sculptor Eric Fischl got the message that his work in a similar vein was premature, at least according to audiences. The mounting of his sculpture "Tumbling Woman" (see Figure 5) in the lower concourse of Rockefeller Center around the first anniversary of 9/11 was met with almost unanimous disgust and the sculpture was soon covered up. Fischl tried to promote the idea that his sculpture was meant to capture the feeling of floating and all of the ways that this might resonate for New Yorkers a year after 9/11, but to no avail.

The line of people who jumped to their deaths during that awful morning of September 11 appeared as a tragic expression of American democracy: a racially and economically diverse mix of bond traders, restaurant workers, and administrative assistants waited at those windows for their chance to escape the punishing heat and suffocating smoke. But when Hurricane Katrina hit in August, almost 4 years later, that heartbreaking vision of equality promoted by the World Trade Center jumpers was washed away by the more compelling vision of the inequities of race and class featured in media coverage of the flood. The democratic appeal of the rising and falling narrative, mostly about the intactness of white families, could not be sustained once Hurricane Katrina revealed the realities of Black suffering in America.

CH/5

Us

"If Osama Bin Laden ever buys a rap album, he'll probably start with a CD by KRS-One." So began a gossip item by regular *New York Daily News* columnists Rush and Molloy on October 13, 2004, about an appearance that KRS-One had made at the New Yorker Festival a week or so earlier during which the legendary rapper had allegedly bragged of having "cheered when 9/11 happened" ("KRS-One, Decency Zero," 2004). Now, excusing the inane set-up of this rhetorical attack (doesn't bin Laden just illegally download the music he wants?), it remains necessary to explore what argument about American identity and racial dissent the former leader of Boogie Down Productions was trying to insert into the conversation at that event in early October of 2004. It matters little, finally, whether KRS-One cheered or not, or whether the *Daily News* misquoted the rapper. Given the opportunity to clarify his position by hip hop activist Davey D, KRS-One insisted on further upsetting the still dominant scripts of national togetherness.

According to KRS-One, when he was asked at the New Yorker Festival to explain why hip hop artists had not "engaged the current situation more (meaning 911)" the rapper explained that 9/11 did not "happen" to African Americans – it only affected "them down the block." KRS-One went on to argue that the "them" he was referring to was "the rich, the powerful, those that are oppressing us as a culture. Sony, RCA or BMG, Universal, the radio stations, Clear Channel, Viacom with BET and MTV, those are our oppressors." From this wide-frame cultural critique, KRS-One also focused in on the racial realities of Twin Tower life: "[W]hen we were down at the trade center we were getting hit over the head by cops, told that we can't come in this building ... because of the way we dressed and talked, and so on, we were racially profiled. So, when the planes hit the building we were like mmmm justice" (Devenish, 2004). It was not only African American artists who demanded that audiences consider that there was more than one way to respond to the tragedy of 9/11. In a short story called "Flight Patterns" (2003b), Native American author Sherman Alexie features a character who after 9/11 feels bitter about his position vis-à-vis the American government: "I am a Native American and therefore have ten thousand more reasons to terrorize the U.S. than any of those Taliban jerk-offs" (112).

After a predictable couple of weeks of call-and-response – right-wing bloggers insisting KRS-One was in cahoots with Al Qaeda, followed by more careful attempts by his supporters to situate his comments – the "we cheered" controversy vanished from the American cultural radar (existing now as only a faint echo of Malcolm X's "chickens come home to roost" summary of President John F. Kennedy's assassination). Three years after the *Tribute to Heroes* telethon and Wyclef Jean's dexterous introduction of the legible history of racism that shaped the modern West with his choice of "Redemption Song," it was still next to impossible for an American artist bluntly to introduce race into any 9/11 equation without being accused of treason – or at least impertinence. The outcry in the spring of 2008 over similar comments made by Jeremiah Wright, pastor at the church attended by presidential candidate Barack Obama, demonstrated that discussions of race and national unity still had no comfortable place in American life.

Jean himself had kept at it with his by-now familiar sly approach. On his 2002 release, *Masquerade*, Jean included a version of Bob Dylan's mournful outlaw farewell, "Knockin' On Heaven's Door." This is a song that has been steadily covered in the past decade – from hard rock band Guns N' Roses' boy-pain ballad, to dying rocker Warren Zevon's darkly comic version (complete with calls to St Peter to "open up, open up"), to Canadian pop sensation Avril Lavigne's girl-pain ballad. It is a remarkably supple song, or a remarkably clichéd one, depending on your point of view.

Jean's *Masquerade* is a record drenched in the sights and sounds of post-9/11 New York, so it comes as no surprise that his approach to "Knockin' on Heaven's Door" is to put it in *his* place. The song begins with an evocation of Brooklyn's Marlborough projects, where Jean lived before moving to New Jersey as a youth. By the end of the song Jean has moved downtown to grieve for "my people in the Twin Tower." Jean's hip hop invocation of the projects is hardly news. From rap's founding days up through our own time, the projects have been a central lyrical and visual sign (on record covers, in videos, and so on) for hip hop artists. What is interesting here is how Jean uses the Dylan song as an occasion to draw a line from the projects to the World Trade Center. This acts, in effect, as Jean's claim to honor all the "ruins" of New York – and not just the officially sanctioned ones.

Jean is not the only young African American artist to connect up the suffering of inner-city communities of color with the suffering of the victims of the 9/11 attacks. Novelist Carl Rux mused in his post-apocalyptic novel *Asphalt* (2004) on how only certain sites of tragedy get sanctified in contemporary America. Rux's narrator surveys his blasted New York landscape (9/11 is not named, but it is the indisputable start-ing point of all this misery, as it is in *'V' for Vendetta*) that is filling up with the official signs of collective grief, even as the more "natural" urban rubble surrounding him goes unmarked:

> They talking about getting the government to expropriate sites of martyr-dom in the neighborhood … I'm not with all these memorials and commem-orative marches and prayers and anniversaries to mark the death of this infantry and that precinct. Ain't nobody commemorating the death of these buildings. These buildings been dying for years. (42)

Rux is posing a rhetorical challenge here, with his embedded (and racialized) questions about how cultures should call attention to their most important sites of suffering and loss. As cultural geographer Kenneth Foote (2003) has suggested, there are certain "invisible" places on the landscape whose "current, unmarked status is not merely a matter of oversight. Their invisibility can be traced to issues of unresolved meaning and to conflicts over memory." Foote explains that things get particularly complicated when questions of racialized violence or neglect are some-how implicated in the shaping of the particular landscape (293).

A number of American novelists and filmmakers have rushed onto the scene in attempts to offer up comforting scripts of racial unity and white superiority. Oliver Stone's *World Trade Center*, for instance, rewrites 9/11 as a kind of World War II foxhole-buddy movie with under-duress cama-raderie offered up as a vision of national togetherness. Stone wrote out of the script an actual African American marine who had participated in the rescue of the Port Authority police officers, in favor of a more familiar vision of white male bravery. More troubling yet was novelist Reynolds

Price's 2005 book *The Good Priest's Son*, which pivots around an involuntary homecoming to North Carolina by Mabry Kincaid, who gets stranded in Nova Scotia as a result of the attacks. While Kincaid pines for his apartment in lower Manhattan (which he cannot immediately return to) he comes to realize that his ailing elderly father can no longer live alone. Luckily, standing at the ready is a sassy but devoted African American woman, Audrey Thornton, who for unknown reasons (well, she is a divinity student) is ready to commit her care to the old white man. Offering his readers a neo-Mammy for the post-9/11 age is Price's method of promoting the specious vision of instant unity after the tragedy.

Lynne Sharon Schwartz, in her 9/11 novel *The Writing on the Wall* (2005), displays a similar investment in creating a vision of cross-racial harmony, but is honest enough to articulate the achievement of this state as temporary and almost magical. Her main character Renata struggles throughout the book to figure out how 9/11 should be memorialized by Americans, but also to reckon with how it has shaped her own individual emotional landscape. Walking along the promenade in Brooklyn with her sometime lover Jack, Renata comes upon an African American man playing a horn: "Everyone understands this is music that can't be ignored or interrupted. But they don't dare get too close. He's playing for all of them, but he's playing in solitude, too, sending his furling riffs through the bluish-gold air like a gift, like water to the parched" (234). As he continues to play it is clear that Schwartz wants her readers to imagine music – music without words – as an antidote to the foulness of political discourse after the attacks:

> Nothing about him could intimate the wry, apocalyptic music he makes … He's playing for the pleasure of it, but he's also a thickset herald, playing to announce what's happened to all of them, playing for the blue glory of the sky that Tuesday morning and how it broke apart, playing the beauty of that day and the horror, oscillating them like figure and ground. He's playing for the city in mourning, for the lost and for those remaining, an elegy and an appeal, playing an antidote to the ugly, nonsensical words that have been the public response. (235)

Before long the music breaks off and Renata is left to realize the transitory effect of the performance and the novel circles back to a realistic admission that the tragedy of 9/11 could not possibly have created or sustained such national unity.

That is the crux of KRS-One's challenge to dominant deracialized enshrinements of Ground Zero as a place of national tragedy. The local knowledge that KRS-One was accessing at the New Yorker Festival encompassed histories of racial profiling and institutionalized oppression. If debate swirled around KRS-One's New York with respect to what should be built at Ground Zero, and with how the dead of 9/11 should be memorialized, virtually no discussion could be heard about the complexities of race and religion, nation and empire that exploded on September 11. In other words, if the prevailing understanding of Ground Zero was as a site where good (race-less) people had met their tragic deaths, KRS-One's provocative rhetoric was an effort to reconceptualize Ground Zero as one of many sites in New York where African Americans were made to feel like second-class citizens. Cultural geographer David Harvey (2002) has written of how "local emphasis upon loss and grief" after 9/11 "feeds on and promotes the idea of innocence" (59). All the columnists and bloggers who piled on KRS-One were working in the service of a nationalistic ideology that depends on illusions of racial and religious union, a mythology that would become increasingly difficult to sustain as rebel voices revealed cracks in the putative alliance.

* * *

The rebel voices did not sing in simple harmony though. They did not just join in and help Wyclef Jean sing another chorus of "Redemption Song." The group conflicts revealed and instensified by the September 11 attacks were anything but simple. If Americans have too often imagined their central "dilemma" as a binary Black–white affair, 9/11 and its aftermath made clear what 50 years of massive immigration (from South Asia, the Middle East, Latin America, and the Caribbean) should have accomplished. The attacks themselves, the wars in Afghanistan and Iraq, the everyday depredations enabled by the Patriot Act, and the horrors of Abu Ghraib and Guantanamo all contributed to an unraveling of the simple "we" that the *Tribute to Heroes* telethon aimed to promote. The only real trouble with KRS-One's rhetorical gambit is that it assumed a binary that had long ago been replaced by triangles (Black–white–Asian, for instance) and even more complex geometries of affiliation and repulsion. (Tensions between African Americans and Korean Americans have been the subject of intense scrutiny at least since the early 1990s and find a defining expression in Ice Cube's 1991 song "Black Korea.")

Martín Espada tried in 2003 to say something about the new math Americans would have to reckon with after 9/11. He did this in a poem titled "Alabanza: In Praise of Local 100," dedicated to the "43 members of Hotel Employees and Restaurant Employees Local 100, working at the Windows on the World restaurant, who lost their lives in the attack on the World Trade Center."

> Praise the great windows where immigrants from the kitchen
> could squint and almost see their world, hear the chant of nations:
> Ecuador, México, Republica Dominicana,
> Haiti, Yemen, Ghana, Bangladesh.

Without romanticizing these workers – up early, working despite illness in order to send money back home – Espada finds them connected through the work that they do and the music that they listen to. Ultimately, it is this music that will also connect them up to the people of Afghanistan:

> When the war began, from Manhattan and Kabul
> two constellations of smoke rose and drifted to each other,
> mingling in icy air, and one said with an Afghan tongue:
> Teach me to dance. We have no music here.
> And the other said with a Spanish tongue:
> I will teach you. Music is all we have.

The poem proposes a dream of music as unreal as the "dream of life" that comes to Springsteen's dead firefighter in "The Rising." The "constellations of smoke" rising from the towers inspired many songs. But the hopeful poetics of communion that Espada employs at the end of "Alabanza" could not conceal for long the always-simmering realities of race as lived in New York and the rest of America.

* * *

Just another year or so after KRS-One's New Yorker Festival experience it would be bizarre to think of asking an African American rapper why there had been so little effort to engage issues surrounding 9/11 in the music. Half a decade after the attacks, it had become a rap commonplace to deny the fantasy that Black–white unity would be an inevitable collateral benefit of the tragedy. But in the first weeks after 9/11 it became a media reflex to outline how African Americans would now forget about any 400-year-old "special grievances" they might have and stand together – "all 300 million of us," Clint Eastwood said at the telethon – in "the conflict that's come upon us." Well-situated African American public figures did reanimate a rhetoric of Black patriotism whose roots stretch back at least as far as the American Revolution and its children's book mythologies of Crispus Attucks, but after 9/11 the concept of unquestioning Black loyalty that had come under some critical scrutiny since the Vietnam War was now deeply contested.

The notion that African Americans would feel an uncomplicated patriotism in moments of American national crisis had never recovered from Muhammad Ali's much-quoted response (whose exact wording is under some debate) when informed that he had been classified as fit to be drafted into the military despite his claims to conscientious objector status: "Man, I ain't got no quarrel with them Vietcong" (Marqusee, 1999: 162). After this statement, which Ali biographer David Remnick (1998) calls extemporaneous, Ali elaborated in a later interview, asking why the United States government should "ask me to put on a uniform and go ten thousand miles from home and drop bombs and bullets on brown people in Vietnam while so-called negro people in Louisville are treated like dogs?" (289).

Of course the elder statesman of 2001 was a very different person than the young fighter of 1966. After 9/11 Ali visited Ground Zero and told reporters that he objected to the demonization of Islam as a "killer religion" but also noted that he would support "100 percent" whatever response the American government made to the attacks (Marqusee, 1999: 300). That this icon of radical Black opposition, the most famous draft resister in American history, was willing to join his voice to the patriotic chorus is an apt shorthand of how utterly, if temporarily, transformative 9/11 was.

By September 26 journalist Lee Hubbard (2001) was able to summarize the consensus under the sanguine headline "Old Glory's New Appeal to Blacks." Hubbard rounded up quotations to demonstrate the cross-generational appeal of this "new" patriotism, and found supporting evidence from a hip hop journalist, the president of the National Black Youth Leadership Council, and journalist Stanley Crouch. No one was more celebratory than Kweisi Mfume, president of the National Association for the Advancement of Colored People (NAACP) and former leader of the Congressional Black Caucus, who argued that 9/11 had "united all of our country" and described how "refreshing" it was "for people to put aside differences and for people to rally around things we have together such as family and faith." With yet more inflated rhetoric, columnist Audrey Edwards (2001), former executive editor of *Essence* and current contributing editor for *More*, only left out smiley-face emoticons:

> Our very diversity will prove to be our strength. Whether it's the "home-boys" on my block who now fly the colors of the American flag with the same defiance they once flew gang colors, or the Irish-American firefighters in the station house two blocks away who lost six men (they were among the first on the scene when the World Trade Center went down), it will take all of America's varied races, cultures and sensibilities, uniting as one, to prevail in the months ahead. Let us hope that, like New York City's some-times-flawed mayor, we will find in our darkest hour, our finest moment, and emerge stronger for having been tested.

What might be more surprising than the certainties of Crouch, Mfume, and Edwards is how quickly the unity they championed would be contested by dissident voices. Boots Riley, of The Coup, published a manifesto in 2002 that reads as if it could be a direct response to Edwards. In this document, Boots writes that "Hip-hop represents people fighting for freedom and justice. The American flag does not. No one will be admitted to a Coup show wearing red, white, and blue. They represent violent gang colors" (Kim et al., 2002: 50).

The objections to the consensus position came hard and fast in hip hop music and were organized first around global concerns. Even in the midst of the relatively popular war in Afghanistan, rap artists, both mainstream and underground, launched critiques of American imperialism and militarism. Nas was one of the first major artists out of the gate with his song "What Goes Around," released in December of 2001. Toward the end of a song that is mostly *not* about 9/11, Nas offers up a spoken interlude that might be taken as a revision of Malcolm X's notorious "chickens come home to roost" speech of December 1963 – the one that Lou Reed would later describe in song as putting "a hex on President Kennedy's tomb" – replacing chickens with a dog:

> Every dog has its day and everything flips around
> Even the most greatest nation in the world has it coming back to 'em
> Everyone reaps what they sow, that's how it goes

A little later in the song Nas recontextualizes a cliché ("what goes up it must come down") and makes it difficult to avoid the implication that the destruction of the towers was inevitable and traceable to American hubris on the world stage. This analysis was made explicit by Native American scholar and activist Ward Churchill just a day after the attacks, in an essay " 'Some People Push Back': On the Justice of Roosting Chickens" (2001).

Boston-based indie rapper Mr. Lif is also more concrete than Nas in the history lesson he offers in his song "Home of the Brave" (2002), which is almost as detailed in its critique as his hometown compatriot Noam Chomsky was in his book *9–11*. Rhyming about the war in Afghanistan, Mr. Lif joined the growing opposition who believed the real motive in Afghanistan was "to build a pipeline to get the oil that they had wanted before": "America supported the Taliban/To get Russia out of Afghanistan/That's how they got the arms in/They're in a war against the Northern Alliance/And we can't build a pipeline in hostile environments." Mr. Lif concludes with a rejection of the most visible sign of patriotism ("you can wave the piece of shit flag if you dare") and an answer to the most ubiquitous and pernicious of post-9/11 nationalistic rhetorical questions: "[T]hey killed us because we've been killing them for years."

Another rap act, Dead Prez, seconded Mr. Lif's anti-imperialist stance in their 2002 song "Know Your Enemy" ("Start with the U.S. imperialists/Ain't no track record like America's") and joined it to a racialized critique of the "United We Stand" impulse: "They wasn't aimin' at us/ Not at my house." Talib Kweli, who has been a major force in independent rap music since the late 1990s, explicitly urged African Americans not to fall for the easy seductions of post-9/11 patriotism. In his 2004 song "Around My Way," Kweli explains how incensed he was to see African Americans "saluting flags, wrapping them around our heads/ When niggaz ain't become American till 9/11."

The anti-imperialist objections did not only come in hip hop, of course. Perhaps the most eloquent musical statement of opposition to post-9/11 American military ventures came in the decision by one giant of African music not to play music in the United States. As critic Robert Christgau (2004) puts it, Youssou N'Dour was "scheduled to undertake the most extensive and expansive American tour of his life" but "did a startling thing: he canceled." In a fascinating brief statement he released at the time, N'Dour (2003) explained that he believed "responsibility for disarming Iraq should rest with the United Nations" but that it was clear to him that the United States government planned to "commence war in Iraq." As a result, he concluded that "coming to America at this time would be perceived in many parts of the world – rightly or wrongly – as support for this policy."

A year later, as the Iraq war raged on, N'Dour released his record *Egypt*, which, as Larry Blumenfeld (2007) explains, is a clear attempt by the Sufi Muslim singer to enact a musical and religious alliance between sub-Saharan Africa and the Arab lands of the North. *Egypt*, recorded with Egyptian musicians, is mostly taken up with praising great Sufi teachers, and stands as a profound effort by one of the most revered Black musicians of the past 20 years to "protect Islam," as N'Dour himself said, "and all the beautiful cultures of Islam." Insofar as N'Dour crosses the popular culture radar in the United States (and his earlier collaborations with Western pop musicians including Peter Gabriel and Neneh Cherry have assured him relatively wide coverage in the mainstream media), his conscientious objection as an African Muslim was met with respectful neutrality.

Opting out was less available to African American cultural actors looking to register their disapproval of the "War on Terror." While there is a long tradition of Black jazz musicians moving to Europe (especially to France and Denmark) to escape and protest the injuries caused by American racism, rap artists have not exercised this option. Since 2002, instead, a wide range of rappers, from obscure independent artists to king of the hill Jay-Z, have responded to post-9/11 jingoism and "Black-and-white together" appeals with scathing indictments of the relationship of home-grown racism and U.S. imperialism. Underground rapper Brother Ali, a (white) albino Muslim, summarized this entire cultural movement in the introduction to his song "Uncle Sam Goddamn" (2007): "The name of this song is Uncle Sam Goddamn. It's a show tune but the show ain't been written for it yet."

What was most galling to this generation of rappers was, perhaps, the virtually compulsory nature of patriotic declarations, and more particularly the culture-wide sanctification of police officers, the most visible figures of racist oppression for many young African Americans. Discussion of harassment by the police has been a staple of rap music at least since 1982 when Grandmaster Flash and the Furious Five released their song "The Message," which ends with a mini-skit that finds the group harassed by police officers who accuse them of being a gang. N.W.A., the Los Angeles act that helped usher in the gangsta rap age with their 1988 album *Straight Outta Compton*, reduced the multiple layers of anti-police rhetoric in hip hop to four syllables, three of which were "tha police."

The New York Police Department (NYPD) had been a particular focus of rap revulsion since the 1997 beating and rape of Haitian immigrant

Abner Louima in the 70th Precinct House in Brooklyn and the 1999 murder of Amadou Diallo, who was killed by police who fired 41 rounds at him as he reached for his wallet outside his Bronx apartment building. Memorials to Diallo abounded in popular music of the late '90s and early '00s with references in numerous rap songs, including "Diallo, Diallo" by Wyclef Jean, which featured a guest vocal by Youssou N'Dour. Bruce Springsteen also weighed in with "American Skin (41 Shots)," a song that puts empathy above all else, and caused the president of the New York chapter of the Fraternal Order of Police to call the New Jersey singer a "dirt bag" (Pareles, 2000).

Firefighters were the heroes of the day on 9/11. Over 300 died in the line of duty that day and hundreds more suffered the trauma of being at Ground Zero and losing so many friends and co-workers. Commemoration of firefighters was relatively simple: from the Naudet brothers' television documentary, to Springsteen's album, to David Halberstam's (2003) book *Firehouse*, nothing really got in the way of celebrating the heroism of the fireman – at least until the advent of the ambivalence of television's *Rescue Me*. (And "fireman" it really should be, notwithstanding our efforts to teach our children to use the gender-neutral term "firefighter"; as Halberstam establishes quite clearly, the firehouse is still almost entirely a male domain.) Questions of racial division in New York were elided in the memorialization of firemen, for the simple reason that most of them were white. African American talk show host Tavis Smiley, in a broad-based critique of media coverage of race and 9/11, suggested in an interview with *Black Issues Book Review* that in the weeks after the attacks it would have been a tall order to "raise the question of why there weren't more black firefighters in the New York fire department" ("What Black America Has to Say," 2002). One brief dust-up ensued when the New York City Fire Department (FDNY) unveiled plans for a statue that would depict the three white firefighters who had been photographed hoisting a flag at Ground Zero, now shown as one Latino, one African American and one white man. Aside from this short-lived controversy, the heroes of the FDNY, as novelist Ken Kalfus (2006) wrote, had "taken on the graces of classical heroes, clear-eyed and broad-chested, manly and kind" (20).

Firefighters were uncomplicated heroes who seemed selflessly interested only in helping others. Police officers were a different story. Once a few months had passed, African American rap artists began to insist that their listeners remember not only Louima and Diallo, but also think about how American racist practices have so consistently been concentrated in police power. J-Live introduced the challenge in early 2002 in his much-praised song "Satisfied." Here he encourages rap fans to "figure out who the enemy is" and describes the police as the same people who had "fun lettin' off forty-one":

> But now it's all about NYPD caps
> And Pentagon bumper stickers
> But yo, you still a nigga
> It ain't right them cops and them firemen died
> The shit is real tragic, but it damn sure ain't magic
> It won't make the brutality disappear
> It won't pull equality from behind your ear

Jay-Z included an anti-police moment in his 2003 song "Ballad for a Fallen Soldier" (a title borrowed from a 1983 Isley Brothers' song about a man remembering his father, who died in the Vietnam War). Here Jay-Z remembers the time before 9/11 when "police were Al Qaeda to Black men." Capital D, an African American Muslim working in the alternative rap sphere, said more or less the same thing, on a larger canvas, in his song "Blowback" (2004): "9–11 was a tragedy/but 9–10 still ain't ancient history."

By the spring of 2004 it was clear that the matter was personal for New York rappers. Stories in a number of mainstream sources reported that the NYPD had been putting figures in the New York hip hop scene under surveillance. Whether or not the department had an official "Hip Hop Task Force" was ultimately not as significant as the admission by the department that members of their intelligence unit were assigned "to monitor the music industry and any incidents regarding the music industry" (Allah, 2004). "Music industry" as used here by a NYPD spokesperson was clearly a dodge: the police were not studying about performers in Broadway musicals. This confirmation of what had long been common knowledge in the rap business was frequently interpreted as an admission that racial profiling was an official policy of the NYPD.

Tavis Smiley recounted visiting with young African Americans in New York soon after the attacks who expressed astonishment that "the same cops who were harassing them pre-9/11 for driving while black, breathing while black, walking while black, doing anything while black" were now "being made heroes" ("What Black America Has to Say," 2002).

Conversations among African Americans – such as the fascinating interview Tavis Smiley gave to *Black Issues Book Review* – reveal a sense of anguish at the both/and scenario of trying to achieve a sort of critical patriotism just after 9/11. Smiley noted ruefully that when "America gets a cold, black America gets pneumonia." He thought it obvious that predictable post-9/11 economic stresses would be felt most deeply by African Americans.

Hip hop artists were in the vanguard again when it came to explaining how misleading (and politically motivated) it was for American government officials and media powers to try to project all post-9/11 evil in the world onto one-dimensional targets – "bin Laden," "the terrorists," or, in the awful neologism of right-wing punditry, "the Islamofascists." A powerful rhetorical move for African Americans was to challenge the common-sense understanding of keywords like "terrorism" and "bin Laden." Capital D did this work of redefinition in his class-conscious 2004 song "Start the Revolution": "think about it tony blair & his people r rich/George bush ... we all know that nigga is rich/osama bin laden yeah that madman's rich/&they all send the poor 2 die." Longtime Washington insider Vernon Jordan employed this "keyword" strategy too, in a speech he gave in 2002 in which he reminded his audience that "Slavery was terrorism, segregation was terrorism, the bombing of four little girls in Sunday school in Birmingham was terrorism" (Mukherjee, 2003: 33). Most efficient of all was bluesman Willie King, a Highlander Folk School-inspired community organizer, who released a song "Terrorized" in 2002 that recounts the history of slavery, lynching, and overall disenfranchisement of African Americans since the original kidnapping of people from Africa. The song begins with a devastating blues line: "You talk about terror/People I've been terrorized all my days."

Careful empirical work done by political scientists Darren Davis and Brian Silver (2004) demonstrates quite convincingly that African Americans have been much less willing than white people or Latinos to give full support to the American's government's "War on Terror." Davis and Silver argue that the post-9/11 increase in "domestic surveillance and restrictions of civil liberties, the invasion of Afghanistan, and the passage of the Patriot Act legislation" were all generally supported by white people and white-run institutions, but were greeted with much greater skepticism by African Americans. African Americans, they suggest, were reluctant "to trade off civil liberties for personal security" perhaps because of "their own experience of terrorism" in the United States (2–4).

No single act of dissent was more eloquent than the speech African American Congresswoman Barbara Lee made on September 14, 2001, as she declared her opposition to the Authorization for Use of Military Force against Terrorists – thus becoming the only member of Congress to vote against what she called "a blank check" for the president.

* * *

One of the most fascinating and culturally complex ways that African American artists responded to the "blank check" of militarism that Congress handed the president to use in South Asia and the Middle East was to incorporate the sights and sounds of Middle Eastern and South Asian culture into their own work. African American political and cultural leaders have long made common cause with the people of the Middle East and South Asia and have been deeply invested in the "cultural stuff" produced by people from those regions. The most familiar entry in this Afro-Asian history is, most likely, the story of how African American civil rights leader Martin Luther King, Jr., found his way to a theory of non-violence by studying the life and work of Indian leader Mathama Gandhi and how Gandhi inspired Black radicals in the United States to envision themselves as part of an international anti-imperialist movement made up of the world's colonized people. The various consequential relationships that have linked Black Americans with the brown people of the Middle East and Asia are far beyond the purview of my work here, but to understand the post-9/11 white–brown–Black triangle it is necessary to have at least a glancing understanding of what pioneering scholar Vijay Prashad has discussed under the rubric of "Afro-Asian connections."

In his book *Everybody Was Kung Fu Fighting* Prashad (2001) traces the Afro-Asian relationship back into antiquity, but for our concerns the important connections begin in the decolonization efforts of the immediate post-World War II era. Inspired by Gandhi's India, and later successful independence movements in Africa, Asia, and the Caribbean, African American intellectuals and activists began a process of redefining themselves as members of the newly defined "Third World." The Bandung Conference, held in the spring of 1955 in Indonesia, brought together leaders from numerous "non-aligned" countries of Asia and Africa (along with individual African Americans) and created a template for the idea that the existence of people of color was to be defined by themselves and not by the interests of the United States, the Soviet Union, or any other imperialist power. African American writer Richard Wright (1956) attended, and later collected his responses in a book called *The Color*

Curtain, making the lessons of Bandung even more available to the rising generation of African American leaders.

By the late 1960s it was a given that a significant number of politically active young African Americans believed in a meaningful connection between their freedom struggle and those of other people of color around the globe. In fact, it has become something of a reflex for scholars studying the relationship of African Americans and American Jews to date the break-up of the "grand alliance" of these two American groups to the moment in the late 1960s when African Americans began to see themselves as having much more in common with the Palestinians struggling against the state of Israel and its Jews for their nationhood, rather than with American Jews who allegedly could tap into some history of persecution that would make them more sympathetic to African American concerns. (This triangle of Jews, African Americans, and Palestinians is what undergirds a fascinating moment in Steven Spielberg's 2005 film *Munich*. There is a tense scene when the group of Jewish assassins has been tricked into staying the night at a "safe" house in Athens that has also been promised to a group of Palestinian radicals. In a simmering moment one of the Jews tunes a shortwave radio to play some treacly French pop music; the Palestinian man gets up and angrily turns to an Arabic-language song. At last, magically, the situation is resolved when a turn of the dial brings peace to all of them in the form of African American singer Al Green's "Let's Stay Together." Steven Spielberg, ever the master of the feel-good *deus ex machina*, here imagines a triangulated moment of unity exactly where dissension was ruling the day.)

There is no straight line connecting the sympathy African Americans felt for postcolonial "brown" people around the world and the racial realities that dominated the scene in the United States just after 9/11. South Asians had long occupied the complicated position of "model minority" in the United States, as Vijay Prashad (2000) explains in another book, *The Karma of Brown Folk*. Indians, and other "good" brown people in the United States, have often been promoted by the dominant culture as the "solution" to the problem of race in America (viii). But after 9/11 South Asians were stitched into a new and more dangerous identity position: "looks Middle Eastern." This category is slippery and flexible and has come to describe numerous South Asians (especially Pakistani and Sikh Americans in the United States) and a variety of Muslim and non-Muslim Arab Americans. The first post-9/11 hate crime victim was a Sikh, Balbir Singh Sodhi, who was shot and killed in front of his gas station in Mesa, Arizona, by Frank Roque. Even the FBI noted a post-9/11 spike in hate crimes: its report for 2001 noted a 1,600 percent increase in bias attacks against Muslims (a category that may well include victims *perceived* to be Muslim) from the previous year. Sikh American men, because of the religious dictates directing them to wear turbans, were particularly visible to bigots who confused them (or didn't) with Arabs and/or Muslims. (See http://www.fbi.gov/ucr/01hate.pdf)

As terrifying and destructive as individual acts of bias and their collective impact were, much more significant was the institutional apparatus created by the United States government in the aftermath of 9/11 to put people who "look Middle Eastern" under surveillance. From a Department of Justice ruling that permitted detention of non-citizens for 48 hours with no charges being filed (and which targeted Pakistanis above all others) through the Patriot Act with its many tentacles, and then later initiatives aimed at investigating, arresting, and deporting Arab and South Asian immigrants (saalt.org has tracked many of these initiatives), the months following 9/11 were perilous times for thousands of people who "looked Middle Eastern."

Scholar Roopali Mukherjee (2003) has argued that in the wake of 9/11 African Americans have been "enabled a claim to Americanness" by "articulating ... distance from Arabs, Arab Americans, and Muslim Americans" (33). There is certainly some evidence for this position. The usual source trotted out to support the notion that African Americans have somewhat opportunistically used 9/11 as an excuse to endorse discrimination against people who "look Middle Eastern" is a Zogby poll, that – as Vijay Prashad has pointed out – used confusing wording that implied that being against racial profiling was equivalent to supporting terrorism ("Interview with Vijay Prashad," n.d.). Anecdotal evidence was frequently trotted out after 9/11 to demonstrate that those who used to suffer from "driving while Black" were now supporting the profiling of those who dared to try "flying while Arab." One journalist even found a young African American who was willing to say it right out: while the police used to harass this young man whenever he hung out with friends, now "it seems like they don't really bother us. They stop everyone that has Middle Eastern features" (Chang, 2002). The harassment went beyond ad hoc profiling. According to one report, a Palestinian American rapper in Brooklyn was put under FBI surveillance "because he had written lyrics calling for peace in the Holy Land" and had criticized "stereotypes of 'irrationally violent' Arabs." "You made us," Lefty rapped, "when you labeled us" (Chang, 2001).

There certainly is reason to believe, as African American writer Kevin Young put it in his 2006 book *Someday We'll All Be Free*, that many African Americans "were simply happy that, for once, the heat was off us and on someone else. Those Arabs. Those Middle Easterners. Those Muslims ... Many Blacks feel that the pressure put on Arabs and Arab Americans since September 11th is somehow a removal of that daily pressure from our shoulders. That we are less likely to be victims of racial profiling, of police brutality, of discrimination" (57). While there is no doubt that hate crimes, racial profiling, and police brutality towards African Americans continue unabated (and may even be on the rise since 9/11), Young's summary seems useful especially when taken in the context of the post-Hurricane Katrina moment in which he was writing.

In some ways the most interesting expression of African Americans' ambivalence about their "new" status after 9/11 came with the strangely out-of-time 2004 Will Smith movie *I, Robot*. The film, which Smith produced and starred in, imagines a time when every American home will have a personal robot. The movie has a paranoid feel, and a number of references are made to the necessity of giving up certain personal liberties in exchange for greater security. It opens with a chase scene in which Smith, a police detective in the year 2035, hunts down a robot he takes for a purse snatcher. Of course the robot is innocent, but Smith explains that he saw a robot running with a purse and "naturally" concluded that it was criminal. With no claims to subtlety, *I, Robot* promotes a vision of Black people as perpetrators of racial profiling, rather than as its victims. The film insists that the audience not indulge in "color blind" viewing to assume that Smith is playing "any" cop: he makes important visits to his grandmother who offers up sweet potato pie and homespun wisdom. Paraphrasing a familiar slogan –"It's a Black thing ... You wouldn't understand" – Smith tells a robot "It's a human thing ... You wouldn't understand"; and parodying moments of romantic angst in Hollywood cinema, Smith tells a cat he is holding, "Look ... this relationship just can't work. I mean you're a cat, I'm Black, and I'm not gonna be hurt again." *I, Robot* wants its viewers to consider a new world that coerces African Americans into an ambivalent position as part of the social machinery of surveillance and discipline.

More pointed yet was African American satirist Aaron McGruder's (2003) set of "We're Number Three!" (172–3) strips for his daily comic

Figure 6 Aaron McGruder's "We're Number Three!" strips. Source: THE BOONDOCKS © 2001 Aaron McGruder. Dist. By UNIVERSAL PRESS SYNDICATE. Reprinted with permission. All rights reserved.

series *The Boondocks* (see Figure 6). By McGruder's own account in the introduction to *A Right to Be Hostile, The Boondocks* was energized by the complexities of 9/11 – given a "new sense of purpose" in his words. McGruder had an especially keen eye for how African Americans were repositioned on the American racial landscape by the new, negative attention being given to people who "look Middle Eastern" (n.p.). In this series McGruder's main character, Huey Freeman, tries to make sense of the news that according to a Newsweek poll African Americans are no longer "America's most-hated ethnic group." As a newscaster tells it, "they fell to third place behind people of Middle Eastern/Arab descent and people of East Indian descent … because they look kind of like people of Middle Eastern/Arab descent." Huey's little brother, an aspirant to the thug life, is particularly distressed by this news, because it cuts into his sense of himself as intimidating to the other kids at school.

In nearly 2 weeks of strips, McGruder works hard to have Huey, Riley, and Michael process this strange news; Riley, in particular, understands the poll as evidence of a demotion – loss of a certain kind of Black cultural capital. With an early reference to the internment of Japanese and Japanese Americans during World War II, McGruder is striving here to remind his readers of the seductive appeal of wartime restrictions on the civil liberties of non-white Americans. Using these young African Americans as his mouthpiece, McGruder issues a special message for African Americans who might want to embrace the benefits of being demoted to "number three": twentieth-century history is a reminder that this social reorganization will likely be temporary and will not, in the long run, serve the interests of any people of color.

It was into this dense thicket of racial and ethnic confusion that a surprising number of African Americans from the world of rap music plunged and the results have been complicated. Since 9/11 dozens of productions that belong to what we customarily call "Black culture" have leaned heavily on musical and visual elements of South Asian and Middle Eastern culture. This is not the first time, of course, that this sort of cultural borrowing has helped to define American youth culture. In our book *Immigration and American Popular Culture*, Rachel Rubin and I (2006) describe a 150-year history of white American interest in the "cultural stuff" of India that peaked in the middle to late 1960s. During the Vietnam War, as we explain, it became appealing for thousands of young Americans to develop a relationship to "Asia" that moved beyond the militaristic and colonial. Of course in adopting wholesale the sounds, styles, and religions of India, these young people flirted with cultural insensitivity at best (the "India" they invented did not often have much to do with the actual place) and with cultural imperialism at worst. Gita Mehta, one of the most acute contemporaneous critics of the cross-cultural encounter, nailed it in the title of her book: *Karma Cola*.

In some respects, then, the young African Americans who were at the controls in the post-9/11 era were simply putting a new date stamp on an old tradition. The assimilation of non-Western sights and sounds lacked specificity; the hip hop artists involved in this cultural movement had no interest in giving geography or history lessons – at least not in any straightforward way. With only a few very significant exceptions, these "looks Middle Eastern" songs are not "political" in any explicit way. The list of the most significant tracks includes work by some of the most important producers and artists in American popular music, including Jay-Z, Timbaland, Missy Elliot, Beyoncé, Erick Sermon, Wyclef Jean, and Truth Hurts, working with DJ Quik.

There have been two main ways that hip hop artists have displayed their determination to reach out to the culture of people who "look Middle Eastern." First, and most important by far, has been to integrate the strings and vocals of India's Bollywood into hip hop and rhythm and blues songs. Less common, but also significant, has been the incorporation of images of Middle Eastern belly dancing into videos by African American performers. This triangulation of American, South

Asian, and Middle Eastern is articulated most fully in the video for Truth Hurts' 2002 song "Addictive," produced by DJ Quik and released on Dr. Dre's Aftermath label. The artist turns out to have been a one-hit wonder, but for some months the song gained a phenomenal amount of attention, and was even the object of a major lawsuit based on its uncredited use of a Hindi-language song. In the video, set in a vaguely "haremesque nightclub," a set of dancers, mostly African American, dance in a manner meant to suggest Middle Eastern styles. Chris Fitzpatrick (2002) has written a blistering attack on the song and its video:

> Although the track is centered on sounds from India, the video features choreographed belly dancing: a Middle Eastern dance form. This odd combination is indicative of a typically totalizing Western mentality: India, the Middle East, what's the difference? The entire "third world" is one big backwards and "underdeveloped" wasteland, right? Wrong, but such assumptions are embedded into every note, chant, beat, image, and dance in "Addictive," relying on the romantic notion that the Middle East and India are inherently mystical and sexy, as if everyone studies the Karma Sutra, practices Tantric Sex, rides magic carpets, and belly dances naked in the moonlight.

Kevin Miller (2004) has seconded Fitzpatrick's argument in part, suggesting that the use of Lata Mangeshkar's Hindi song "Thoda Resham Lagta Hai" ("It Looks Silky") as one of many contemporary "decontextualized samples" ends up creating "an indulgent fantasy space" that folds together "two or more distinct cultures" with little care for specificity or authenticity (6).

Erick Sermon's song "React," also from 2002, inspired similarly disapproving responses. "React" is organized around a Bollywood musical excerpt that the rapper and his producer, Just Blaze, then rang changes on. In the song and its video, Erick Sermon offers up a seemingly indiscriminate mix of sampled Hindi vocals with images that borrow equally from an imagined harem scene and a familiar rap-video quasi-porn vocabulary. The Hindi vocalist is described as an "Arabian chick" in the narration of the song, a narrative move that is supported by the settings and costumes in the video. Indian American journalist Raj Beri, according to Kevin Miller, has complained that this sort of conflation is "especially dangerous after 9/11, and contributes to the public's lack of knowledge about the regions – evidenced by how South Asian Sikhs and Arabs are all the same in America's eyes" (Miller, 2004: 7).

In "React," Erick Sermon (formerly of EPMD) participates in what ultimately sounds like a duet with the female Hindi singer he has sampled. Most significant is a sampled vocal line in Hindi that has been translated as "If someone wants to commit suicide, so what can you do?" Interestingly, the "call" in this call-and-response comes from the sample: after each featured line in Hindi, the rapper responds "Whatever she said, then I'm that." Kevin Miller (2004) and Tina Chadha (2003) have written negative appraisals of this song and video, based on this juxtaposition. Both suggest that Indian American listeners are bound to find this call-and-response "stupid": "If you're not Indian it sounds fine, but *I* understand and everyone I know thinks it sounds stupid" (Chadha, 2003). (This criticism is surely undercut by the video, which makes a joke out of the reflexive repetition of "Whatever she said, then I'm that"; it includes cartoon air bubbles next to women who "look Middle Eastern" which include translations of the Hindi sample in a number of ways to mock Erick Sermon and guest rapper Redman – "He need deodorant" and "He think he cute" and so on.) It is also worth noting that for a song released less than a year after the 9/11 hijackings, there is something more than slightly subversive about a rapper using "Middle Eastern" sounds to structure a song whose hook is a philosophical acceptance of suicide.

The critiques of "Addictive" and "React" are valuable and harmonize with much of what Rachel Rubin and I wrote about white American youth culture in the 1960s and 1970s. Indian Americans have rightly complained that the mining of Bollywood sounds has rarely been joined by scrupulous efforts to find and pay original copyright owners or to employ actual Indian Americans in promotional videos (Chadha, 2003). (Iranian American comedian Maz Jobrani warned his fellow actors who "look Middle Eastern" to be careful what they wish for when it comes to working in the post-9/11 industry: "You're out of work, in a ditch, and someone brings you a turban and says 'Hey, put this on and make some money.' What do you do?" [Timiraos, 2007])

Evaluations of this post-9/11 musical activity need to take into account that this new culture is being promoted by young African Americans and not by the white Americans who "discovered" India previously. With a history of meaningful Afro-Asian political association behind them and a current scene on which any unity move among young people of color runs counter to the dominant scripts of purity, scapegoating, and cultural atomization, the hip hop "turn to the East" seems conspicuously distinct from earlier instances of Karma Cola. The critical appraisals of the contemporary scene, while sincere and likely motivated by a progressive politics, also betray a fundamental misunderstanding of hip hop's most basic musical premise. Rooted in an aesthetics of pastiche, an approach that takes as a given that new songs can be constructed from the shards of earlier creations, rap music has always promoted the cultural ideals of cut-and-mix. The central activities of rap music-making – "digging in the crates" for sounds, sampling them, and recombining them – are based on a shared culture of "recontextualization" as opposed to a simple act of decontextualization. Putting old sounds in a new place can mean a lot of different things, and can (at the worst) seem to mean "nothing" or something insulting. The fact that African Americans in the centralized corporate world of hip hop in the early 2000s are no longer signifying from below, as their predecessors were in the late 1970s and early 1980s, complicates any notion that this is a simple alliance of colonized people of color. And the songs (and videos for) "Addictive" and "React" certainly indulge in imperialist and sexist fantasies that severely undercut whatever positive outreach work they might also be doing. Erick Sermon and other rap artists give no indication that they are thinking about Bandung. But for African Americans in the years after 9/11 to announce that their music *needs* South Asia and the Middle East must be heard as a cultural declaration of interdependence. Unlike the fossil fuel that is the source of so many Western interventions in the Middle East, music has always been a renewable resource. "Looking for the perfect beat" is not only the title of an early rap song, it is standard operating procedure. There are, nevertheless, major issues of intellectual property and remuneration that always have to be worked out in and around rap music sampling: the appearance of "Addictive" was met with a major lawsuit filed by Bappi Lahiri, the holder of the copyright of its main sample.

African American hip hop artists working in the aftermath of 9/11 have insisted (or admitted) that their culture relies on cultural synergies created by reaching out to (or into) the various cultures of South Asia and the Middle East. As Tina Chadha (2003) has reported, Timbaland – the rap producer at the heart of this new hybrid – "says he spends five grand on Indian albums every time he steps into Tower Records" and was, for a time, working with an Indian American protégé. Making sure that less powerful artists get paid for their work would go even farther than

Timbaland's declaration of love when it comes to forging connections between African Americans and other people of color.

While Timbaland has made large claims for his primacy in this Afro-Asian musical activity, it is Jay-Z who has made the most impressive cultural and political moves by building on the now-familiar Bollywood samples with actual thematizing of the 9/11 attacks and their aftermath, and in a thrilling collaboration with a British Indian, Panjabi MC. Jay-Z's *Blueprint* record, of course, was released on September 11, 2001, and that coincidence alone granted the rapper and entrepreneur ("I'm not a businessman, I'm a business, *man*" he rapped on Kanye West's "Diamonds from Sierra Leone") cultural and actual capital that he drew from in the ensuing years.

On his follow-up record, *The Blueprint 2: The Gift and the Curse,* Jay-Z promoted his own 9/11 legend, in a song "The Bounce," that featured a Hindi lyric sung by Raje Shwari (Timbaland's protégé). On this track, Jay-Z begins "Rumor has it *The Blueprint* classic/Couldn't even be stopped by bin Laden/So September 11th marks the era forever/of a revolutionary Jay Guevara." Bragging has been a central activity of rap record-making since the inception of the form; promoting one's skills and achievements is simply normative in rap rhetoric. But Jay-Z's interesting move on *The Blueprint 2* is to plot his self-promotion onto a national map. Breaking from the common "hood"-based landscape of hip hop music, Jay-Z here competes with Bruce Springsteen as he nominates himself as America's most important post-9/11 musical artist. This same record also featured "Ballad for a Fallen Soldier" and a lead-off track, "A Dream," which dramatically samples Notorious B.I.G.'s 1994 song "Juicy," inserting a silence where earlier the rapper had made reference to the 1993 bombing of the World Trade Center. Naming the whole record as a sequel was part of Jay-Z's strategy of declaring himself as the defining rapper of the moment – as a way of marking "the era forever."

A year later Jay-Z contributed to a remixed version of "Mundian To Bach Ke," now retitled "Beware" a track by British Indian musician Panjabi MC. Here the triangulation of African American–South Asian–Middle Eastern goes far beyond the work of Truth Hurts and Erick Sermon. As with so many collaborations in hip hop, the two principal musicians never actually met while making the song. Sending digital files to each other, Panjabi MC and Jay-Z created a new song (a track that borrows from northern India's Bhangra music and other contemporary dance styles) that is explicitly anti-war. After detailing his various world travels, Jay-Z raps "We rebellious, we back home, screaming leave Iraq alone" and adds "only love kills war/When will they learn?"

Also of interest is that in the same verse Jay-Z brags that he has "been havin' the flow/Before bin Laden got Manhattan to blow/Before Ronald Reagan got Manhattan to blow." This boast literally means that the rapper is holding Ronald Reagan responsible for the foreign policy (i.e. as "blowback") that resulted from U.S. support of the Taliban in Afghanistan as an anti-Soviet strategy that ultimately led to the rise of Al Qaeda and the destruction of the towers. But it is intriguing to consider that Jay-Z is also representing a more local form of knowledge here – the widely held belief that crack cocaine reached African Americans in the United States as a consequence of CIA involvement in the American support for the Contras in Nicaragua in the early 1980s. (Interestingly, the claim that the government purposely promoted crack in Black communities was given mainstream attention again in the spring of 2008 during the Jeremiah Wright controversy. Wright, it seems, had repeated this charge as part of a larger indictment of the racism of the United States' government.)

With either reading of "Beware of the Boys" it is clear that Jay-Z is using the post-9/11 complexities of American life as an opportunity to create at least provisional alliances with people of color in South Asia and the Middle East. The same could certainly be said of Ozomatli, a West Coast band that has always privileged hybridity and global reach in their music. On their 2004 release, *Street Signs*, Ozomatli wove Middle Eastern sounds into their already complex mix of hip hop, salsa, and rock and roll.

* * *

Of course it was not only African Americans who utilized South Asian and Middle Eastern sounds, themes, and images in their musical work. Britney Spears got into the act in 2003 as well with her song "Toxic," which features stirring Bollywood strings and was later parodied in the film *Music and Lyrics* (2007) as "an orgasm set to the *Gandhi* soundtrack." Bruce Springsteen's major 9/11 record *The Rising* (2002) features one song that somewhat sympathetically narrates from the point of view of a suicide bomber in the Middle East ("Paradise") and another that actually employs Asif Ali Khan, a Pakistani Sufi Muslim qawwali singer, to help him tell a post-9/11 *Romeo and Juliet* tale of star-crossed lovers. More interesting was Steve Earle's "John Walker's Blues," also from 2002, which sings from the point of view of John Walker Lindh,

"The American Taliban." While right-wing bloggers and talk radio hosts went mad over Earle's audacity – that he dared to humanize the young white American who received training in Yemen and then joined the Taliban forces – missing from Earle's song is the convoluted racial identification that defined Lindh's situation. Earle's "John Walker's Blues" presents this John as "just an American boy, raised on MTV," an echo of Earle's own earlier "I'm an American, boys" that leads off his "Johnny Come Lately" (1988), a song about a Vietnam veteran musing on his grandfather's much different experience returning from World War II. With this Earle was striving to dignify Lindh by placing him in a recognizable tradition of young white American men who hear a lofty call, and respond.

Earle's Lindh is lost in the world until he hears "the word of Mohammed, peace be upon him." But according to many accounts, most of them demonizing of rap music, the first thing Lindh heard that made sense to him was rap music, especially that made by "Five Percenters," followers of a radical form of Islam whose roots are in Clarence 13X's break from the Nation of Islam in the early 1960s (Miyakawa, 2005: 9). Following a trail from more mainstream rappers like Nas into the complex teachings found in the music of the Five Percenters, Lindh's triangulation of white–Black–Middle Eastern landed him ultimately as a prisoner of war, after fighting for the Taliban in Afghanistan. But before his adventures in the Middle East and Asia, Lindh had already taken fascinating trips in cyberspace: according to James Best's (2003) investigative reporting in the *East Bay Express*, Lindh had regularly participated in early internet message boards – usenet groups – on which he often masqueraded as an African American. Lindh started as a white teenager and traveled through a Black identity to find a Middle Eastern one, and then was put on trial as a white traitor. Becoming radicalized by an encounter with Islam has been, since the 1960s, a recognizable route for young people of color in the United States to register their disaffection from the normative white, Christian, and colonial practices of their home country.

There was a brief flurry of media handwringing after Lindh's arrest about how the event should serve as a wake-up call to white parents who had indulged in overly permissive childrearing practices, and about the dangers of radical hip hop and radical Islam. Lindh's capture in 2001, and the strange tale his life told of racial and religious ambivalences, did not interfere long with the real headline stories of racial confusion that were to dominate the American scene in the immediate post-9/11 era. The terrifying demonization of people who "look Middle Eastern" after the attacks had to be incorporated into the reigning American racial system that is at once rooted in a binary and hierarchical system of white and Black and yet is complicated by a meaningful history of Afro-Asian association in the United States. Moustafa Bayoumi (2002), in his heartrending essay "Letter to a G-Man," reminds readers that Arab settlements in New York City predate the twentieth century and were centered around the part of lower Manhattan now marked as Ground Zero; further, he notes that the first generations of Arab merchants in the United States would go "places others would not, namely into the warm hearths of African American homes" (135).

But this relatively forgotten trace of Black–brown relations offered little to the present generation of African Americans and Arab Americans or the other thousands of Americans and visitors who "look Middle Eastern." Even as Huey Freeman of *The Boondocks* celebrated the demotion of African Americans on the "most hated" charts (and his little brother Riley mourned his dwindling "thug" status), real Black people struggled with how to position themselves in political life, personal relations, and in the public marketplace vis-à-vis the increasingly visible brown denizens of the United States. Alternating currents of rapprochement and division characterized this complex set of relationships that had been thrust upon African Americans, South Asians, and Arab Americans. Hisham Aidi (2002) has noted that Zacarias Moussaoui and Richard Reid, the "two most notorious accused terrorists ... in US custody," are both Black Europeans. Aidi goes on to argue that the "ubiquitous mug shot" of Moussaoui in "orange prison garb" has "intrigued many and unnerved some". Aidi quotes African American journalist Sheryl McCarthy who suggested that the last thing "African Americans need is for the first guy to be tried on terrorism charges stemming from this tragedy to look like one of our own."

Even so, some major players in African American cultural life have worked hard to resist the lure of creating Black distance from South Asian and Middle Eastern people, and African American rap musicians have been out front in this. While much about hip hop music's "turn East" can be chalked up to the kind of opportunistic exoticization that marked late 1960s corporate raids on the storehouse of Asian textiles, music, and religions, there have also been moments of meaningful collaboration that act as a repudiation of what too often is sold as a zero sum game of American racial politics. Jay-Z's collaboration with Panjabi MC and Timbaland's plan to work with M.I.A. – maker of dance music and the daughter of an Indonesian radical – both point to a desire felt by powerful African American cultural figures to identify themselves with brown people who have much less celebrity muscle to flex than their African American counterparts. That the Timbaland/M.I.A. project was stalled by M.I.A.'s immigration woes (according to her because she was this "citizen of the Other World" and matched "the profile of a terrorist" ["The Best Albums of 2007"]) only underscores how important it has been for African Americans to make common cause with other people of color.

This is not to say that we can track a consistent narrative of Black–brown unity across the cultural landscape or even through individual works of popular art. Spike Lee's *Inside Man* (2006), for instance, is framed by opening and closing credits that use versions of A. R. Rahman's Bollywood soundtrack song "Chaiyya, Chaiyya" (over the close, it is a remixed version by Panjabi MC). This usage seems to function as an effort on the director's part to join his counterparts in the hip hop world who have been reaching out to the music of South Asia as a gesture of intergroup affiliation. Inside of the movie's Bollywood frame, however, we find a bit of dialogue that has become perhaps the emblematic statement of complexity summarizing the relationship of African Americans to people who "look Middle Eastern." When one of the hostages in the film's bank heist, a Sikh American named Vikram, is apprehended by the police he is called "Arab" by them, and they remove his turban. Vikram refuses to offer any information to the police until they return his turban. "What happened to my fucking civil rights?" Vikram asks, as he catalogs all the freedom being denied him in this moment of crisis. The sharp reply, allegedly ad-libbed by Denzel Washington? "Bet you can get a cab though."

White artists were much less likely to enter the post-9/11 arena with the relationships among African Americans, South Asians, and Arabs on their mind. One ambitious attempt came with Sara Paretsky's 2003 mystery novel *Blacklist*, whose plot invites readers to understand the Patriot Act's assault on civil liberties in the light of the anti-Communist hysteria of the post-World War II era. Most interestingly, Paretsky's complex plot lines link the persecution of radical African Americans in the era of the House Un-American Activities Committee with the contemporary demonization of a young Egyptian man living in Chicago.

When the desperate-to-seem-relevant novelist John Updike (2006) tried to implement some comparative racial group shorthand in his wretched snatched-from-the-headlines novel *Terrorist*, this came off as perfunctory at best, explicitly racist at worst. With a cast that included cardboard cutouts of a tortured half-Arab, an oversexed African American teenager, and an embittered but noble Jew, Updike revealed mostly that the new math of race relations in the United States after 9/11 held little real weight for him. With its emphasis on the psychological suffering of Ahmad, a high school student in New Jersey who is wracked by self-doubt as a result of his abandonment by his Egyptian father and is saved by a surrogate Jewish father (his guidance counselor), *Terrorist* makes clear that its post-9/11 concern surrounds gender role, and not race. As with so many of his male contemporaries in the United States, what truly animated Updike's work was a sense – a fear really – that the 9/11 attacks were both the result and the cause of some major problems in contemporary gender arrangements in the United States. Attempts to right the applecart of traditional gender roles became, as we will see, an almost obsessive focus of American literary and popular culture in the years after 9/11.

CH/6
Tools

According to some fan accounts, the pop punk band Blink-182 were finishing up work on their video for the song "Stay Together for the Kids" on September 10 and 11 of 2001. The video opens with a black screen and text that tells us that "50 percent of American households are destroyed by divorce." The video begins to tell its tale of "broken homes" as shots of the band are intercut with literal images of a building in ruins; before long we see a wrecking ball destroying what remains of the physical structure that has been housing the band and the sad-looking kids who we understand represent their audience. News of the attacks allegedly reached the band as they wrapped up work on the video, and with their director they decided to reshoot because they feared that the images of destruction would seem too close to what was being obsessively broadcast on television and circulated on the internet on that day and in the days after.

Ultimately Blink-182 released the original video on DVD and it is now widely available on YouTube and other sites. This seems fitting, because in many ways the original video for "Stay Together for the Kids" acted as a premature "first responder": it is an emblem of the cultural backlash that helps set 9/11 in time and place for us – a backlash whose first principle was that the attacks were a startling wake-up call for Americans to shore up proper gender behavior and renounce the "liberty" that the hijackers and their backers supposedly found so infuriating. Here the pop punk band anticipate much of what Susan Faludi (2007) was later to chronicle as America's "terror dream" – recent history as a nightmare that Americans need to awake from in order to reinstate traditional gender roles. The video tells us that the "house divided against itself

[that] cannot stand," which Abraham Lincoln spoke of in 1858 with reference to the nation, now must be understood as each "broken home" in the United States destroyed by divorce. This was a call to unity to heterosexual American mothers and fathers, and a call to behave according to a very tight and traditional script. Fearing that their video might be too incendiary or upsetting for the immediate post-9/11 scene, Blink-182 could not recognize that the video "Stay Together for the Kids" was actually exemplary 9/11 art, *avant la lettre*.

Writing in the introduction to his unclassifiable work *In the Shadow of No Towers* ("The Sky is Falling"), Art Spiegelman (2004) describes how in the weeks after 9/11 he found himself living on the edge of panic:

> I tend to be easily unhinged. Minor mishaps – a clogged drain, running late for an appointment – send me into a sky-is-falling tizzy. It's a trait that can leave one ill-equipped for the sky when it actually falls. Before 9/11 my traumas were all more or less self-inflicted, but out-running the toxic cloud that had moments before been the north tower of the World Trade Center left me reeling on that faultline where World History and Personal History collide. (n.p.)

It is an evocative phrase that Spiegelman uses here – "the faultline where World History and Personal History collide" – and in his book he works hard to keep both terms in the foreground. He reminds us that one of the major challenges facing artists working in the post-9/11 context has been to develop meaningful strategies for balancing the local and the global in their efforts.

A few artists have made that test their first principle. From Steven Spielberg in his 9/11 trilogy (*Minority Report*, *War of the Worlds*, and *Munich*) to the British-Sri Lankan-Baltimore-Brooklyn dance music artist M.I.A. on her record *Kala* (2007), there have been some satisfying attempts to reckon with the most complex questions of post-9/11 personal identity and political reality. But where the feminists of the late 1960s and 1970s held as a key principle that the "personal is political" (i.e. that everything that happens to us individually shapes and has meaning in the larger field of social relations), the art of 9/11 has been much more intent on reflecting on how the political becomes personal. To put it plainly, one of the defining features of the post-9/11 cultural landscape has been to translate the violence of the day as a simple assault on the proper functioning of American masculinity and femininity. Spike Lee's allegorical *25th Hour*, for instance, gains much of its narrative energy not only from its basic premise – that tomorrow Monty Brogan will go to jail – but that his life as a man will surely end then, because his good looks will make him a target for rape in prison. In the film's climax Monty convinces his best friend to beat him up, to render him ugly, as a possible inoculation against this injury. In a much different register (with puppets!) *Team America: World Police* features an action-hero main character whose degradation in the film comes when he is coerced to perform oral sex on Spottswoode, the commander of the team.

A startling level of cultural work has been put into play on the American scene since, and in response to, the attacks, whose main animus seems to be pushing "reset" on American gender roles and relations. Critic Richard Goldstein (2003) noticed this wave as early as 2003 in an essay on what he calls the "Neo-Macho Man." Acknowledging that a decades-long cultural "flight from feminism" has characterized the 1990s, Goldstein still can find numerous consequential challenges to this well-documented backlash. But then even these challenges disappear and to Goldstein the explanation (at least the short version) is simple: 9/11 happened. To Goldstein, no figure better emblematizes the rush to promote "patriarchal vitality" than the rapper Eminem, whose semi-autobiographical film *8 Mile* was released late in 2002. Here, Marshall Mathers' rap persona was reorganized: now, Eminem delivers no anti-gay or anti-woman lyrics. In fact, as Goldstein puts it, in *8 Mile* Eminem "never busts a rhyme against a bitch, not even his mom" and comes to the defense of a gay co-worker. As Goldstein explains, *8 Mile* worked to "firemanize" Eminem "by placing him in the tradition of working-class heroes and blunting his sexism with stirring images of racial harmony." The work of celebrating "real men" after 9/11 has been done across many media and in political discourse, but nowhere in so focused or sustained a manner as in mainstream Hollywood film.

* * *

Upon retiring in 1991 *New Yorker* film critic Pauline Kael is reputed to have said that the "prospect of having to sit through another Oliver Stone movie" was simply "too much" (Wolf, 1997). Stone's most vociferous critics throughout his career have been right-wing writers and public figures who see in his body of work a sustained left-wing critique of the evils of the United States government and social institutions. But Stone has never been as committed to any ideology so much as that of masculinism. His films are, above all else, epics of besieged manhood. From *Platoon* (1986), his breakthrough film, through *World Trade Center*, Stone has revealed a consistent – or better yet, obsessive – interest in men under attack. Jonathan Rosenbaum is one of the few working film critics to challenge Stone's gender politics. In "It's All About Us" Rosenbaum (2006b) writes:

> Many critics seem to see no contradiction between the progressive mantle Stone wears and the blatant misogyny of his *Born on the Fourth of July* and *Nixon* (which blame the warmongering instincts of Ron Kovic and the corruptions of Nixon on castrating mothers); the human Barbie dolls of *Wall Street* and *The Doors*; the homophobia of *JFK*; the adolescent patriarchal hang-ups of *JFK*, *Nixon*, *Platoon*, and *Wall Street*; or the cynical exploitation of sex and violence in *Midnight Express* and *Natural Born Killers*.

As one of the most important post-1970s American film directors, Stone's major work has been to reconstruct the authority of American men at moments of extreme vulnerability.

This would seem to be a tough sell in *World Trade Center*, which focuses on John McLoughlin and Will Jimeno, the two Port Authority police officers trapped in the rubble of the towers and later rescued by two volunteers at the site. McLoughlin and Jimeno are not characters per se, but types. McLoughlin's is the stolid and humorless hero-as-career-man; Jimeno the wise-cracking upstart who ultimately enables and emulates the noble dedication of his leader. Together they act out an update of the kind of patriotic "we're all in the same foxhole" drama that was deployed so significantly as a propaganda weapon during World War II. The hole that McLoughlin and Jimeno are trapped in stands in for the military front. After McLoughlin warns Jimeno not to fall asleep because he might not wake up, Jimeno asks his sergeant "How long's this internal bleeding take?" When McLoughlin expresses guilt for having led some of his men to their death, Jimeno reassures him that "they did what they had to do, Sarge." Here in the hole the men are fighting the war, while back home the women and children wait for news of daddy's return.

The final dedication of the film is to all who "fought, died, and were wounded that day." Stuart Klawans (2006) has perceptively noted that *World Trade Center* is a barely sublimated cry for war. Stone's characterization of Dave Karnes, a former Marine who helps rescue McLoughlin and Jimeno, acts as the vehicle for Stone's translation of victimhood into a species of military volunteerism. Stone's men are down, for sure, but not only will they get back up, they will be joined by a legion of other Christian soldiers (with Karnes at the front of the line) marching as to war.

Rosenbaum (2006b) has written aptly of these two main characters that "it's hard to imagine any two men on the planet could be as conventional as the filmmakers make these heroes." *World Trade Center* must necessarily rely on flashback to imbue McLoughlin and Jimeno with Stone's requisite amount of male power, because the present they occupy is one in which they literally cannot move; seriously injured and immobilized by the crumbling of the tower they have bravely rushed into, Jimeno and McLoughlin can *do* nothing in the hours after the attack. They cry, suffer from survivor's guilt, and reminisce. The future holds diminished possibilities. An epilogue shows us the men retired from the Port Authority, with serious permanent injuries.

But the past, as the now proverbial line by L. P. Hartley puts it, is a foreign country. The pre-9/11 world of McLoughlin and Jimeno, as Stone presents it, is a PG-13 version of *Father Knows Best*. With the help of lots of soft-focus shots we are encouraged to forget about the current helplessness of the men and experience them as endowed with plenty of phallic power. Art Spiegelman has written in his introduction to *In the Shadow of No Towers* of how he considered putting a "terror sex" sequence into the work: he wanted to capture the rumors he heard about women rushing "into the wreckage to give comfort to rescue workers at night" and include the testimony of a friend who reminisced – as firefighter Franco does in the pilot episode of television's *Rescue Me* – about all the opportunities for great sex that existed in the days after the attacks. Ultimately Spiegelman abandoned his plan for the "terror sex" panels because he personally "couldn't imagine anything more detumescent" than the two towers falling (n.p.). Stand-up comic Margaret Cho has parodied this whole post-9/11 masculinist preoccupation with male power in the opening moments of her film *Notorious C.H.O.*: "I have been in New York a lot and I actually got a chance to go down to Ground Zero and I was there day after day, giving blowjobs to rescue workers ... Yeah. Because we all have to do our part."

Much of the flashback material in *World Trade Center* focuses on the men as baby makers. Jimeno's flashback scenes mostly have to do with his wife's pregnancy and the naming of their daughter-to-be (their second child). The first time we see Will and a very-pregnant Allison Jimeno, they are post-coitally discussing the coming baby. While in other contexts it might be cheering to see an unusually misogynist director presenting a pregnant woman as a sexual being, here the effect feels more desperate: look, *World Trade Center* seems to shout, he has her all knocked up and he is still at it! (Steven Spielberg's *Munich*, too, features an early sex scene between lead assassin Avner and his pregnant wife Daphna; the effect is to underscore the difference between making babies and raising them. As Naturelle Riviera says to Monty Brogan as they take a bath together in *25th Hour*, "Well, I could see you *fathering* children ...") Pregnancy in *World Trade Center* consistently functions as Stone's reminder of the main contribution women make to social life. Maggie Gyllenhaal's Allison Jimeno works outside the home, but strokes her belly so obsessively that it begins to seem that her hands might not be free for any other tasks.

McLoughlin gets much more "back story" attention than Jimeno. In the opening scene of the movie we see him rising for work at 3:29 a.m. and looking in on all of his children – four, it seems, but it is hard to keep count. McLoughlin's flashback scenes are so clichéd that when I screen this film for my students – not an irreverent bunch overall – they tend to laugh. An ongoing concern for McLoughlin, the thematic pivot that ultimately brings his intact past and broken present together in *World Trade Center*, has to do with his unfinished promise to build a new kitchen for his wife Donna. (The kitchen theme was to be played out even more insipidly in Adam Sandler's 2007 film *Reign Over Me*, in which the widowed Charlie Fineman is shown frantically redoing his kitchen because it is what his wife wanted before she died in one of the planes on 9/11.)

John McLoughlin has tools and knows how to use them. In an emblematic flashback, McLoughlin is in his basement workshop, teaching his eldest son how to use the tools as his wife looks on, beaming, in the background: "Nice and easy," he tells his son as the boy pushes the saw through the wood. "Don't force anything." In another scene Donna folds (and smells!) unbelievably white sheets in the bedroom, seeming to be transported to a near ecstatic state by her household chore, until she hears McLoughlin just outside the bedroom window. He has injured his hand while working on the roof and they take a moment to exchange loving glances – Donna in her proper place, McLoughlin in his. Another flashback shows us John and Donna waiting for the results of a home pregnancy test. The results are positive, of course, even though the couple did not plan to have any more children.

With its tense insistence on the power of these two fathers, Stone's movie barely hides its central anxiety – the one shared by so many 9/11 films – that the father has been rendered powerless by the attacks, or, worse yet, is revealed to have been powerless all along. Once Stone selected his text, it became impossible for these men to operate as standard issue male heroes; one way or another they were leaving the ruins on stretchers. As with much of what Susan Faludi (2007) has taught us to understand as the art of "backlash," the proper functioning of gender is lodged in the past. The present, with its deeply unsettling evidence of unmanned and/or absent fathers cannot compete with the gender certainties of the past. It is not surprising that following the terrible attack filmmakers would express instant nostalgia for the recent past. What is striking is how much this nostalgia has been articulated as a desire for powerful daddies.

Denis Leary's television drama *Rescue Me* (which debuted in 2004) is one of the few offerings in mainstream culture to attempt to move beyond a simple glorification of male power. While Susan Faludi is surely correct to argue that even as late as 2007 "virtually no film, television drama, play, or novel on 9/11 had begun to plumb what the trauma meant for our national psyche" (2), *Rescue Me*, with a dramatically wavering level of commitment, searched for a nuanced and intricate representation of wounded masculinity. Faludi's central argument in *The Terror Dream* has to do with how a perceived male weakness in the moment of the attacks got translated into a familiar idiom of female helplessness and active male bravery. The post-9/11 cultural landscape, in Faludi's account, is littered with tales of vulnerable women and heroic men; these stories draw from captivity narratives – that originary form of American literature that deals with white women endangered by darker men.

This cultural bait and switch, in Faludi's account, grows from a central challenge posed by the 9/11 attacks: what is "a rescuer without someone to rescue?" (53) Leary's show, from the title on down, repudiates the simple pleasures of male rescue fantasies. The show's title will be most familiar to audiences from Fontella Bass's 1965 song narrated by a woman desperate for her roaming man to return. In its first few episodes *Rescue Me* established that it is Leary's Tommy Gavin who is most in need of rescue: he is an alcoholic, heartbroken about the dissolution of his marriage, and seeing visions of his best friend (and cousin) who died in the towers on 9/11. While *Rescue Me* is consistently willing to look carefully at the costs of male bravado, it also regularly revels in masculine privilege – most notably the objectification of women and the delights of locker-room talk.

But what the show most productively plumbs is male loneliness. In her study Susan Faludi properly calls our attention to how 9/11 stories draw from a deep well of popular culture sources having to do with the rescue of women – from the original Indian captivity narratives through movie Westerns of the 1950s (most notably *The Searchers*). But missing from her account is an acknowledgment of how consistently such narratives have presented audiences with the image of the rescuer as a solitary figure: the iconic image here is John Wayne's Ethan Edwards, at the end of *The Searchers*, standing in the doorway of his rescued niece's home, unable to cross the threshold of the family space. So too does Leary's character in *Rescue Me* find himself protecting other people's family, but unable to fully engage with his own.

The fullest expression of the post-9/11 father fantasy came, perhaps, with *Chicken Little*. The first thing to remember about this movie is that unlike its centuries of folkloric antecedents, in this version the sky is falling. The second thing to know is that, as I have already discussed, the falling sky will not do any lasting damage. The major impulse of *Chicken Little* is therapeutic; its objective is to reassure its audience that ultimately fathers will be there for their sons, especially when the sky is falling. For much of the movie Chicken Little and his father find it impossible to understand each other. When Chicken Little causes a ruckus in Oakey Oaks early in the film by shouting his famous line, his father treats him as embarrassingly hysterical. Over the course of the film, the little chicken-boy ventures to be tough (and good at sports) in order to please his jock of a dad. Along the way *Chicken Little* makes visual reference to Steven Spielberg's *War of the Worlds* (2005) and with this it tips its hand. As with the Spielberg movie it is clear that *Chicken Little* will offer up a spectacle of previously clueless fathers learning from their sons how to be better dads. In *War of the Worlds* Tom Cruise's Ray Ferrier, a divorced working-class father, has barely existed for his children, who – defying the sociological realities of divorce in the United States – seem to have moved up the class ladder since their parents split up. Ferrier knows nothing about his children; he can competently "ferry" them away from the invading force but is immobilized by his daughter's food allergies and panic disorder and his son's desire to be a man.

In *Minority Report* (2002), the first of his 9/11 trilogy, Steven Spielberg presents an even darker picture of besieged fatherhood. In this, John

Anderton has become a "pre-crime" officer because he lost his son, kidnapped before the movie begins telling its story. Anderton spends much screen time viewing old home movies of his lost child and Lara, his estranged wife. He has been deeply wounded by the attack on his family, we see, but by movie's end Anderton is back with his wife, now obviously pregnant with their new child.

Both *Chicken Little* and *War of the Worlds* promise a post-attack reconfiguration of the father's role – with a little careful guidance coming from the younger generation. What *Chicken Little* offers children in particular is a fairy tale based on a fable. In the movie, the reason Chicken Little thinks the sky is falling is that a small panel from an alien space ship has fallen to earth. When it falls a second time, much panic ensues, but Chicken Little is able to stay calm enough to help reunite the cute furry little alien child with its desperate parents. In the climactic scene of reunion, the alien father is chided by his wife for using his "big voice": he needs to learn to speak softly and stop scaring people. The movie replaces the right-wing vision of 9/11 as a symptom of the "clash of civilizations" and replaces it with a child-friendly picture of battling fathers who can be humanized by the innocence of their children.

The search for "good enough" fathers, to borrow a concept from British psychoanalytic theorist D. W. Winnicott, has become a major framework for 9/11 arts, and not only in Hollywood films like *Chicken Little* and *War of the Worlds*. One of the most dramatic articulations of this find-a-father-at-all-costs approach came in Sherman Alexie's perplexing 2007 novel *Flight*. In this book, narrated by a boy without a name ("Call me Zits"), Alexie introduces a time-traveling protagonist who occupies numerous bodies across history, including that of a flight instructor who inadvertently trains a terrorist. The novel is about terror across the years, from a modern-day bank robbery back through Custer's Last Stand. Ultimately, this boy, who has been shuffled from one foster home to another, literally occupies the body of his own father, a homeless and alcoholic Native American man.

This journey to the absent Indian father was not new to Alexie's writing, but in *Flight* the narrative takes a surprising turn to a conventional vision of benign white fatherhood. In what has to be one of the strangest conversions of the post-9/11 age, Alexie has seemingly become a proponent of uncritical togetherness. In the book (and in publicity interviews done for it), Alexie argues that violence begets violence, and that those who commit it are victims too, of loneliness and misunderstanding. In *Flight*

Alexie offers up two white fathers as the ultimate solution to all of the pain Zits has suffered. The boy is ultimately placed with the brother and sister-in-law of "Officer Dave," the policeman who has taken an interest in the case. In fitting post-9/11 fashion, his final rescuer, the brother, "is a fireman." Zits notices too that "the wife is wearing a nurse's uniform." After completing the placement, Dave tells Zits that after "work today, I'm thinking all of us men should go to the Mariners game." Rebellious and prickly throughout his many transformations in the book, Zits embraces this development: "Dave is going to take care of me, too. That makes sense, I suppose ... I need as many fathers as possible." The "wife" packs "fruits and vegetables" for the men to take along, teaches Zits how to clear up his skin condition, and the farm is saved (174–6).

This is not a young adult novel; that was to come next for Alexie with his *The Absolutely True Diary of a Part-Time Indian*. Joyce Maynard *has* written a 9/11 YA book, *The Usual Rules*, and it too is organized around the search for fathers. In this work, the 13-year-old main character has lost her mother, who was working at the World Trade Center on 9/11. Having lived for years with her mother and caring stepfather Josh, Wendy is now thrust into a new life with her biological dad Garrett, who has reappeared to claim her. As with *Flight*, the post-9/11 panacea in *The Usual Rules* is *two* fathers. After moving from New York to California to live with Josh (and like her namesake in *Peter Pan*, this Wendy is also expected to be a replacement mother), by novel's end Wendy and her fathers have figured out how they can all be a family together. As with so much post-9/11 popular art, Maynard's novel assumes that American fathers are at once deeply flawed, crucial to contemporary child-raising, and capable of experiencing redemption of the deepest sort.

But the 9/11 arts have granted space to many more nuanced visions of manhood and fatherhood than this catalog of redeemed dads might suggest. A number of major works in the developing 9/11 canon have used the occasion of the attacks to prosecute flawed fathers. No one went at the father-worship that rose so quickly from the ashes of Ground Zero with more vitriol than Sherman Alexie, who, in his 2003 short story "Can I Get a Witness?," allows a character to imagine the death of a monstrous father in the World Trade Center as a species of triumphant collateral damage. In this story Alexie presents a nameless character who lives through a suicide-bomb attack in a pan-ethnic restaurant in Seattle. She is unhinged – perhaps she was before the attack – and wanders through the streets, before being "rescued" by a man who takes her back to his apartment.

Here, as I began to suggest in the introduction to this book, Alexie blows away every piety of post-9/11 American rhetoric that he can get in his scope. The rescuer is not noble: he is a software developer who at the time of 9/11 was working on a first-person shooter computer game, one in which the player pretends to be a terrorist, attacking either "a shopping mall, an Ivy League college, or the World Trade Center" (87). His company had not only anticipated controversy, but had figured a dollar amount in sales that would grow from that controversy. This man has been living in the aftermath of a broken marriage – a relationship that failed, at least in part, because of his desire to put being funny above all else.

The woman he "saves" from the Seattle bombing is not a noble or grateful victim. She is an acute critic of American ways of speech and being in response to the attacks. She remembers being at her law firm's office on September 11 and watching on television as the first tower collapsed. Rather than simply repeating the mantra "it looked like a movie," this woman goes much farther: "She remembered how ... she'd closed her eyes and listened to her colleagues' anguished moans and wondered why they sounded so erotic. We're so used to sex on TV that everything on TV becomes sexy" (88). She is disgusted by her husband's reflexive patriotism after the attacks and cannot believe he does not die of "toxic irony" after placing flags in "every window of our house." "What kind of Indians," she wonders, "put twenty-two flags in their windows?" (91).

Alexie's protagonist goes much further as she rants her truths to her rescuer, and they come to seem less and less connected in a specific way to 9/11 and drawn more from years of living as a woman under patriarchy. With a clueless husband and two clueless sons, this woman has been on the verge of a nervous breakdown for quite some time. As an experiment, the injured woman recounts that she started moving dinner back 5 minutes every night, until ultimately her oblivious men were eating at 11 p.m., still screaming at the sports program on the television. "Men have walked on the moon and written *Hamlet* and painted the Sistine Chapel and played the piano like Glenn Gould," and still other men, like her husband and sons, "have the need to hang antlers and flags on their walls." Taking measure of the noxious masculinity that has ruined her life, the wounded woman finds it unsurprising that other men have "crashed jets into buildings" (92). Rather than falling for some nostalgic vision of the home front as a place of romantic love and gentle nurture, Alexie insists here that the domestic is the sphere of first bloodshed, the place where men are taught to express domination and commit violence as their natural right.

"Can I Get a Witness?" climaxes by breaking the ultimate 9/11 taboo, the one that says we must all follow the media lead and understand every person who died on that day as a hero. In essence, Alexie's character puts a hex on the victims of 9/11 and deconsecrates Ground Zero. She asks her companion "Didn't you get sick of all the news about the Trade Center? Didn't you get exhausted by all the stories and TV shows and sad faces and politicians and memorials and books? It was awful and obscene, all of it, it was grief porn" (91). Turning *America: A Tribute to Heroes* and "Portraits of Grief" inside out, Alexie's protagonist finds that the heart of darkness is found not outside, but in the American home.

Starting generically, the injured woman reminds the software designer that the "towers were filled with bankers and stockbrokers and lawyers. How honest do you think they were?" (89). From here the woman devises a new and frightening math of 9/11 that supports her hypothesis that maybe "September eleventh means things nobody has thought of yet."

> Let's say twelve hundred men died that day. How many of those guys were
> cheating on their wives? A few hundred probably. How many of them were
> beating their kids? One hundred more, right? Don't you think one of those
> bastards was raping his kids? Don't you think, somewhere in the towers,
> there was an evil bastard who sneaked into his daughter's bedroom at night
> and raped her in the ass? (89)

"After the Trade Center," she thinks, "it was all about the innocent victims, all the innocent victims, and I kept thinking – I knew one of those guys in the towers was raping his daughter. Raping her. Maybe he was raping his son too. And beating his wife" (92). Compounding the horror, this bomb survivor imagines this character is "a hero at work." But as the initial television reports speak of possible survivors this man's wife and children "are praying to God he died. That he burned to death or jumped out a window or was running down the stairs when the tower fell." Concluding her rant and then falling into a swoon the woman offers up this final flourish: "Don't you think there's some daughter walking around who whispers Osama's name with tenderness and affection?" (93).

This narration by a deeply hurt woman is not meant to be realist and the story that frames it should not be held to the standards of documentary.

It is not "9/11 Truth" that Alexie proposes here, but 9/11 possibility. The church-based title "Can I Get a Witness?" functions as an imaginary call-and-response; the only appropriate response, of course, is "Amen." Alexie's charge to his readers here is quite simple and profound: look through another lens than the one that has been offered by the media and government officials up until this moment. This woman's script is no more "true" than the dominant one that turns all victims into heroes and all of the dead into saints. The shocking moral of this story is that not every father can be redeemed after 9/11. The reality occupied by Alexie's protagonist is every bit as "virtual" as that of the "first person shooter" game developed by her rescuer and it is no less reprehensible. But given that her real goal is to get someone to pay attention to the terrors of her daily life – the utter sense of powerlessness she feels as her Indian husband turns her Indian sons into U.S. Marines – it becomes clear why an attack on the "father myth" of 9/11 becomes so compelling for her.

In "Can I Get a Witness?" Alexie's main character suggests that perhaps some of these brokers and traders did "deserve to die." This woman has just survived a bomb attack and readers are given every indication that she should not be held accountable for all her words. But the demythologizing impulse at the heart of her rant should not be dismissed simply as crazy talk. Alexie is attempting to carve out some cultural space for a discussion of what the World Trade Center was *for*, and how that should shape our understanding of the violence of 9/11.

No single organization lost as many employees on 9/11 as the brokerage house Cantor Fitzgerald. But even this company's complicated role in the world economy (described by Monty Brogan in *25th Hour* during his mirror speech as devoted to "figuring out new ways to rob hard-working people blind") has been crowded out of post-9/11 commentary by the lead story of CEO Howard Lutnick. According to widely circulated press accounts, and a fawning book about Cantor Fitzgerald's rise from the ashes of Ground Zero written by a college friend of Lutnick, the CEO only lived that day because he had taken his son to school for his first day of kindergarten.

From this serendipitous "second chance" beginning, the Cantor Fitzgerald story then gained power as a tale of Howard Lutnick as a caring dad – not only of his son, but of his whole company. Building on the popular post-industrial rhetoric that reconfigures the workplace as a "family" or team, Lutnick was able to rebrand Cantor Fitzgerald as the post-9/11 brokerage house with a heart. Wrapping himself in the cloak of the good father, Lutnick positioned himself above the doubting critique of David Harvey and the angry denunciation of "Can I Get a Witness?" and instead occupied the same sacred space inhabited by the men of *World Trade Center*, *Chicken Little*, and *War of the Worlds*.

Spike Lee's *25th Hour* is the one major work of 9/11 art that offers up a father who is at once deeply flawed and, at least in the extended fantasy sequence I have discussed in the introduction, fantastically able to care for his son. James Brogan is a recovered alcoholic who owns a bar. His bar is a shrine to firefighters, with their pictures and regalia on the walls. James himself used to be a firefighter, but apparently left the department because of his drinking problem. When Monty has dinner with his father the night before the younger man is to enter prison, James at once reminds Monty of how the boy worshipped his dad (and used to sleep with a fireman's helmet in his bed) and was fatally let down by this weak father, who could not raise Monty well when the boy's mother died. When Monty enters the bathroom for his now infamous mirror scene (inspired by Robert DeNiro's "You looking at me?" speech in *Taxi Driver* and by Spike Lee's own *Do the Right Thing*) his father is included in the litany of the cursed: "Fuck my father with his endless grief, standing behind that bar, sipping on club sodas, selling whiskey to firemen, cheering the Bronx Bombers."

The next morning, Monty's dad shows up at his apartment to drive him upstate to prison, even though Monty has asked him not to. The father claims he needs this favor – that the son must do this for the father. But soon it becomes clear that the father has a last gift for Monty, a boy's Western story that James can make real, if only Monty gives the word. As they drive up the West Side Highway, Monty's dad tells Monty to give him the word, and he will go over the George Washington Bridge (the one named for the "father" of the country), head West, and drive for days until he can leave Monty in some small town in the desert. This fantasy sequence goes on and on: James finds his voice as a father as he imagines the 25th hour that Monty will never truly get. "These towns out in the desert," he asks Monty, "you know why they got there? People wanted to get away from somewhere else. The desert's for starting over." James Brogan's "desert" is another name for Huck Finn's "territory" – the place you light out for when civilization closes in on you.

The awful present melts away as James Brogan invents a great future for his son. We see Monty getting a new black-market ID card and renaming himself "James," becoming his own father (just as Zits does). In this vision Monty does become a father. After a few years in the desert he sends for his girlfriend Naturelle and together they make a whole slew of beautiful brown babies. The fantasy sequence ends; there is no 25th hour. Monty is left bloody and slumped as his father drives him off to prison in his SUV with an American flag flying from the antenna. A more reflective piece of art than, say, *World Trade Center* or *Chicken Little, 25th Hour* is willing to indulge the post-9/11 father-fantasy, but then ultimately pull the plug on it.

This collective national dream of the good father has necessitated, not surprisingly, a tacit agreement to render mothers as absent or insignificant. In the popular press there was a relatively brief period of idealizing 9/11 widows (and 9/11 babies) but this honeymoon was short-lived. When four of the widows (three of them married to employees of Cantor Fitzgerald) began agitating together for an inquiry into how the terrorists could have pulled the attacks off with the U.S. government remaining clueless, they were transformed from "grieving widows" into the Jersey Girls. The activism of the Jersey Girls is widely credited with leading to the creation of the 9/11 Commission, chaired by former New Jersey governor Thomas Kean, and they have been alternately lionized (by *Ms.* magazine, for instance, who named them Women of the Year in 2004) and excoriated by right-wing talk radio hosts. In either case, it was their dead spouses and not their living children or their political acumen defining them in the public arena.

Mothers who matter cannot compete with powerful fathers – living or dead – in post-9/11 American arts. The culture industries have produced mostly heroic fathers and just-right surrogate fathers. The most laughable examples – John Updike's Johnny-on-the-spot guidance counselor Jack Levy comes to mind – pretend that it is enough to throw a man, any man, at all the problems facing young Americans in the years after 9/11. Updike's Ahmad Mulloy thirsts for his absent father, hates his mother Teresa because she has sex, and averts disaster only when Jack Levy's steadying hand literally takes the wheel.

Of course few working male artists reach quite the level of misogyny that characterizes Updike's work and some have even managed to resist the cultural decree to idealize fathers and efface mothers. Perhaps the most complex and rewarding rendering of the post-9/11 father myth comes in Jonathan Safran Foer's (2005) *Extremely Loud and Incredibly Close*. Here we follow a 9-year-old boy who is hunting for some final connection to his father, who died in the attacks. Oskar, to begin with, is a boy who upsets all sorts of expected behavioral norms. He is puzzled when the other kids at school laugh at him for referring to his cat as "my pussy." He knows all kinds of things he wishes he didn't know, but doesn't know the one thing (he thinks) he wants to know: exactly how his dad died. A good part of the novel, as I have discussed in chapter 4, is taken up with Oskar's search through New York to find a lock that will be opened by a key he has found among his father's possessions. All he knows at first is that the lock belongs to someone named Black.

The details of the search do not matter so much. What does signify is that Foer constructs a both/and scenario that allows Oskar to continue worshipping his dead father and gain a number of surrogate fathers along the way (old Mr. Black upstairs, his actual long-lost grandfather, various doormen and drivers, and the final Mr. Black) while also allowing the boy a meaningful reconciliation with his mother at the end of the novel. The whole search, it turns out, has been stage managed by Oskar's mother. For much of the book his loneliness and terror are compounded by the sense that his mother has forgotten to notice him. As it turns out, Oskar's mother knows about every step he has taken and kept him safe. What she has given him, above all, is the space in which to create imaginative memorials to his father, through the retelling of stories and jokes, and ultimately through the flipbook-in-reverse that ends the novel and allows the son to resurrect the father. Unlike *World Trade Center*, and so many other superficial post-9/11 projections of facile togetherness, *Extremely Loud and Incredibly Close* announces itself as anti-realist: the heart of the book is a dream of a culture that protects and nurtures all children.

If *Extremely Loud and Incredibly Close* is concerned finally with endowing the post-9/11 mother with the power to represent security and nurture in the family (a steeper challenge in this cultural field than might seem reasonable), Steven Spielberg's *Munich* draws the circle more broadly. In this anguished film, motherhood is murderously tied up with nation-hood. Avner is handpicked by Israeli leader Golda Meir as the movie begins; he is to lead a team of assassins to avenge the deaths of the Israeli athletes at the Munich Olympics in 1972. The movie is a long investigation into the meaning of revenge and the compromises, as Meir's character puts it, that "every civilization finds it necessary to negotiate ... with its own values." This sets the 9/11 framework, and Spielberg makes it clear from the media-saturated opening scenes of the kidnapping, through a final shot of the Twin Towers standing ominously in New York in the early 1970s, that the movie is really about America's post-9/11 military ventures.

At its heart *Munich* is an investigation of what happens when family feeling is displaced into the national arena. From early on, viewers are instructed by Daphna, Avner's wife, to understand his commitment to the Israeli cause as a kind of compensatory behavior that grows from having been left at a kibbutz by his mother after his hero father went missing. As with *Extremely Loud and Incredibly Close,* the search for the absent father in *Munich* (less literal here, but no less consequential) is facilitated by the powerful mother. Avner's mother is trotted onscreen a few times in the movie, essentially to tell him to do whatever he must to kill Palestinians; doing so, she tells him, is a way to honor the Jewish dead of the Holocaust who wanted only that there should be an Israel, and an Avner. "You are what we prayed for," Avner's mother tells him. Filiopietism, in the vision of Avner's mother, is inseparable from murder. When Avner meets with the Palestinians in the Greek safe house and asks Ali "Do you really miss your father's olive trees?" it becomes clear that the Israeli has begun to doubt his own blind allegiance to his father's original mission.

Saying no to the (absent) father is one of *Munich*'s major contributions to American arts after 9/11. Avner also says no to a surrogate father, refusing to call the mercenary patriarch who has been supplying his team with information by the honorific "Papa." The brave innovation of *Munich* is to turn away from the easy father worship of so much 9/11 art and insist instead that Avner's work is to become a real father to his own child. Off Israel's payroll, Avner settles in Brooklyn, with the World Trade Center in view just across the water as a reminder that, as Avner himself says, "There is no peace at the end of this."

* * *

So much 9/11 father-art has operated on the same simple, affective level as that wrought by Stanley Stearns' famous photograph of John-John Kennedy saluting his father's casket that it has become thrilling sport to find exceptions that help trace the outlines of the larger story. The exceptions include, of course, significant mothers and surrogate mothers, and mostly (and not suprisingly) these characters have been created by women. These 9/11 mothers include the narrator of punk band Sleater-Kinney's 2002 song "Faraway" who nervously nurses her baby while contemplating the horrible reality that as she does this President Bush is hiding and rescue workers are rushing into the towers to their deaths, as well as Lynne Sharon Schwartz's Renata (from *The Writing on the Wall*: 2005) who tries to become a surrogate mother to a homeless teen she finds on the streets of New York after the attacks and pretends is the niece she lost years ago. At the same time that Renata is saving – or kid-napping – this young woman, she is also teaching herself Arabic. When her boyfriend Jack asks her to say something in Arabic, so that he can hear how it sounds, Renata voices a significant speech act. What she says in Arabic is about her private life: "I lost my niece when she was seven … and now I've found her. So many dead and one brought back to life" (231). When Jack asks what she has said, Renata translates this personal message into the degraded public language of male power that has so oppressed her in the novel, saying "We will fight the evil ones to the death to preserve our sacred way of life."

Tracking these exemplary "mothers" rounds out our understanding of the popular rhetorics of post-9/11 popular arts and may feel like a spiritual necessity to all who have been served a glut of heroic fathers. But as American literary, film, and musical artists have wrestled with the fallout from 9/11 it has been relatively rare for them to give serious attention to mothers. Nor has American popular culture made much space in the post-9/11 heroic pantheon for non-white fathers, and certainly not for the "gentle Arab daddies" that Naomi Shihab Nye (2001) has written of, who "laugh around the table, who have a hard time with headlines, who stand outside in the evenings with their hands in their pockets staring toward the far horizon" (288).

Of course, it is not fathers per se who even constitute the main focus of this cultural discourse: it is just men. Using the social construct of fatherhood is a shorthand way of indicating the proper functioning of manhood. There are, of course, other ways to achieve this aim, as when *Rescue Me* broadcast an episode titled "Inches" in September of 2004. "Inches" tracks a number of stories, but the episode's central plot has to do with a contest at the station house to determine which firefighter has the biggest penis. After much arguing about proper measuring tech-nique, the contest is won by Billy, who has recently died while fighting a fire. Soon after his death, one of his sex partners informs the other firefighters of Billy's winning measurements. The first real line of dialogue in *Rescue Me*'s pilot episode featured Tommy Gavin screaming at a bunch of new recruits "Do you know how big my balls are?" Now, with only the barest degree of sublimation, *Rescue Me* tells its viewers that nobody has a bigger dick than a dead firefighter. At once a critique and an expression of post-9/11 American masculinism, *Rescue Me* has helped establish the reconstruction of American manhood as a major task for agents of popular art.

Country singer Toby Keith participated as fully as anyone in the attempt to reconstruct American manhood after 9/11. His "Courtesy of the Red, White, and Blue" (2002) was at once a celebration of his father's own bravery (he lost an eye during training in the U.S. military) and a promise to put a "boot in the ass" of America's unnamed enemy. Even more pernicious was a follow-up duet with Willie Nelson, "Beer for My Horses," which mourned the loss of a sort of rough-and-tumble masculinity and promoted lynching as the answer to all of America's woes.

All this man-art could not obliterate the reality that the brute power of American manhood was not enough to neutralize the anxieties of the post-9/11 world. From Bruce Springsteen's "Nothing Man," a rescue worker who now feels his only remaining courage will be to commit suicide, to the devastated parents of Michael Moore's *Farenheit 9/11* who have lost their son to war (while members of Congress refuse to imagine their own children participating in the fight), 9/11 and its fallout resonate more and more as a challenge to more traditional notions of "proper" gender behavior. The most tragic imaginable punctuation to the 9/11 story of heroic fatherhood came in 2004 in the real world, when Carlos Arredondo set himself on fire and burned over half of his body after learning that his first-born son had died in Iraq.

CH/7
Shout-Outs

In June of 2005, a little-known Seattle area band called SEAN released their first record, titled *Singers Ruin Perfectly Good Bands*. The group are purely instrumental, featuring only Mike Peterson on drums and Luke LaPlante who, according to their MySpace page, plays "piano run through a noise gate into guitar amplification." SEAN are generally classified as grindcore or, as the band put it, "Jerry Lee Lewis inspired grindcore without the incest." The second song on *Singers Ruin Perfectly Good Bands* seemed like it might be a similarly insular statement of purpose developed by this keyboard-driven band somewhere a little further along in the night: "Everyone and bin Laden Plays Guitar." At first glance this song title does seem simply an argument in support of the piano-as-guitar that defines the band's sound. But by 2005 SEAN's transformation of the idiom "everyone and his brother" into "everyone and bin Laden" seemed like it was making a broader argument about the status of 9/11 citation in America's popular culture.

In the familiar idiom "his brother" is at once appositive and redundant. Once you say "everyone" you have already included "his brother" but the work of the idiom is to make clear just how firmly settled this collective is. In essence, "his brother" has no meaning of its own; it simply works as emphasis – a way to underscore, or italicize "everyone." Using "bin Laden" in place of "his brother" is a fascinating rhetorical move. Since "bin Laden" has come to function clearly as a metonym for "9/11" and all of its aftershocks, SEAN's song title ultimately works to suggest how "9/11" can be – and has been – emptied of definite content since 2001. The song title "Everyone and bin Laden Plays Guitar" reminds us that "9/11" has been transformed in only a few years since the attacks from a key sacred term in a new American language into something much more diffuse and unstable. The *Doonesbury* strip I wrote of in the introduction to this book posited "9/11" as a totalizing response to all cultural questions. But by 2005, when SEAN released their song, "9/11" had lost this full power.

Now, references to September 11 were often as not working on the level of the "shout-out" – an acknowledgment of something important that helps establish context and gravity, but that does not necessarily work as a free-standing artistic, political, or spiritual expression. "9/11" does remain a thing-in-itself on the contemporary American cultural scene (as the 9/11 truth movement and the ongoing dissension surrounding the Ground Zero rebuilding project make plain) but it is coming more and more to work like a pair of 3-D glasses at the movies. Attaching "9/11" to any cultural product is a quick way to add dimension to what might otherwise appear flat or lifeless. To use a slightly different "glasses" analogy: sometimes celebrities arrange to have their picture taken while wearing glasses, although their vision needs no correction. They wear them because they think doing so will make them look more serious and formidable and they usually do it just as they are promoting themselves in roles that are more weighty than their usual fare.

So too with the American popular and literary arts, which have taken to using "9/11" as a vehicle rather than a destination. This was certainly the animating principle of the presidential campaign (briefly, in 2007) of former New York City mayor Rudolph Giuliani, who hoped to ride 9/11 to the White House. Giuliani was a crucial player in the original consecration of Ground Zero. He spoke in late December of 2001 at the opening of the first viewing platform at Ground Zero and referred to the site as "hallowed ground, sacred ground" ("Public Viewing Platform Opens," 2001). In doing so he was participating in what cultural geographer Kenneth Foote (2003) has termed the "sanctification" of a landscape after a major trauma (7). But by the fall of 2007, Giuliani was to be widely mocked for running a presidential campaign that seemed to many to depend on promiscuous invocations of September 11. When Pakistani leader Benazir Bhutto was assassinated in late December of 2007, Giuliani responded by suggesting that this tragedy was for him a "particularly personal experience ... because I lived through Sept. 11, 2001" (Cooper, 2007). Senator Joe Biden, then also running for president, most efficiently satirized Giuliani's rhetorical practices by suggesting that in Giuliani's campaign, there are "only three things he mentions in a sentence: a noun, a verb and '9/11'" ("Biden," 2007).

In surveying the contemporary cultural landscape of America's 9/11 arts it has become necessary to sort out those works that are directly involved in understanding and analyzing the attacks and their cultural consequences from those that use September 11 as a shout-out. In 2003 Mark Hamm surveyed the mp3.com website and found 520 songs with 9/11 in their title, plus another 83 that had September 11 or something similar in the title (Hamm, 2003). All told, he counted some 1,500 songs about the attacks. Once the 9/11 popular arts achieved this density, it became possible to see that not all 9/11 mentions were operating with the same intention or effect. Calling a 9/11 reference in art a "shout-out" is hardly an insult; it is, rather, an attempt to index a shift from a relatively sacralized and bounded use of the attacks in American cultural expression to a more complex and unpredictable set of artistic practices.

Casting a wide net around American culture, it is easy to drag in all sorts of shout-outs to 9/11, ranging from respectful asides to the most grotesque marketing schemes. Nappy Roots, a Southern rap group, used the fall of the towers as part of a narrative of personal growth on their 2002 song "Po' Folks": "somethin' happen to me on last Tuesday night/ It's plain as day, man they ... with this World Trade/Naw, brave ain't the word I'm looking for." Less pious was the 2003 song "Bin Laden," by Three 6 Mafia, where an especially potent strain of marijuana (a combination of three other kinds, actually) is celebrated as a necessary element of life, "straight from the Taliban." Other hip hop efforts to incorporate the 9/11 attacks were undeniably offensive. New York rapper Cam'ron worked hard, for instance, to get attention for an effort he was making to work with a group called The Diplomats, whose 2003 release (*Diplomatic Immunity)* made claims for itself as somehow representing "9/11 music." More direct still was the New York radio station that promoted a record release event on September 11, 2007 that pit Kanye West against 50 Cent as a battle of the Twin Towers of Hip Hop; flyers promised that on this day the towers would be rebuilt.

Rap musicians were not the only ones trying to capitalize on shout-outs to 9/11. On their 2002 release 3, the metal band Soulfly released a track entitled "9-11-01" which was simply one minute of silence. In 2003, we could find offerings ranging from alternative rockers Yellowcard, with their inspirational song "Believe" (which ends with lines quoted from the Gettysburg Address), to alt-country mainstays the Bottle Rockets, who offered up the is-it-satire-or-is-it-for-real "Baggage Claim," which bemoans the fact that lovers can no longer have their reunions at airport gates. (See Appendix 2 for a list of 9/11 related songs.)

A case can be made that a number of the most popular television shows of the past decade have taken advantage of explicit references to 9/11 or at least clear allusion. *24*, obviously, with its heart-pounding landscape of terror, and *Lost*, with a basic set-up that includes a post-airplane crash society on an island, both draw energy from the frisson of the 9/11 attacks and their aftermath. Since so much television (from situation comedies to "reality" shows) draws its power from how the serial format builds on an unchanging first principle, the 9/11 shout-out has functioned perhaps most significantly in the rudimentary structure of various shows, rather than as sustained citation.

One indication of how pervasive 9/11 shout-outs have become is the number of satires *of* 9/11 shout-outs that have been circulated in the culture. As early as 2002, as I discussed in chapter 4, Lev Grossman was already exploring the possibility that people in Hollywood were "pitching 9/11": in this story a variety of 9/11 ideas are floated, including one for a documentary on the ironies of cumin being harvested in Afghanistan and then being used to spice food served that fateful morning at Windows on the World. During season five of the animated show *Family Guy*, when Lois runs for mayor, she learns to say "9/11" whenever possible to gain her audience's attention and support. In early 2008, when *The Boston Globe* reviewed the monster movie *Cloverfield*, the paper included its usual sidebar with the movie's basic stats, including running time, director, and why it received its PG-13 rating: "violence, terror, disturbing images; sublimated 9/11 fears." No single moment of 9/11 "shout-out" critique was more efficient or devastating than a brief bit of dialogue in the 2007 suspense film *Gone Baby Gone*. A South Boston mother has just been reunited with her little daughter, who had been kidnapped months earlier. The police bring Amanda back to Helene McCready, who hugs her child as the news microphones are shoved in her face: "Thank you to all the policemen and firemen," she triumphantly says. "I feel like 9/11 right now."

* * *

The "shout-out" is, of course, derived from hip hop practices of naming friends, family, and God in song performance, and in liner notes and other promotional materials, as well as in radio dedications. This is not to say that rap musicians invented the cultural practice of naming friends in an attempt to "borrow" some of their cultural power, market share, and so on. In contemporary American culture the practice continues in a variety of forms, from the much parodied Academy Award winner's speech to the academic's acknowledgment page.

But it is in hip hop culture that the shout-out has been most fully formalized as part of the package and as part of the art. Hip hop liner notes have, since the 1980s, featured such extensive lists of shout-outs that in order to fit them all in, font sizes have at times rivaled the Oxford English Dictionary. In the liner notes and in the music itself the shout-out usually functions "first and foremost," as Queen Latifah puts it on *All Hail the Queen*, as a devotional – a reminder to the audience that none of this great music would exist without the guiding hand of God. On his ferocious 1990 song "Mama Said Knock You Out," LL Cool J reveals the pro forma nature of the God shout-out as he follows up verse after verse of hyperbolic threat and violence with "I gotta thank God, 'cos he gave me the strength to rock hard."

Shout-outs function as expressions of humility and gratitude, of course, but they also work to delineate context. Every time a rapper mentions another rapper approvingly – or disapprovingly, for that matter – on record there is significant boundary work being done. For one performer to cite another in a print list of posse members or with a vocal mention is a way to establish frameworks of reception for the audience. In the late 1980s and early 1990s, for instance, the Native Tongues movement in hip hop (which included, among others, A Tribe Called Quest, the Jungle Brothers, De La Soul, and Queen Latifah) "announced" itself through interviews, guest spots on each others' records, and also through numerous cross-referenced shout-outs.

The shout-out has become positively inescapable in the age of Web 2.0. With user-generated tagging, bloggers promoting other bloggers, and long lists of Facebook "friends," it has become a cultural commonplace to establish one's identity by naming others. Running parallel to all of these individual and personal shout-outs has been the increasing use of 9/11 as a shout-out, a key term whose precise definition is much less significant than its function as an intensifier. In the cultural life of the United States since 2001, "9/11" has become important as a constituent of American grammar, put into action not only (or even mostly) for what it *means* but also for what it *does*. While numerous cultural actors have participated in using 9/11 as a shortcut to artistic gravity, it is worth noting too how 9/11 "shout-outs" have worked to deny the events of

September 11 the aura of exceptionalism – the "day of infamy" tag Clint Eastwood put on the attacks at the *America: A Tribute to Heroes* telethon – that helped to organize the nation for war.

* * *

Using "9/11" (or one of its many representatives – e.g. "World Trade," "the Towers," "bin Laden," and so on) as a shout-out in hip hop has functioned both as a statement of serious purpose but also as a way to domesticate the attacks and their awful singularity: in short, the hip hop 9/11 shout-out is a way to put 9/11 into hip hop, rather than vice versa. When Missy Elliott included the "World Trade families" in a litany that opens up her 2002 album *Under Construction*, it became clear that even this early on, an attempt was being made to incorporate 9/11 into an ongoing history of hip hop life and, in effect, deny the tragedy its aura of complete (and white) distinctiveness:

> Yeah, what's the deal, y'all? This Missy Elliott givin' y'all magazine writers, radio cats, listeners, or plain old haters a small piece of my album which is titled *Under Construction*. *Under Construction* simply states that I'm a work in progress, I'm working on myself, you know. Uh, ever since Aaliyah passed I view life in a, uh, more valuable way looking at hate and anger an' gossip or just plain ol bullshit became ignorant to me when you realize in a blink of a eye you walking down a church aisle an' that was meant for weddings and happiness but realizin' those same church aisles are used to view a loved one for the last time. from the World Trade families to the Left Eye family, Big Pun family, you know, Biggie family 'Pac family, to the hip hop family we all under construction trying to rebuild, you know, ourselves ...

What Missy Elliott offers up here is an alternate history of modern times, that stretches not, as so many would have it, from 9/11 onward, but from 1996 to 2002. *Under Construction*'s history begins with Aaliyah, who died in a plane crash a few weeks before the September 11 attacks. Aaliyah's music was Missy Elliot's entry to the big time; appearing as writer, producer, and guest vocalist on Aaliyah's record *One in a Million* (1996) helped Elliott establish herself as a major player in contemporary rhythm and blues and hip hop.

Elliott's wonderfully narcissistic hip hop history of the world puts Aaliyah's death first and the World Trade Center second. In this litany, the shout-out to 9/11 makes it clear that the World Trade Center deaths are just as significant – no more, no less – than the deaths of Tupac Shakur, Biggie Smalls, Lisa "Left Eye" Lopes (of TLC), and Big Pun.

Claiming "rebuilding" as a life activity for all within range of her voice, Missy Elliott's shout-out to 9/11 represents a decentering of the day, a way to deny the event its generally unquestioned status as epoch-defining. At the same time, Elliott's 9/11 mention allows her to grab a bit of its cultural gravity, a way to juice her title trope without being subsumed by its narrative requirements (of grief, piety, and so on).

My chapter heading and introductory comments to this section are obviously misleading. While some 9/11 references in popular and literary culture are easy to read as crass exploitation, the shout-out is such serious business in hip hop music, so central to its constructed personae and public stances, that we need to take special care in parsing the music's 9/11 mentions. Some of the most complex 9/11 allusions in hip hop have come from Eminem, the white rapper who has made his own unruliness a main text of his art. On his May 2002 release *The Eminem Show,* and in one music video accompanying it, Eminem went even further than Missy Elliott in rejecting the compulsory regulations of 9/11 art then under construction. After a brief opening skit that literally features Eminem clearing his throat, the first song on the record, "White America," starts with the MC shouting "America" followed by the sounds of an airplane rushing by. When a few songs later (in "Business") Eminem declares that "hip hop is in a state of 911" it is impossible not to hear the double meaning of the numbers. Eminem's 9/11 shout-outs on the record are messy and sometimes contradictory: in separate verses of one song, "My Dad's Gone Crazy," he builds images around both a hijacker about to crash a plane into a (the?) tower *and* a little girl who is on a plane about to crash into the World Trade Center.

If Eminem's 9/11 shout-outs seem to act, as one critic has commented, as "cynically calculated bids for controversy" (Radosh, 2002) they also operate as a repudiation of the sensationalism, short attention-span, and politically consequential myth-making of America's media culture. For instance, in "Business," Eminem introduces a Batman-and-Robin theme that includes a rhyme of Robin and "Laden" (as in bin Laden). It seems, well, stupid, as does his tasteless boast that he has a private plane that can "blow college room doors off the hinges." Two verses after this, Eminem muses, as he so often does in rhyme, about how easy it is for him to gain attention (and market share) through cheap controversy: "How can this shit be so easy/How can one Chandra be so Levy?" The seemingly nonsensical non-rhyme that finishes this couplet is where Eminem's 9/11 shout-outs come into some focus. Chandra Levy was the Washington intern whose disappearance dominated national news in the spring of 2001 well up through that summer. The story of her relationship with Gary Condit, a California congressman, and his possible role in her vanishing, was only displaced by the September 11 attacks. With this apparently cheap shout-out to the Chandra Levy case, what Eminem accomplishes, parallel to Missy Elliott's stitching of 9/11 into hip hop history, is a reminder of how 9/11 fits into the recent history of tabloid journalism. Again, the shout-out functions to resituate 9/11 while also acknowledging its huge cultural power.

The same move is made in the video for "Without Me," in which Eminem actually dresses as Robin in order to deliver an unedited version of his CD to a young fan. The song reiterates many of the main themes of "Business": ultimately it is about Eminem's ability to stir up controversy. In this light, when he appears in the video as a dancing Osama bin Laden, it is as if Eminem is gloating about how much easier his job is going to be in post-9/11 America.

The 9/11 shout-outs and the boasts implicit in them would be much harder to abide if Eminem didn't undercut himself at so many turns. *The Eminem Show* begins with the MC coming "onstage" to applause, tapping the microphone, and clearing his throat; it finishes with him coming back onstage for "Curtains Close" which finds an elderly Eminem walking onstage, tapping the microphone again (with feedback noise) and trying to figure out "where'd everybody go?" The record ends with the grizzled-sounding rapper pathetically imitating the younger self – the Real Slim Shady: "Guess who's back, back again" before trailing off with "rub my back, rub my back."

The 9/11 shout-outs on the *The Eminem Show* demonstrate how thorny our job will be as we try to sort out the base exploitations of 9/11 – what Sherman Alexie (2003a) calls "grief porn" – from sincere exploration and genuine critique of the "9/11 industry." So much about Eminem – his misogyny and homophobia above all – make it politically necessary to bracket *every* word out of his mouth as part of a larger cultural backlash against women and sexual minorities. While acknowledging that reality, it is also interesting to see how the rapper attempts to repudiate some of the masculinist privileges expressed in so much 9/11 art, particularly those having to do with heroic fatherhood. "My Dad's Gone Crazy," which opens with his daughter Halie Mathers interrupting Eminem while he snorts a line of cocaine, is just the climax of an extended meditation by the rapper on his failures as a father.

Clever and complex 9/11 shout-outs do not absolve the rapper (or his listeners) of taking responsibility for the damage he inflicts elsewhere, but they do act as a compelling reminder of how difficult it will be to construct moral or aesthetic taxonomies of 9/11 art in the short run. While diverse commentators have already outlined mini-manifestos for 9/11 art, one thing that Eminem's work makes clear is that these artistic guidelines are going to need to be in the form of wikis and not single-authored works. Shout-outs, with their ephemeral yet deeply allusive potential, demand that we approach the fullness of 9/11 art with no expectation that we will come upon traditional markers of monumental art. The mysteries of subjectivity and the complexities of reception embedded in shout-outs undercut the illusion of superficiality that might otherwise doom them to a quick trip to the dustbin of history.

* * *

The instability of the 9/11 shout-out, the difficulty of figuring out when 9/11 is being invoked in a meaningful and sustained way, is the theme of "Gelato is Gelato," a devastating short story by Jennifer Belle, published in 2002. In this story, the narrator recounts going to her first Weight Watchers meeting after September 11: "One by one the women in the group raised their hands and said how much weight they'd gained since September 11" (37). The leader of the group, Estelle, shocks the group by enumerating a list of "forbidden" foods and then admitting that in the past week "I ate them all" (38). Invoking the Holocaust in an attempt to frame the enormity of the recent attacks, the maternal Estelle tells the assembled dieters that she has "enough kinds of ice cream so every one of you could take your pick" (38).

This soon after the attacks the fearless leader of this group is intent on invoking the tragedy as augury of a total cultural paradigm shift. "Eat!" she tells her charges. "Do whatever it takes to make you feel better" (39). A brownie is a brownie. Gelato is gelato. The story's narrator embraces the new realities outlined by Estelle. She stays in "bed the rest of the week eating and watching television." She looks forward to returning to Weight Watchers, to weigh in and proudly not care about her added pounds. The return to Weight Watchers is devastating: "the old Estelle was back. The anarchy had ended. But we wouldn't ever be the same. Estelle had said 'Eat'! and for a moment I had known what it felt like to be completely free, to be thin, to fly. It was like Hitler opening the camp gates. It was like my shrink telling me to just go ahead and kill my parents" (39).

Estelle, in a week, has converted 9/11 from a landscape-altering and generation-defining event into a simple validation of all that had been in place previously. " 'Think of all the people who died in the towers who were on Weight Watchers, working hard to follow the plan, keeping track of their points,' Estelle said ... 'They would have wanted us to stay on the program,' one woman said, wiping tears from her eyes. 'Do it for them,' Estelle said" (39). Jennifer Belle's work here is to demonstrate how quickly 9/11 could be transformed from the Holocaust into an advertisement for Weight Watchers. This is fiction, of course, and satire at that. But in her poignant story Belle is indexing a cultural phenomenon just taking shape around her – not simply the branding and selling of 9/11 but its incorporation into the surrounding culture as a relatively non-specific marker of grief and of American resolve.

This is just how a number of television advertisements have shouted out to 9/11. The first major 9/11 shout-out ad was made by Budweiser and aired once, during the Super Bowl of 2002. Budweiser has loudly trumpeted its good taste in showing the ad only one time, as if that qualifies the beer company for some kind of community service award. In the televised ad, a team of Budweiser's trademark Clydesdale horses are shown preparing for work. They lead an empty wagon across the snow-covered heartland of America – presumably these are amber waves of grain that will reappear when the snow melts. The only human figure we see in a frontal shot is a Norman Rockwell-inspired barber, peering out through the glass of his shop at the noble horses. The horses leave the barber's small town and the camera soon pans up, revealing the Brooklyn Bridge from an angle that projects its architecture as two towers. The Budweiser horses make it into lower Manhattan and stop: they are in place to see the Statue of Liberty in the harbor and the lead horse, in fine trick-pony fashion, bends its forelegs and "bows." The screen goes black and the Budweiser logo appears. It would take a heart of stone, as Oscar Wilde's infamous quip put it, not to laugh.

This 9/11 shout-out, as vulgar as it is, draws on a deep tradition of venerating the Brooklyn Bridge. While the advertisement seems to be, at first glance, a knee-jerk pastoral reaction to the assault on the towers, those most visible symbols of late twentieth-century global capitalism, the focus on the Brooklyn Bridge actually supplies a more complex message. The bridge, when built, was the tallest structure in New York City and it acted, as Alan Trachtenberg (1979) has argued, as a symbol of America's change "from a predominantly rural to an overwhelmingly urban and industrial society" (ix). With this surprising focus on work horses at the Brooklyn Bridge, the Budweiser commercial shouts out to 9/11 with a patriotic call to get the nation back to work: we are all under construction.

One thing that the 9/11 shout-outs demonstrate inarguably is that William Gibson's framing of the attacks as an "experience outside of culture" (in his 2003 novel *Pattern Recognition*) was more wishful thinking than accurate description. In this book Gibson follows a "cool hunter," Cayce Pollard. who is hired by corporations to work as a kind of marketing empath. Pollard has an uncanny ability to "read" brand identities (through corporate logos and so on) and determine which will be successful. But Pollard is stymied by the images she saw on television on 9/11; she thinks that the visuals she was subjected to on that day are somehow remaining apart from the globalized image-production machine that employs her. One result for Pollard is that she becomes obsessed with some spectral film imagery (and the fan community growing up around it) that has been posted on the internet since the attacks. These short films seem "outside of culture" (137) and speak to Pollard's deep need to believe that the 9/11 attacks fundamentally challenged the commercialization of all human experience and emotion.

But from the 9/11 shout-outs in Robert De Niro's American Express advertisement to the Budweiser Clydesdale spot, there is no doubt that American corporations were more than willing to incorporate the tragedy as a potential commodity into extant marketing structures. Seth Stevenson (2006) has argued that one of the most egregious of such usages came in the 2006 Chevy Silverado ad scored by John Mellencamp's song "Our Country" – which debuted in the advertisement months before appearing on a CD release of his own. Here is Stevenson:

> Singer John Mellencamp leans on the fender of a Chevy pickup, strumming an acoustic guitar. He sings, among other things, "This is our country." Meanwhile, a montage of American moments flies by: Rosa Parks on a bus. Martin Luther King preaching to a crowd. Soldiers in Vietnam. Richard Nixon waving from his helicopter. And then modern moments: New Orleans buried by Katrina floodwaters. The two towers of light commemorating 9/11. As a big, shiny pickup rolls through an open field of wheat and then slows to a carefully posed stop, the off-screen announcer says, "This is our country. This is our truck. The all-new Chevy Silverado."

The advertisement actually has two 9/11 shout-outs – the towers of light and a later shot of some tired-looked FDNY firefighters sitting on the front bumper of their truck.

Clearly Chevrolet thought it was using this 9/11 imagery as a simple evocation of American vitality. But the montage is just not that decisive and ends up having a much more extreme message: with shots of hula hoops and sock hops giving way to images of Muhammad Ali knocking out an opponent, American soldiers in Vietnam, Nixon entering the airplane after resigning, and Hurricane Katrina visiting devastation upon New Orleans, the 9/11 shout-outs end up feeling much more like part of a warning than a celebration. Bad things happens all the time, the Silverado ad reminds us. You better have a good truck. This Silverado advertisement is an unstable text, one that telegraphs its purpose but is not able to sustain an uncomplicated message. That said, its intentions are clear, and its usages of 9/11 (and Rosa Parks and Katrina, and so on) have pushed a number of guerrilla filmmakers to post their own "edits" of the ad. One montage puts a Chevy at the scene of various crimes, from Kent State, to the assassination of Martin Luther King, Jr., to the abuses at Abu Ghraib prison. Another remix runs with the tag "This is our country" and offers a set of images with new tags, from "This is our delusion," over a picture of John Wayne, to "This is our secret," over a picture of Glenn Hughes, the gay leatherman character in the Village People.

Using 9/11 as a shout-out is a tricky business. When Marsh & McLennan ran their subway ad "There's Another Side of Risk" in 2007 they were quickly taken to task by the *New York Post*, which quoted family members of 9/11 victims who believed that the ad consciously evoked the Twin Towers by placing beams of light in the eyes of each model (Mangan, 2007; see the advertisement at http://www.nypost.com/seven/06112007/news/regionalnews/9_11_kin_rip_evil_eye_ads_regionalnews_dan_mangan.htm). MMC had lost nearly 300 people in the 9/11 attacks and attempted to take the high ground in the controversy: "The mere suggestion that MMC would include, suggest or disregard 9/11 imagery in its ad campaign is not only wildly wrong, but cruel and despicable" ("Marsh & McLennan Blasts," 2007). Perhaps having its cake and eating it too, the risk and insurance company took refuge in the safety of plausible deniability. If this was in fact the plan, Marsh & McLennan may have been building on the bizarre success of the *Aqua Teen Hunger Force* guerilla marketing ploy of January 2007, when a set of Lite-Brite-like electronic gadgets placed around the Boston area were taken for explosive devices, causing something of a panic. This viral marketing 9/11 shout-out should be understood as "blowback" from the more traditional efforts to market 9/11, rather than as the irresponsible and context-free prank it was taken to be. Actual commercials in the mainstream media that feature 9/11 shout-outs will continue to come under critical scrutiny – since their job is, obviously, to move product, and there is no consensus yet as to how 9/11 branding can or should be implemented.

But in some ways the most exploitative usages of 9/11 appear in those artifacts that make claims to artistic seriousness while delivering very little. In a discussion of the built-in failure of much September 11 art (as opposed to what he calls the more satisfying art of September 12), Mark Lawson (2002) has written that "we know in advance what every moment will be." In *The Guys*, a play about delivering eulogies for fallen members of the FDNY, the author "merely dramatizes an unarguable platitude: firefighters were brave on 9/11." But *The Guys*, whatever else it accomplishes, has good intentions. I am not sure that is the case with such works as Updike's *Terrorist* or the Adam Sandler film vehicle, *Reign Over Me*. In these texts, the invocation of 9/11 is a shortcut and a dodge, a way to insist on the gravity of the mission without ever revealing what that mission is. After an opening scene of Charlie Fineman (Sandler) riding his lonely scooter through Manhattan, *Reign Over Me* next offers up the office of a dentist (Don Cheadle's Alan Johnson) where the plastic divider separating the receptionist's station from the waiting room looks like a close-up of the World Trade Center – particularly as it appeared as a backdrop in the famous photograph of the "falling man."

The 9/11 references in *Reign Over Me* function as the coarsest sort of shout-out, the sort where the naming functions only as a desperate attempt to accrue cultural capital that the product itself cannot otherwise earn. *Reign Over Me* is just a buddy movie, and its only real twist is that the slightly off-center white person will act as the redemptive force for the uptight Black person rather than the other way around, as is more usual. Fineman is a mess, of course, spending his days riding the scooter and playing *Shadow of the Colossus*, a video game in which giants keep tumbling to the ground. But Johnson is in equally bad shape, buttoned up so tightly that he seems like he might burst, unhappy with the routines of job and home. The WTC divider in his office is a bit of visual foreshadowing to prepare us for the film's moral: many men are sad. Some are dissatisfied with jobs and relationships; others have lost their children and life partners in a world-historical inferno. Same difference. *Reign Over Me* does not want to say anything about 9/11 but was trotted out only in an effort to rebrand Adam Sandler. It is a desperate strategy at work here, an attempt to turn Sandler into a portrait of grief. The major flaw in *Reign Over Me*'s approach is the faith it puts in generalized grief, the notion that everyone in the audience will activate the same exact 9/11 emotions as those Sandler mopingly telegraphs on the screen. Jess Walter attacks the assumption of generalized grief in his 2006 novel *The Zero,* in which a character complains "I suppose you'd rather I behave like everyone else and grieve generally. Well I'm sorry. I'm not built that way. General grief is a lie ... a fleeting emotion, like lust. It's a trend, just some weak shared moment in the culture, like the final episode of some TV show everybody watches" (34). Celia Streng has written similarly, in a passage that serves as an epigraph to Lynne Sharon Schwartz's (2005) *The Writing on the Wall,* that the

> public reports about the shock and grief suffered after the attacks on September 11, 2001, implied that those feelings were uniform and generic in everyone. And probably extremes of shock and grief, like extremes of hunger and desire, do feel the same in everyone. Yet the people who endured the transforming effects of that day were not blank slates ready to be imprinted with the same images. They brought to that moment all the events of their lives until then, and the new events, by their very force, called forth earlier shocks and reconfigured them in a new context. So the collapse of the buildings made a different sound for everyone who heard it, and for each the noise echoed in a different key. (n.p.)

9/11 shout-outs do not usually intend to open interesting questions or pose difficult challenges. They are ready-mades, easily digestible.

The shout-outs to 9/11 at once add to the overall currency of the tragedy, but sacrifice its deeper dimensions in the process – they have become a kind of obsessive handwashing that the culture is indulging in. The ritual is not carried out with a definite purpose, but rather operates on the level of magical thinking, meant to inoculate creator and audience. But inoculate against what? As an evolving expressive practice, the shout-out seems aimed at protecting its "users" from the fear of forgetting. The job of the shout-out, I think, is to sustain the sense of collectivity that so many found to be a positive outgrowth of the attacks and to intensify all manner of human experiences. No one has captured this aspect of the crisis more poignantly than Judy Budnitz, in her 2005 short story "Preparedness." In this story, as I have explained in the introduction, Budnitz describes a president who plans a false crisis in an attempt to exert social control over the populace. When he sounds a national emergency alarm "people's first instincts were to touch each other: women embraced, strangers clasped hands, men slapped each other on the back and said, 'Guess this is it, big guy'." The president continues to "play 9/11" in an attempt to terrify the people and get them to feel that they need his protection. But it doesn't work and the people continue to respond, as the cliché puts it, by affirming life: "in the parks, on benches, on the grass, on bridges, floating on the ponds in stolen paddleboats, in phone booths, on sofas, on the hoods of cars, up against trees and walls, people were making love" (253). In its (just barely) allegorical form, "Preparedness" argues that we want somebody to "cry 9/11" because of how pleasurably it brings us together.

Shouting out 9/11 does not simply bring Americans together, it allows them (as "Preparedness" suggests) to access dimensions of emotional and physical satisfaction that they might not otherwise be able to reach. John Cameron Mitchell makes just this claim in his 2006 film *Shortbus*. When queer cabaret performer Justin Bond is asked in the movie why so many young people keep flocking to New York, despite the prohibitive expense of the city, Bond answers simply "9/11." "It's the only real thing," he adds "that's ever happened to them." Trying to recapture (i.e. "fake") the intensity of that "real thing" is what so many 9/11 shout-outs aim to do. The only thing more terrifying than remembering the attacks is acknowledging the possibility that we might forget them. Lynne Sharon Schwartz gets at this worry, that 9/11 might end up meaning less than it originally seemed to, toward the end of her devastating novel *The Writing on the Wall*. Renata is watching a live television broadcast from Ground Zero when the announcer says, "I don't know what we'll see when the smoke clears ... but I fear it may be nothing" (270). If the manifest meaning here is obvious (i.e. the buildings are gone), Schwartz also seems intent on reminding her readers that they will not always be able to draw emotional substance from the drama of that day. The reflex of shouting out 9/11 may be, then, a way to stave off that inevitability.

William Langewiesche (2002) has written of the construction of the World Trade Center and the "prodigious energy originally required to raise so much weight." When the towers were hit, and then collapsed, "they released that energy back into the city" (4). Langewiesche is writing of actual kinetic energy – steel beams flying through the air like spears, and fires that could not be put out. As these physical forces were unleashed on the city, so too were cultural forces. Art critic Arthur Danto (2002) has written that the attack turned New York into a "mourning site" and that in response all New Yorkers should become "memorial artists." Some responded by turning their own bodies into memorials, as with the dozens

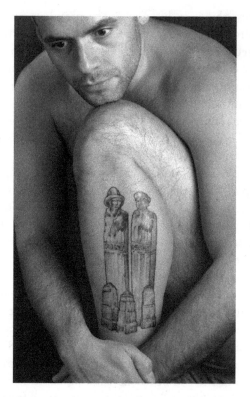

Figure 7 Vinnie Amessé's photograph of Francis Coppola's "Twin Towers." Source: © Amessé Photography

of New Yorkers featured in Vinnie Amessé's photographs of 9/11 tattoos that ran at the Staten Island Historical Society. None was more poignant, perhaps, than the photograph of Francis Coppola, a New York City policeman who lost his life partner, a fireman, on September 11. His tattoo shows two towers, pictured as a firefighter and a police officer (see Figure 7).

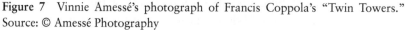

If 9/11 will continue to matter in American popular and literary arts it will be because the memorial artists will move from the personal to the social and from the reactive to the reflective. The power of 9/11 as immediate and profound intensifier cannot last much longer. Foxhole movies had their moment during and just after World War II, but it is *Catch-22* (1961), with its broad satire of wartime bureaucracy, that became a crucial part of the American vernacular. The September 11 attacks will continue to resonate in American arts – in music, film, television, literature, and the visual arts – only insofar as they are stitched into history and mapped onto an expansive landscape.

The rubble of the World Trade Center was referred to by workers at the site as the pile, but by popular acclaim (and by September 16) its name was "Ground Zero." This naming connected the 9/11 attack, through time and space, to the World War II-era atomic testing sites in the Nevada desert, and to America's bombing of Hiroshima. The tacit agreement made by the American people, their government officials, and their media to call the World Trade Center site "Ground Zero" was one acknowledgment that 9/11 was neither outside of culture nor outside of history. But it did not take long for September 11 to gain the aura of exceptionalism, and that exceptionalism is the burden that 9/11 art has been carrying since the first few weeks after the attacks. Flattening out the dimensions of meaning in and around this American tragedy has ultimately rendered 9/11 less artistically valuable. The American novelist Henry James wrote in an 1879 study of Nathaniel Hawthorne that "the flower of art blooms only where the soil is deep," adding that it "takes a great deal of history to produce a little literature." Whether in the personal back-stories of Lynne Sharon Schwartz's *The Writing on the Wall* and Spike Lee's *25th Hour* on the one hand, or Eugene Hutz (lead man of Gogol Bordello) banging on an FDNY bucket as he sings gypsy "immigrant punk" songs and Steven Spielberg offering up the Olympian world history of *Munich* on the other, plotting 9/11 in history has formed the basis of the richest 9/11 art to date.

It seems possible that the pivotal moment for our study of 9/11 art will turn out to have been the moment of the next American tragedy, Hurricane Katrina's devastation of New Orleans and other sites on the Gulf Coast and the abandonment of the region and its people by the United States federal government. While questions of race, privilege, and power have been largely submerged in artistic conversations surrounding 9/11, Katrina forced artists in the United States to confront America's central dilemma. It is interesting to track how a few musicians worked hard to link up the very different realities of 9/11 and Katrina. Jay-Z, for instance, offered up a Katrina song in the fall of 2006 that he called "Minority Report." Using this title was, no doubt, the rapper's strategy to argue that Black disenfranchisement was the headline story in the U.S. government's neglect of Katrina's most vulnerable victims, as well as to muse on his own position of relative privilege. But it was also a way for Jay-Z to invoke Steven Spielberg's 9/11-themed movie of that name, with its obsessive circling around the question of prior knowledge. Whether the 9/11 attacks could have been predicted or not, Jay-Z's use of "Minority Report" as his title for a song about Hurricane Katrina works as a loud 9/11-inspired rebuke of the federal government's unwillingness to prepare for the breach of the levees that so many knew was coming.

Bruce Springsteen did not tie 9/11 and Katrina together so directly, but he did draw from the cultural capital he developed with *The Rising* to mount a much more radical effort after Katrina. Pulling back from the arena-scale rock and roll sound of *The Rising*, Springsteen next released the much more intimate *Devils and Dust* in 2005 (followed by a solo tour) and then *The Seeger Sessions* in 2006. With this latter, an homage to the music of Pete Seeger, Springsteen also mounted a major band tour – but not with his usual E Street Band. Now Springsteen drew mostly on younger players and crafted a sound with deep roots in New Orleans. He made an appearance at Jazz Fest in New Orleans in April of 2006 and played a rewritten version of Blind Alfred Reed's Depression-era song "How Can a Poor Man Stand Such Times and Live?" Decrying the "criminal ineptitude" of the Bush administration and FEMA, Springsteen here moved beyond the bromides of *The Rising*, and found an angry voice to sing with as he tried to capture the situation of Katrina's victims – the "poor folks" the president in his song gives "a little pep talk" to before he takes "a little walk" out of town. Springsteen is aware in this moment that there will be no portraits of grief for the dead and wounded of New Orleans, and offers up a vision of a nation – not quite 4 years out from 9/11 – cleft by the familiar and tragic divisions of race and class.

Working similar terrain, and with a sing-along buoyancy and political optimism worthy of Pete Seeger himself, the young string band Old Crow Medicine Show powerfully connected up 9/11 and Katrina with their 2006 song "I Hear Them All." If Springsteen literally reached back into the Depression for his modern protest song, Old Crow Medicine Show instead hinted at the proletarian art of the period, especially the books *You Have Seen Their Faces*, with text by Erskine Caldwell and photographs by Margaret Bourke-White, and *12 Million Black Voices*, with text by Richard Wright and photographs by Dorothea Lange, Walker Evans, and others working for the Farm Security Administration.

The song, as originally recorded, never attracted the wrath of right-wing bloggers or talk show hosts, but represented a radical reproach to the unity scripts that so dominated initial responses to the attacks. With a gentle jug band sound, lyrics that invoke Seeger's "Where Have All the

Flowers Gone?" and cadences borrowed from "If I Had a Hammer" (written by Seeger and Lee Hays), the song starts generally enough with images of hungry people crying in the desert. What comes next is stunning:

> I hear the sound of tearing pages and the roar of burning paper
> All the crimes in acquisitions turn to air, and ash, and vapor

Questioning the innocence of 9/11's World Trade Center victims is a provocative move; few in American popular or literary culture have dared this. Soon the song makes clear its anti-war agenda:

> I can hear the flowers a-growin' in the rubble of the towers
> I hear leaders quit their lying
> I hear babies quit their crying
> I hear soldiers quit their dying one and all.

Even with the pan-religious invocations that end the song "I Hear Them All" functions, on record, as a piece of radical art that keeps company with Sherman Alexie's "Can I Get a Witness?" and Immortal Technique's "Cause of Death."

The video for "I Hear Them All" tells a whole different story, and it is a Katrina story. The "plot" of the video is simple: some members of Old Crow Medicine Show are waiting for a bus with a crowd of African American people in New Orleans. They all wait and wait, checking their watches and leaning into the street to see if the bus is coming. Finally, the bus arrives, driven by George Porter, Jr., (bassist for the important New Orleans instrumental band, The Meters), and off they roll. It is a simple twist on Civil Rights art: "We Shall Not Be Moved" turned, by necessity, into "We Shall Be Moved" – but all together. Collective memories of Rosa Parks and the Montgomery Bus Boycott of 1955 are accessed here, as Old Crow's white band members leave the front seats of the bus for New Orleans' African Americans. Text appears as the scene fades, reminding viewers of the toll Katrina took on New Orleans and its people, along with information on how to contribute to ongoing rebuilding efforts. In translation from song to video, "I Hear Them All" travels from the frozen moment of 9/11 to the challenging future of post-Katrina New Orleans. With song lyrics that continue to undercut any easy unity promised by the "bus of freedom" visuals, "I Hear Them All" begins to map a route for a post-tragedy, anti-war American art that is "under construction," equal parts buoyant hope and loyal opposition.

Bibliography

Aidi, Hisham. 2002. "Jihadis in the Hood: Race, Urban Islam and the War on Terror." *Middle East Report*. October 27.

Alexie, Sherman. 2003a. "Can I Get a Witness?" In *Ten Little Indians*. New York. Grove, 69–95.

Alexie, Sherman. 2003b. "Flight Patterns." In *Ten Little Indians*. New York. Grove, 102–23.

Alexie, Sherman. 2007. *Flight*. New York. Grove.

Allah, Dasun. 2004. "NYPD Admits to Rap Intelligence Unit." *Village Voice*. March 16, 2004. http://www.villagevoice.com/2004-03-16/news/nypd-admits-to-rap-intelligence-unit/1

"Among the Missing." 2001. *New York Times*. October 14. http://query.nytimes.com/gst/fullpage.html?res=9507E4DB133FF937A25753C1A9679C8B63

Andrews, Robert. 2006. *The Birth of the Blog*. In *Wired*, September 11. http://www.wired.com/techbiz/media/news/2006/09/71753

"At O'Hare, President Says 'Get on Board'." 2001. http://www.whitehouse.gov/news/releases/2001/09/20010927-1.html

"Banned Songlist Revealed As Fake." 2001. *The Guardian*. September 20. http://www.guardian.co.uk/world/2001/sep/20/september11.usa12

Baraka, Amiri. 2001. "Somebody Blew Up America." http://www.amiribaraka.com/blew.html

Bayoumi, Moustafa. 2002. "Letter to a G-Man." In Michael Sorkin and Sharon Zukin, eds. *After the World Trade Center: Rethinking New York City*. New York. Routledge, 131–42.

Beigbeder, Frédéric. 2004. *Windows on the World*. New York. Hyperion.

Belle, Jennifer. 2002. "Gelato is Gelato." In Ulrich Baer, ed. *110 Stories: New York Writes After September 11*. New York. New York University Press, 37–9.

Berman, Marshall. 2002. "The Lives of the Saints." In Michael Sorkin and Sharon Zukin, eds. *After the World Trade Center: Rethinking New York City*. New York. Routledge, 1–12.

Best, James. 2003. "Black Like Me: John Walker Lindh's Hip-Hop Daze." *East Bay Express*. September 3. http://www.eastbayexpress.com/news/black_like_me/Content?oid=285804

"The Best Albums of 2007." 2007. *Blender*. http://www.blender.com/articles/default.aspx?key=10512&pg=5

"Biden: Rudy's Sentences Consist of 'A Noun, A Verb And 9/11.' " 2007. *The Huffington Post*. October 30. http://www.huffingtonpost.com/2007/10/30/biden-rudys-sentences-c_n_70509.html

Blumenfeld, Larry. 2007. "Exploding Myths in Morocco and Senegal: Sufis Making Music after 9/11." In Jonathan Ritter and J. Martin Daughtry, eds. *Music in the Post-9/11 World*. New York. Routledge, 209–24.

Boehlert, Eric. 2004. "The Passion of Howard Stern." *Salon.com*. http://dir.salon.com/story/news/feature/2004/03/04/stern/print.html

Budnitz, Judy. 2005. "Preparedness." In *Nice Big American Baby*. New York. Knopf, 245–61.

Burr, Ty. 2006. "The Capital of Brashness Finds Itself Suddenly Humbled." *The Boston Globe*. September 3. http://www.boston.com/news/globe/living/articles/2006/09/03/the_capital_of_brashness_finds_itself_suddenly_humbled/

"Bush Gives Update on War Against Terrorism." 2001. http://archives.cnn.com/2001/US/10/11/gen.bush.transcript/

Cave, Damien. 2002. "Forbidden Thoughts about 9/11." *Salon.com*. September 7. http://dir.salon.com/story/must/feature/2002/09/07/forbidden/print.html

Chadha, Tina. 2003. "Mix This." *Village Voice*. July 1. http://www.villagevoice.com/2003-07-01/news/mix-this/

Chang, Jeff. 2001. "Time to Elevate: Hip-Hop Resists Terror and War." *AlterNet*. November 26. http://www.alternet.org/story/11961/?page=2

Chang, Jeff. 2002. "9/11: The Fallout." *Bad Subjects*. February. http://bad.eserver.org/issues/2002/59/chang.html

"Chat Room Review of *America: A Tribute to Heroes*." 2001. *Ape Culture*. http://www.apeculture.com/television/telethon.htm

Chin, Frank and Jeffrey Paul Chan. 1972. "Racist Love." http://www.modelminority.com/article1026.html

Christgau, Robert. 2004. "Facing Mecca." *Village Voice*. May 25. http://www.villagevoice.com/music/0422,christgau,53980,22.html

Churchill, Ward. 2001. " 'Some People Push Back': On the Justice of Roosting Chickens." http://www.kersplebedeb.com/mystuff/s11/churchill.html

Cooper, Michael. 2007. "Giuliani, Seeking to Gain Ground, Returns to a Familiar Theme: 9/11." *New York Times*. December 29. http://www.nytimes.com/2007/12/29/us/politics/29giuliani.html

Danto, Arthur. 2002. "The Art of 9/11." *The Nation*. September 5. http://www.thenation.com/doc/20020923/danto

Davis, Darren and Brian Silver. 2004. "Civil Liberties vs. Security: Public Opinion in the Context of the Terrorist Attacks on America." *American Journal of Political Science.* Volume 48 (1): 28–46.

DeLillo, Don. 2001. "In the Ruins of the Future." *The Guardian.* December 22.

DeLillo, Don. 2007. *The Falling Man.* New York. Scribner.

Denning, Michael. 1987. *Mechanic Accents: Dime Novels and Working Class Culture.* New York: Verso.

Devenish, Colin. 2004. "KRS-One: 'I Cheered 9/11.'" *Rolling Stone.* October 14. http://www.rollingstone.com/news/story/6559895/krsone_i_cheered_911

Du Bois, W. E. B. 2004. "Close Ranks." In Ronald Bayor, ed. *The Columbia Documentary History of Race and Ethnicity in America.* New York. Columbia University Press, 505. (Original work published 1918.)

Edwards, Audrey. 2001. "What I Saw: Brooklyn." http://www.washington.edu/alumni/columns/dec01/911_brooklyn.html

Engelhardt, Tom. 2006. "9/11 in a Movie-Made World." *The Nation.* September 10. http://www.thenation.com/doc/20060925/engelhardt

Espada, Martín. 2003. "Alabanza: In Praise of Local 100." http://www.martinespada.net/alabanza.htm

Faludi, Susan 2007. *The Terror Dream: Fear and Fantasy in Post-9/11 America.* New York. Metropolitan.

Feldschuh, Michael. 2002. *The September 11 Photo Project.* New York. Regan Books.

Fitzpatrick, Chris. 2002. "Boom Go the Bombs, Boom Goes the Bass." *PopMatters.* June 11. http://www.popmatters.com/music/videos/t/truthhurts-addictive.shtml

Foer, Jonathan Safran. 2005. *Extremely Loud and Incredibly Close.* Boston. Houghton Mifflin.

Foote, Kenneth. 2003. *Shadowed Ground: America's Landscapes of Violence and Tragedy.* Austin. University of Texas Press, 1997.

Friedman, Thomas. 2007. "9/11 is Over." *New York Times.* September 30. http://www.nytimes.com/2007/09/30/opinion/30friedman.html

Gabler, Neal. 2001. "This Time, The Scene Was Real." *New York Times.* September 16. http://query.nytimes.com/gst/fullpage.html?res=9D01E6DA163BF935A2575AC0A9679C8B63

Gibson, William. 2003. *Pattern Recognition.* New York. G. P. Putnam's.

Giese, Rachel. 2006. "The War at Home: Ken Kalfus Pens the First Satirical 9/11 Novel." http://www.cbc.ca/arts/books/kenkalfus.html.

Goldstein, Richard. 2003. "Neo-Macho Man: Pop Culture and Post-9/11 Politics." *The Nation.* March 14. http://www.thenation.com/doc/20030324/goldstein/2

Goodman, Robin and Andrea Henderson Fahnestock. 2002. *The Day Our World Changed: Children's Art of 9/11.* New York. Harry N. Abrams.

Grossman, Lev. 2002. "Pitching September 11." In Ulrich Baer, ed. *110 Stories: New York Writes After September 11.* New York. New York University Press.

Guilfoile, Kevin. 2002. "I Know You're Lonely for Words That I Ain't Spoken." *The Morning News*. August 5. http://www.themorningnews.org/archives/opinions/i_know_youre_lonely_for_words_that_i_aint_spoken.php

Halberstam, David. 2003. *Firehouse*. New York. Hyperion.

Hall, Rashaun. 2004, "Jadakiss Single Courts Controversy." *Billboard.com*. July 9. http://www.billboard.com/bbcom/news/article_display.jsp?vnu_content_id=1000574096

Hamm, Mark. 2003. "Agony and Art: The Songs of September 11." In Steven Chermak, Frankie Bailey, and Michelle Brown, eds. *Media Representations of September 11*. Westport, CT. Praeger.

Harnden, Toby. 2001. "Bin Laden Is Wanted: Dead or Alive, Says Bush." London *Telegraph*. September 18. http://www.telegraph.co.uk/news/main.jhtml?xml=/news/2001/09/18/wbush18.xml

Harris, Daniel. 2002. "The Kitschification of 9/11." In Editors of *Salon.Com*. *Afterwords: Stories and Reports from 9/11 and Beyond*. New York. Washington Square Press, 203–20.

Harvey, David. 2002. "Cracks in the Edifice of the Empire State." In Michael Sorkin and Sharon Zukin, eds. *After the World Trade Center: Rethinking New York City*. New York. Routledge, 57–67.

Heim, Joe. 2004. "Rapper Ups the Anti on Bush and 9/11." *Washington Post*. July 17. http://www.washingtonpost.com/wp-dyn/articles/A56356-2004Jul16.html

Heller, Dana. 2005. "Introduction: Consuming 9/11." In Dana Heller, ed. *The Selling of 9/11: How a National Tragedy Became a Commodity*. New York. Palgrave Macmillan, 2–26.

Hoberman, J. 2006. "The New Disaster Movie." *Village Voice*. May 9. http://www.villagevoice.com/2006-05-09/film/the-new-disaster-movie/

Hornaday, Ann. 2003. "25th Hour: Stunningly True to Its Time." *Washington Post*. January 10. http://www.washingtonpost.com/wpdyn/content/article/2003/01/10/AR2005033116234.html

Hubbard, Lee. 2001. "Old Glory's New Appeal to Blacks." *AlterNet*. September 26. http://www.alternet.org/story/11595/

"Interview with Vijay Prashad." (n.d.) http://www.frontlist.com/interview/Prashad-Interview

James, Henry. 1879. *Hawthorne*. Chapter 1. http://www.ibiblio.org/eldritch/hjj/nhhj1.html

Junod, Tom. 2003. "The Falling Man." *Esquire*. September 11. http://www.esquire.com/features/ESQ0903-SEP_FALLINGMAN

Kahane, Claire. 2003. "Uncanny Sights: The Anticipation of the Abomination." In Judith Greenberg, ed. *Trauma at Home: After 9/11*. New York. Bison, 107–116.

Kalfus, Ken. 2006. *A Disorder Peculiar to the Country*. New York. Harper Perennial.

Kim, Jee et al. 2002. *Another World Is Possible: Conversations in a Time of Terror*. New Orleans. Subway and Elevated.

Klawans, Stuart. 2006. "Virtual Catastrophe." *The Nation*. August 24. http://www.thenation.com/doc/20060911/klawans

"KRS-One, Decency Zero." 2004. *New York Daily News*. October 13. http://web.archive.org/web/20061211170831/http://www.nydailynews.com/front/story/241988p-207504c.html

Krugman, Paul. 2003. "Channels of Influence." *New York Times*. March 25. http://query.nytimes.com/gst/fullpage.html?res=9B02E1DD1230F936A157 50C0A9659C8B63

Langewiesche, William. 2002. *American Ground Unbuilding the World Trade Center*. New York. North Point.

Langlois, Janet. 2005. "Celebrating Arabs: Tracing Legend and Rumor Labyrinths in Post-9/11 Detroit." *Journal of American Folklore*. Volume 118 (468): 219–36.

Lawson, Mark. 2002. "After the Fall." *The Guardian*. August 16. http://arts.guardian.co.uk/film/2002/aug/16/artsfeatures.september11

Levine, Lawrence. 1998. "The Historian and the Icon: Photography and the History of the American People in the 1930s and 1940s." In Carl Fleischhauer and Beverly Brannan, eds. *Documenting America, 1935–1943*. Berkeley. University of California Press, 15–42.

Limerick, Patricia Nelson. 1987. *Legacy of Conquest: The Unbroken Past of the American West*. New York. W. W. Norton.

Lhamon, W. T. 2000. *Raising Cain: Blackface Performance from Jim Crow to Hip Hop*. Cambridge, MA. Harvard University Press.

"Lost Children of Babylon Interview." 2006. http://my.opera.com/hiphopheadz/blog/show.dml/163049

Mangan, Dan. 2007. "9/11 Kin Rip 'Evil' Eye Ads." *New York Post*. June 11. http://www.nypost.com/seven/06112007/news/regionalnews/9_11_kin_rip_evil_eye_ads_regionalnews_dan_mangan.htm

Marcus, Greil. 1991. *Dead Elvis: A Chronicle of a Cultural Obsession*. New York. Doubleday.

Marcus, Greil. 2002. "Days Between Stations." *Interview*. February 2002. http://findarticles.com/p/articles/mi_m1285/is_1_32/ai_82352407

Marqusee, Mike. 1999. *Redemption Song: Muhammed Ali and the Spirit of the Sixties*. New York. Verso.

"Marsh & McLennan Blasts N. Y. Post Criticism of Ad Photos." 2007. *Insurance Journal*. June 12. http://www.insurancejournal.com/news/national/2007/06/12/80742.htm

Maynard, Joyce. 2003. *The Usual Rules*. New York. St. Martin's Press.

"McCain: Bush Should Have Urged Enlistment." 2007. http://www.msnbc.msn.com/id/21118179/

McGruder, Aaron. 2003. *A Right to Be Hostile: The Boondocks Treasury*. New York. Three Rivers Press.

Miller, Kevin. 2004 "Bolly'hood Remix." *Institute for Studies in American Music Newsletter*. Volume 33 (4): 6–7, 15.

Miller, Nancy K. 2003. " 'Portraits of Grief' ": Telling Details and the Testimony of Trauma." *Differences*. Volume 14 (3): 112–35.

Miyakawa, Felicia. 2005. *Five Percenter Rap: God Hop's Music, Message, and Black Muslim Message*. Bloomington, IN. Indiana University Press.

Mukherjee, Roopali. 2003. "Between Enemies and Traitors: Black Press Coverage of September 11 and the Predicaments of National 'Others.' " In Steven Chermak, Frankie Bailey, and Michelle Brown, eds. *Media Representations of September 11*. Westport, CT. Praeger, 29–46.

N'Dour, Youssou. 2003. "Youssou N'Dour Cancels US Tour Over Threat of War." March 7. http://soundingcircle.com/newslog2.php/__show_article/_a000195-000040.htm

Nuzum, Eric. 2004. "Crash Into Me, Baby: America's Implicit Music Censorship Since 9/11." June 3. http://www.freemuse.org/sw7005.asp

Nyberg, Amy Kiste. 2003. "Of Heroes and Superheroes." In Steven Chermak, Frankie Bailey, and Michelle Brown, eds. *Media Representations of September 11*. Westport, CT. Praeger, 175–85.

Nye, Naomi Shihab. 2001 "To Any Would-Be Terrorists." http://poetry.about.com/library/weekly/aa100901a.htm

O'Carroll, Lisa. 2002. "9/11 Makers 'Refused to Film the Dying'." *The Guardian*. September 12. http://www.guardian.co.uk/media/2002/sep/12/september112001.usnews

Pareles, Jon. 2000. "Born to Run, Or At Least to Be Redeemed." *New York Times*. June 14. http://query.nytimes.com/gst/fullpage.html?res=9C00EEDF123EF937A25755C0A9669C8B63

Pareles, Jon. 2002. "His Kind of Heroes, His Kind of Songs." *New York Times*. July 14. http://query.nytimes.com/gst/fullpage.html?res=9D03E5DB1430F937A25754C0A9649C8B63

Paretsky, Sara. 2003. *Blacklist*. New York. Penguin.

"Paris Gets a Bad Rap." 2003. *Political Affairs*. October 1. http://www.politicalaffairs.net/article/view/51/1/27

Pegley, Kip and Susan Fast. 2007. "*America: A Tribute to Heroes*: Music, Mourning and the Unified American Community." In Jonathan Ritter and J. Martin Daughtry, eds. *Music in the Post-9/11 World*. New York. Routledge, 27–42.

Poffenberger, Nancy. 2002. *September 11ᵗʰ, 2001: A Simple Account for Children*. Cincinnati, OH. Fun Publishing.

Powell, Kevin. 2006. *Someday We'll All Be Free*. New York. Soft Skull.

Prashad, Vijay. 2000. *The Karma of Brown Folk*. Minneapolis. University of Minnesota Press.

Prashad, Vijay. 2001. *Everybody Was Kung Fu Fighting: Afro-Asian Connections and the Myth of Cultural Purity*. New York. Beacon.

Price, Reynolds. 2005. *The Good Priest's Son*. New York. Scribner.

"Public Viewing Platform Opens at Ground Zero." 2001. http://archives.cnn. com/2001/US/12/30/rec.viewing.platforms/index.html

Radosh, Daniel. 2002. "Eminem Makes Steve Earle Look Like Toby Keith. Why Hasn't Anyone Noticed?" *Radical Society*. October. http://findarticles. com/p/articles/mi_qa4053/is_/ai_n9085960

Rall, Ted. 2006. "The Legend of United 93." *Common Dreams*. March 8. http:// www.commondreams.org/views06/0308-26.htm

Rees, David. 2002. *Get Your War On*. New York. Soft Skull Press.

Remnick, David. 1998. *King of the World*. New York. Random House.

Rosenbaum, Jonathan. 2006a. "Hijacking the Hijacking: The Problem with the United 93 Films." *Slate*. April 27. http://www.slate.com/id/2140676/

Rosenbaum, Jonathan. 2006b. "It's All About Us." *Chicago Reader*. August. http://www.chicagoreader.com/features/stories/moviereviews/060811/

Rosenblatt, Roger. 2001. "Closing Thoughts." *Online NewsHour*. September 16. http://www.pbs.org/newshour/bb/terrorism/july-dec01/essayists_9-16.html

Roten, Robert. 2002. "Is Hollywood Responsible for 9/11?" http://www.lariat. org/AtTheMovies/essays/moviesand911.html

Roth, Philip. 2004. *The Plot Against America*. Boston. Houghton Mifflin.

Rourke, Constance. 2004. *American Humor: A Study of the National Character*. New York. NYRB Classics. (Original work published 1931.)

Rubin, Rachel. 2003. *Cyberspace Y2K: Giant Robots, Asian Punks*. Boston. Institute for Asian American Studies.

Rubin, Rachel and Jeff Melnick. 2006. *Immigration and American Popular Culture: An Introduction*. New York. New York University Press.

Rux, Carl Hancock. 2004. *Asphalt*. New York. Simon and Schuster.

Scanlon, Jennifer. 2005. " 'Your Flag Decal Won't Get You into Heaven Anymore: U.S. Consumers, Wal-Mart, and the Commodification of Patriotism." In Dana Heller, ed. *The Selling of 9/11: How a National Tragedy Became a Commodity*. New York: Palgrave, Macmillan, 174–99.

Schulman, Helen. 2007. *A Day at the Beach*. Boston. Houghton Mifflin.

Schwartz, Lynne Sharon. 2005. *The Writing on the Wall*. New York. Counterpoint.

Scott, A. O. 2002. "The Poet Laureate of 9/11." *Slate*. August 6. http://www. slate.com/id/2069047/

Sella, Marshall. 2001. "Missing." *New York Times*. October 7. http://query. nytimes.com/gst/fullpage.html?res=9801E5DE123DF934A35753C1A9679 C8B63&sec=&spon=&pagewanted=2

Shulan, Michael. 2004. "Introduction." *Here is New York*. http://hereisnewyork. org/gallery/bookintro.asp

Smith, Judith. 2006. *Visions of Belonging: Family Stories, Popular Culture, and Postwar Democracy, 1940–1960*. New York. Columbia University Press.

"Snapshots of Their Lives, Told with the Pain of Those Who Loved Them." 2001. *New York Times*. September 16. http://query.nytimes.com/gst/fullpage.html? res=9A06E1D9163BF935A2575AC0A9679C8B63

Soults, Franklin. 2004. "Ghetto Blasting." *The Boston Phoenix*. August 13–19. http://www.bostonphoenix.com/boston/music/other_stories/documents/ 04046019.asp

Spiegelman, Art. 2004. *In the Shadow of No Towers*. New York. Viking.

Stevenson, Seth. 2006. "Can Rosa Parks Sell Trucks? Chevy's Icky, Exploitative New Ad." *Slate*. October 9. http://www.slate.com/id/2151143/

Sturken, Marita. 2007. *Tourists of History: Memory, Kitsch, and Consumerism from Oklahoma City to Ground Zero*. Durham. Duke University Press.

Tate, Greg. 2001. "Intelligence Data." *Village Voice*. September 25. http://www. villagevoice.com/2001-09-25/music/intelligence-data/1

Timiraos, Nick. 2007. "Want to Play a Terrorist?: Actors Face a Dilemma." *Wall Street Journal*. April 11. http://doctorbulldog.wordpress.com/2007/04/11/ want-to-play-a-terrorist/

Trachtenberg, Alan. 1979. *Brooklyn Bridge: Fact and Symbol*. Chicago. University of Chicago Press.

Trachtenberg, Alan. 1988. "From Image to Story: Reading the Archive." In Carl Fleischhauer and Beverly Brannan, eds. *Documenting America, 1935–1943*. Berkeley. University of California Press, 43–73.

Turner, Patricia. 1993. *I Heard It Through the Grapevine: Rumor in African American Culture*. Berkeley. University of California Press.

Tyrangiel, Josh. 2001. "Did You Hear About…" *Time*. September 30. http://www. time.com/time/magazine/article/0,9171,1101011008-176941,00.html.

Updike, John. 2006. *Terrorist*. New York: Alfred A. Knopf.

"The 4,000 Jews Rumor." 2005. U.S. Department of State. January 14. http:// usinfo.state.gov/media/Archive/2005/Jan/14-260933.html

Volpp, Leti. 2003. "The Citizen and the Terrorist." In Mary Dudziak, ed. *September 11th in History: A Watershed Moment?* Durham. Duke University Press, 147–62.

Walter, Jess. 2006. *The Zero*. New York. Regan.

"What Black America Has to Say about 9/11." September/October 2002. *Black Issues Book Review*. http://findarticles.com/p/articles/mi_m0HST/is_/ ai_91913264

White, Armond. 2002. "Citizen Jay-Z." *First of the Month*. June 12. http://www. firstofthemonth.org.

White, Emily. 2002. *Fast Girls: Teenage Tribes and the Myth of the Slut*. New York. Scribner.

Wolf, Jaime. 1997. "Oliver Stone Doesn't Want to Start An Argument." *New York Times*. September 21. http://query.nytimes.com/gst/fullpage.html?res=9D0DE ED81438F932A1575AC0A961958260&sec=&spon=&pagewanted=2

Wright, Richard. 1956. *The Color Curtain: A Report on the Bandung Conference*. Cleveland. World Publishing.

Yates, Brad. 2005. "Healing a Nation: Deconstructing Bruce Springsteen's *The Rising*." http://www.westga.edu/~byates/Healing%20a%20nation-Deconstructing%20Bruce%20Springsteen's%20The%20Rising.pdf

Žižek, Slavoj. 2001. "Welcome to the Desert of the Real." *Reconstructions*. http://web.mit.edu/cms/reconstructions/interpretations/desertreal.html

Appendix 1: 9/11 in Film and on Television

9/11 (Naudet brothers)
11'9"01
24
25th Hour
Battle for Haditha
Body of War
The Cats of Mirikitani
Charlie Wilson's War
Chicken Little
Civic Duty
Cloverfield
Control Room
Diary of the Dead
Family Guy ("It Takes a Village Idiot, And I Married One")
Farenheit 9/11
Flight Plan
Ghosts of Abu Ghraib
Gone Baby Gone
Grace is Gone
The Great New Wonderful
The Guys
The Happening
Harold and Kumar Escape from Guantanamo Bay
Hijacking Catastrophe
Home of the Brave

I Am Legend
I Now Pronounce You Chuck & Larry
I, Robot
Inside Man
In the Valley of Elah
The Kingdom
King Kong (2005)
Kite Runner
Land of Plenty
Liberty Kid
Lions for Lambs
Live from Shiva's Dance Floor
Looking for Comedy in the Muslim World
Lost
Loose Change
Masked and Anonymous
A Mighty Heart
Minority Report
The Mist
Munich
Notorious C.H.O.
Panic Room
Parallel Lines
Postal
Protocols of Zion
Red Eye
Redacted
Reign Over Me
Rendition
Rescue Me
The Road to Guantanamo
The Saint of 9/11
Shortbus
Sleeper Cell
Snakes on a Plane
Sorry, Haters
South Park ("Mystery of the Urinal Deuce," "Osama bin Laden Has Farty Pants," and others)
Standard Operating Procedure

Stop Loss
Stuart Little 2
Taxi to the Dark Side
Team America: World Police
Transformers
United 93
"V" for Vendetta
War of the Worlds
War, Inc.
The War Within
Where in the World Is Osama bin Laden?
Why We Fight
World Trade Center
WTC View
You Don't Mess with the Zohan

Appendix 2: 9/11 Music

Songs with 9/11 Content

Dan Bern, "Talkin' Al Kida Blues"
Dan Bern, "Thanksgiving Day Parade"
Black Eyed Peas, "Where is the Love?"
Blue Sage, "Flight 93"
Bon Jovi (with Jennifer Nettles), "Who Says You Can't Go Home"
Bottle Rockets, "Baggage Claim"
Bright Eyes, "When the President Talks to God"
Brother Ali, "Uncle Sam Goddam"
Henry Butler, "Homeland"
Canibus, "Draft Me"
Chuck D, "Son of a Bush"
Clarity, "Buddy Buddy"
Leonard Cohen, "On That Day"
Charlie Daniels, "This Ain't No Rag"
Kimya Dawson, "Fire"
Kimya Dawson, "Parade"
Kimya Dawson, "Anthrax"
Dead Prez, "Know Your Enemy"
Zach de La Rocha, "We Want it All"
Kevin Devine, "Noose like a Necklace"
Ani DiFranco, "Self Evident"
The Diplomats, "Ground Zero"
The Diplomats, "I Love You"
Dixie Chicks, "Travelin' Soldier"

DJ Krush, "Song for John Walker"
Everclear, "New York Times"
Everclear, "Blackjack"
Donald Fagen, "Security Joan"
Five For Fighting, "Superman"
Fleetwood Mac, "Illume (9/11)"
Radney Foster, "Everyday Angel"
Barry Thomas Goldberg, "Homeland"
Nanci Griffith, "Good Night, New York"
Merle Haggard, "America First"
Merle Haggard, "Where's All the Freedom"
Immortal Technique, "Bin Laden"
Immortal Technique, "Cause of Death"
Immortal Technique, "Homeland and Hiphop"
Alan Jackson, "Where Were You (When the World Stopped Turning)"
Jadakiss, "Why"
Jay-Z, "Minority Report"
Jay-Z, "Ballad for a Fallen Soldier"
Jay-Z, "Bounce"
Jay-Z, "A Dream"
Wyclef Jean, "Knockin' on Heaven's Door"
Wyclef Jean (with Buju Banton), "Who Gave the Order"
Wyclef Jean, "War No More"
J-Live, "Satisfied"
Toby Keith, "Courtesy of the Red, White and Blue (The Angry American)"
Toby Keith, "The Taliban Song"
Toby Keith, "Beer for My Horses"
Toby Keith, "American Soldier"
Willie King, "Terrorized"
Know Boundaries, "Homeland Security"
Jenny Lewis, "With Fists Raised"
Lightning Bolt, "Two Towers"
Lonestar, "I'm Already There"
Lynyrd Skynyrd, "Red White and Blue"
Masterminds, "September in New York"
George Michael, "Shoot the Dog"
Buddy Miller, "Water When the Well is Dry"
Buddy Miller, "With God on Our Side"

John Michael Montgomery, "Letters"
Nappy Roots, "Po' Folks"
Nappy Roots, "Right Now"
Nas, "What Goes Around"
Nas, "Rule"
The Nightwatchman, "No One Left"
Old Crow Medicine Show, "I Hear Them All"
Panajabi MC (with Jay-Z), "Beware of the Boys"
Papa Roach, "Lovehatetragedy
Dolly Parton, "Hello God"
Pearl Jam, "World Wide Suicide"
The Perceptionists, "Memorial Day"
Prince, "Cinnamon Girl"
Public Enemy, "Hannibal Lecture"
Public Enemy, "The Enemy Battle Hymn of the Public"
Public Enemy, "Hell No, We Ain't Alright"
Dan Reich, "Homeland Security"
Sunny Riddell, "Hey Osama"
Rush, "Peaceable Kingdom"
Jill Scott, "My Petition"
SEAN, "Everyone and Bin Laden Plays Guitar"
Michael Sherry, "9/11"
Sleater Kinney, "Far Away"
Sleater Kinney, "Combat Rock"
Soulfly, "9-11-01"
Andre Tanker, "Food Fight"
Three 6 Mafia, "Bin Laden"
Various Artists, "What's Going On?"
Loudon Wainwright, "President's Day"
Loudon Wainwright, "No Sure Way"
Loudon Wainwright, "Here Come the Choppers"
Tom Waits, "Hoist that Rag"
Yeah Yeah Yeahs, "Our Time"
Yellowcard, "Believe"
Yo La Tengo, "Nuclear War"
Neil Young, "Let's Roll"

Plus countless other Flight 93, Osama, Twin Tower, and "homeland" songs.

Full-Length Works with 9/11 Content or Resonances

John Adams: *On the Transmigration of Souls*
Addek: *Hip Hop 9/11*
Laurie Anderson: *Live at Town Hall, New York City, September 19–20, 2001*
Arcade Fire: *Neon Bible*
Beastie Boys: *To The Five Boroughs*
Tlee Brooks: *9/11–911*
Capital D: *Insomnia*
The Coup: *Party Music*
The Coup: *Pick a Bigger Weapon*
Steve Earle: *Jerusalem*
Steve Earle: *The Revolution Starts Now*
Missy Elliott: *Under Construction*
Eminem: *The Eminem Show*
Mark Erelli: *Hope and Other Casualties*
Merle Haggard: *Chicago Wind*
Immortal Technique: *Revolutionary, Vol. 2*
Rickie Lee Jones: *The Evening of My Best Day*
The Klezmatics: *Rise Up!*
Living Things: *Ahead of the Lions*
The Lost Children of Babylon: *The 911 Report: The Ultimate Conspiracy*
The Mekons: *OOOH! (Out of Our Heads)*
Mr. Lif: *Emergency Rations*
Moby: *18*
Youssou N'Dour: *Egypt*
NOFX: *War Against Errorism*
Ozomatli: *Street Signs*
Paris: *Sonic Jihad*
Elvis Perkins: *Ash Wednesday*
Suzzy and Maggie Roche: *Zero Church*
Sonny Rollins: *Without a Song (The 9/11 Concert)*
Bruce Springsteen: *The Rising*
Bruce Springsteen: *The Seeger Sessions*
Bruce Springsteen: *Devils and Dust*
Bruce Springsteen: *Magic*

Wilco: *Yankee Foxtrot Hotel*
Neil Young: *Greendale*
Neil Young: *Living with War*

Tribute Albums/Collections

Rock against Bush Volumes 1 and 2
Vigil: N.Y. Songs Since 9/11
America: A Tribute to Heroes
Concert for New York
Wish You Were Here
Songs and Artists that Inspired Farenheit 9/11
Hip Hop Against Terrorism

A Note to Teachers

I have been fortunate to have the opportunity to teach a course on 9/11 in American culture regularly since the winter of 2004. But calling it "a course" is misleading. In these 4 years it has been many courses, even while a number of major themes and works have traveled through all of its versions. One of the thrilling, if sometimes challenging, aspects of teaching this course on American culture after 9/11 is that the subject will not stay still for even a moment. While some attempts at canonizing 9/11 art are already being made (and my work here certainly participates in that effort to some degree) teachers interested in exploring the arts of September 11 can feel pretty free to pick texts as they wish. From children's books and movies up through complex works of literary fiction and avant-garde film, the list of available works to share with students is now dauntingly long.

Much of the work I assign in my class is built on the fact that my students (and I) have access to good and fast internet connections. We spend quite a bit of time studying 9/11 rumors, for instance, and this relies completely on web work. So too with our investigation of the snapshot culture of 9/11, which is built on surveys of the *Here is New York* site as well as a number of other digital archives. Throughout the course we study music and I am able to make the assumption that my students have various ways of accessing the relevant songs. Our class discussions, not surprisingly, often veer into investigations of how 9/11 and the development of Web 2.0 are inextricably linked.

So I want to make a plea for instructors to use the study of 9/11 also as an occasion to explore with students the thrilling and sometimes baffling shifts in production and consumption that are altering some of the most familiar paradigms of American popular (and literary) culture. Whether every student has a laptop (as they do at my college) or even regular access to the internet, it is important, I think, for teachers from the primary grades on up to try to orient their students to developing the skills they need to navigate these digital waters. I know that my experience of teaching privileged students at a private college will not be shared by all of the instructors who want to teach courses or units on 9/11 culture. 9/11 culture offers up all kinds of opportunities to teach in fairly traditional ways about fiction and poetry, film and music; close readings are still close readings, after all. But I also think we have a responsibility to try to acknowledge that, for many of our students, what reaches them as "culture" at all comes to them through a computer screen – or on some even smaller screen. At a moment when the most exciting revenue stream for music companies is the licensing of cell phone ringtones, it has become necessary for teachers to figure out how our older models of singular "great works" of art are being replaced by more fragmented models of cultural transmission.

It has been scary for many critics and teachers to move away from our training in order to come to terms with the new atomized realities of cultural production. The near-universal praise of Don DeLillo's novel *The Falling Man* in the spring of 2007 reached me as a sort of relief on the part of people of a certain age that we could still turn to the pleasures of unified works of literary fiction as representative of the best response to the tragedies of September 11. That DeLillo's book might also have been taken as a somewhat exhausted rehash of novels he had been writing for decades was of less moment than the simple fact that *here was a DeLillo novel about 9/11*. With ambiguity and symbols and complex motivations! For many of us, this kind of work is just the kind of text we have been taught to understand as significant on the face of it. How can we measure some amateur Flash animation against the work of this master?

The work, I think, is to embrace the chaos (as the title of Ozomatli's September 11, 2001, release put it). 9/11 culture is everywhere and is reaching our students through the internet, in song, on television, in graffiti on the train and on the bumper of the car we are stuck behind in traffic. One of the most gratifying aspects of teaching my class on 9/11 has been seeing how quickly students can come to feel like they are already experts in the field – or at least in some corner of the landscape we are studying. That sense of empowerment brings its own challenges of course, but it is a refreshing change from how the study of literature and history can so often leave students feeling disenfranchised and alienated. When I teach this class, students are constantly bringing me bits of 9/11 culture they have found on their own; the evidence of that runs through this book and I am only sorry that I have not been able to track who gave me this song or that television episode. Please email me (melnick.jeffrey@gmail.com) if you want to share syllabi or ideas for assignments.

Here is the text list from the first time I taught this class:

Bruce Springsteen: *The Rising*
David Rees: *Get Your War On*
Michael Feldschuh, ed.: *The September 11 Photo Project*
Paul West: *The Immensity of the Here and Now*
William Langewiesche: *American Ground*
Salon.com Editors: *Afterwords*

And here is my most recent one:

Ken Kalfus: *A Disorder Peculiar to the Country*
Lynne Sharon Schwartz: *The Writing on the Wall*
Moshin Hamid: *The Reluctant Fundamentalist*
David Rees: *Get Your War On*
Dana Heller, ed.: *The Selling of 9/11*
Susan Faludi: *The Terror Dream: Fear and Fantasy in Post-9/11 America*

Index

Note: numerals in headings are arranged as though spelled out; e.g. "9/11" is filed as if "nine eleven"

Everybody Was Kung Fu Fighting (book), 107
"Everyone and bin Laden Plays Guitar" (song), 141–2
exceptionalism, 157
Extremely Loud and Incredibly Close (novel), 85–7, 136–7

fables, 85–9, 130
Fahrenheit 9/11 (documentary), 48, 140
falling, representation, 78
falling bodies, 80–1, 86, 87, 90–3
falling man image, 21, 87
Falling Man, The (novel), 9, 91, 178
falling paper, 89–90
Faludi, Susan, 55, 79, 122, 128, 129
Falwell, Jerry, 7
families, 122–3, 125–8, 129–39
Family Guy (television show), 144
"Faraway" (song), 138
fascism, "*V*" *for Vendetta*, 7–8
Fast Girls (book), 27
Fast, Susan, 57
fatherhood, 123, 126–8, 129–38, 139–40, 148
federal government *see* government
Feldschuh, Michael, 68, 70, 72
femininity, 123–4
feminism, 123, 124
film
    American identity–race relations, 108, 110, 120
    falling bodies, 80–1
    falling paper motif, 90
    gender roles and relations, 123–8, 129–30, 135–6, 137–8
    9/11 attacks like, 65–6, 80
    with 9/11 content (list), 169–71
    rising narratives, 87–9
    shout-outs, 144, 153–4, 155
    violence, 50–1

war, 55, 56
firefighters
    American identity–race relations, 104
    gender roles and relations, 126, 135
    memorial art, 156
    9/11 questions, 9–10
    rising narratives, 84–5
Fischl, Eric, 92
Fitzpatrick, Chris, 113
Five Percenters, 118
Flight 93 narrative, 78–9
Flight (novel), 130–1
"Flight Patterns" (short story), 95
flying fantasies, 89
Foer, Jonathan Safran, 85–7, 136–7
Foote, Keneth, 76, 96, 142
"Forbidden Thoughts" (*Salom*.com), 23, 35
Friedman, Thomas, 18
Furious Five, 103
"Fuse, The" (song), 11, 83

Gabler, Neal, 67
Gallen, Joel, 52, 56
Gandhi, Mahatma, 107
gay people, 7–8
"Gelato is Gelato" (short story), 149–50
gender parity, celebrity telethon, 54, 56
gender roles and relations, 121, 122–40
Get Your War On (comic strip), 15–16
Gibson, William, 80, 151
Giuliani, Rudolph, 142–3
global–local balance, 123
"go shopping" directives, 32–3, 34
Goldstein, Richard, 124
Gone Baby Gone (film), 144
González Iñárritu, Alejandro, 80–1